Understanding Society

A Collection of Essays

Mehrdad Mashayekhi

Howard F. Taylor
Princeton University

Kim A. Logio
Saint Joseph's University

Margaret L. Andersen
University of Delaware

Patricia A. Adler
University of Colorado

Peter Adler
University of Denver

Leonard Cargan
Wright State University

Jeanne H. Ballantine
Wright State University

WADSWORTH

™

THOMSON LEARNING

Wadsworth/Thomson Learning
10 Davis Drive
Belmont, CA 94002-3098
USA

For information about our products, contact us:
Thomson Learning Academic Resource Center
1-800-423-0563
http://www.wadsworth.com

International Headquarters
Thomson Learning
International Division
290 Harbor Drive, 2nd Floor
Stamford, CT 06902-7477
USA

UK/Europe/Middle East/South Africa
Thomson Learning
Berkshire House
168-173 High Holborn
London WCIV 7AA

Asia
Thomson Learning
60 Albert Street, #15-01
Albert Complex
Singapore 189969

Canada
Nelson Thomson Learning
1120 Birchmount Road
Toronto, Ontario MIK 5G4
Canada
United Kingdom

ISBN 0-534-19803-1

The Adaptable Courseware Program consists of products and additions to existing Wadsworth Group products that are produced from camera-ready copy. Peer review, class testing, and accuracy are primarily the responsibility of the author(s).

Custom Contents

1

The Sociological Imagination

C. WRIGHT MILLS

First published in 1959, C. Wright Mills' essay, taken from his book, The Sociological Imagination, *is a classic statement about the sociological perspective. A man of his times, his sexist language intrudes on his argument, but the questions he posed about the connection between history, social structure, and people's biography (or lived experiences) still resonate today. His central theme is that the task of sociology is to understand how social and historical structures impinge on the lives of different people in society.*

Nowadays men often feel that their private lives are a series of traps. They sense that within their everyday worlds, they cannot overcome their troubles, and in this feeling, they are often quite correct: What ordinary men are directly aware of and what they try to do are bounded by the private orbits in which they live; their visions and their powers are limited to the close-up scenes of job, family, neighborhood; in other milieux, they move vicariously and remain spectators. And the more aware they become, however vaguely, of ambitions and of threats which transcend their immediate locales, the more trapped they seem to feel.

Underlying this sense of being trapped are seemingly impersonal changes in the very structure of continent-wide societies. The facts of contemporary history are also facts about the success and the failure of individual men and women. When a society is industrialized, a peasant becomes a worker; a feudal lord is liquidated or becomes a businessman. When classes rise or fall, a man is employed or unemployed; when the rate of investment goes up or down, a man takes new heart or goes broke. When wars happen, an insurance salesman becomes a rocket launcher; a store clerk, a radar man; a wife lives alone; a child grows up without a father. Neither the life of an individual nor the history of a society can be understood without understanding both.

Yet men do not usually define the troubles they endure in terms of historical change and institutional contradiction. The well-being they enjoy, they do not usually impute to the big ups and downs of the societies in which they live. Seldom aware of the intricate connection between the patterns of their own lives and the course of world history, ordinary men do not usually know what this connection means for the kinds of men they are becoming and for the kinds of history-making in which they might take part. They do not possess the quality of mind essential to grasp the interplay of man and society, of biography and history,

From: C. Wright Mills. *1959. The Sociological Imagination.* New York: Oxford University Press, pp. 3–11. Reprinted with permission.

of self and world. They cannot cope with their personal troubles in such ways as to control the structural transformations that usually lie behind them. . . .

The sociological imagination enables its possessor to understand the larger historical scene in terms of its meaning for the inner life and the external career of a variety of individuals. It enables him to take into account how individuals, in the welter of their daily experience, often become falsely conscious of their social positions. Within that welter, the framework of modern society is sought, and within that framework the psychologies of a variety of men and women are formulated. By such means the personal uneasiness of individuals is focused upon explicit troubles and the indifference of publics is transformed into involvement with public issues.

The first fruit of this imagination—and the first lesson of the social science that embodies it—is the idea that the individual can understand his own experience and gauge his own fate only by locating himself within his period, that he can know his own chances in life only by becoming aware of those of all individuals in his circumstances. In many ways it is a terrible lesson; in many ways a magnificent one. We do not know the limits of man's capacities for supreme effort or willing degradation, for agony or glee, for pleasurable brutality or the sweetness of reason. But in our time we have come to know that the limits of 'human nature' are frighteningly broad. We have come to know that every individual lives, from one generation to the next, in some society; that he lives out a biography, and that he lives it out within some historical sequence. By the fact of his living he contributes, however minutely, to the shaping of this society and to the course of its history, even as he is made by society and by its historical push and shove.

The sociological imagination enables us to grasp history and biography and the relations between the two within society. That is its task and its promise. To recognize this task and this promise is the mark of the classic social analyst. . . .

No social study that does not come back to the problems of biography, of history and of their intersections within a society has completed its intellectual journey. Whatever the specific problems of the classic social analysts, however limited or however broad the features of social reality they have examined, those who have been imaginatively aware of the promise of their work have consistently asked three sorts of questions:

1. What is the structure of this particular society as a whole? What are its essential components, and how are they related to one another? How does it differ from other varieties of social order? Within it, what is the meaning of any particular feature for its continuance and for its change?

2. Where does this society stand in human history? What are the mechanics by which it is changing? What is its place within and its meaning for the development of humanity as a whole? How does any particular feature we are examining affect, and how is it affected by, the historical period in which it moves? And this period—what are its essential features? How does it differ from other periods? What are its characteristic ways of history-making?

3. What varieties of men and women now prevail in this society and in this period? And what varieties are coming to prevail? In what ways are they

selected and formed, liberated and repressed, made sensitive and blunted? What kinds of 'human nature' are revealed in the conduct and character we observe in this society in this period? And what is the meaning for 'human nature' of each and every feature of the society we are examining?

Whether the point of interest is a great power state or a minor literary mood, a family, a prison, a creed—these are the kinds of questions the best social analysts have asked. They are the intellectual pivots of classic studies of man in society—and they are the questions inevitably raised by any mind possessing the sociological imagination. For that imagination is the capacity to shift from one perspective to another—from the political to the psychological; from examination of a single family to comparative assessment of the national budgets of the world; from the theological school to the military establishment; from considerations of an oil industry to studies of contemporary poetry. It is the capacity to range from the most impersonal and remote transformations to the most intimate features of the human self—and to see the relations between the two. Back of its use there is always the urge to know the social and historical meaning of the individual in the society and in the period in which he has his quality and his being.

That, in brief, is why it is by means of the sociological imagination that men now hope to grasp what is going on in the world, and to understand what is happening in themselves as minute points of the intersections of biography and history within society. In large part, contemporary man's self-conscious view of himself as at least an outsider, if not a permanent stranger, rests upon an absorbed realization of social relativity and of the transformative power of history. The sociological imagination is the most fruitful form of this self-consciousness. By its use men whose mentalities have swept only a series of limited orbits often come to feel as if suddenly awakened in a house with which they had only supposed themselves to be familiar. Correctly or incorrectly, they often come to feel that they can now provide themselves with adequate summations, cohesive assessments, comprehensive orientations. Older decisions that once appeared sound now seem to them products of a mind unaccountably dense. Their capacity for astonishment is made lively again. They acquire a new way of thinking, they experience a transvaluation of values: in a word, by their reflection and by their sensibility, they realize the cultural meaning of the social sciences.

Perhaps the most fruitful distinction with which the sociological imagination works is between 'the personal troubles of milieu' and 'the public issues of social structure.' This distinction is an essential tool of the sociological imagination and a feature of all classic work in social science.

Troubles occur within the character of the individual and within the range of his immediate relations with others; they have to do with his self and with those limited areas of social life of which he is directly and personally aware. Accordingly, the statement and the resolution of troubles properly lie within the individual as a biographical entity and within the scope of his immediate milieu—the social setting that is directly open to his personal experience and to some extent his willful activity. A trouble is a private matter: values cherished by an individual are felt by him to be threatened.

Issues have to do with matters that transcend these local environments of the individual and the range of his inner life. They have to do with the organization of many such milieux into the institutions of an historical society as a whole, with the ways in which various milieux overlap and interpenetrate to form the larger structure of social and historical life. An issue is a public matter: some value cherished by publics is felt to be threatened. Often there is a debate about what that value really is and about what it is that really threatens it. This debate is often without focus if only because it is the very nature of an issue, unlike even widespread trouble, that it cannot very well be defined in terms of the immediate and everyday environments of ordinary men. An issue, in fact, often involves a crisis in institutional arrangements, and often too it involves what Marxists call 'contradictions' or 'antagonisms.'

In these terms, consider unemployment. When, in a city of 100,000, only one man is unemployed, that is his personal trouble, and for its relief we properly look to the character of the man, his skills, and his immediate opportunities. But when in a nation of 50 million employees, 15 million men are unemployed, that is an issue, and we may not hope to find its solution within the range of opportunities open to any one individual. The very structure of opportunities has collapsed. Both the correct statement of the problem and the range of possible solutions require us to consider the economic and political institutions of the society, and not merely the personal situation and character of a scatter of individuals.

Consider war. The personal problem of war, when it occurs, may be how to survive it or how to die in it with honor; how to make money out of it; how to climb into the higher safety of the military apparatus; or how to contribute to the war's termination. In short, according to one's values, to find a set of milieux and within it to survive the war or make one's death in it meaningful. But the structural issues of war have to do with its causes; with what types of men it throws up into command; with its effects upon economic and political, family and religious institutions, with the unorganized irresponsibility of a world of nation-states.

Consider marriage. Inside a marriage a man and a woman may experience personal troubles, but when the divorce rate during the first four years of marriage is 250 out of every 1,000 attempts, this is an indication of a structural issue having to do with the institutions of marriage and the family and other institutions that bear upon them.

Or consider the metropolis—the horrible, beautiful, ugly, magnificent sprawl of the great city. For many upper-class people, the personal solution to 'the problem of the city' is to have an apartment with private garage under it in the heart of the city, and forty miles out, a house by Henry Hill, garden by Garrett Eckbo, on a hundred acres of private land. In these two controlled environments—with a small staff at each end and a private helicopter connection—most people could solve many of the problems of personal milieux caused by the facts of the city. But all this, however splendid, does not solve the public issues that the structural fact of the city poses. What should be done with this wonderful monstrosity? Break it all up into scattered units, combining residence and work? Refurbish it as it stands? Or, after evacuation, dynamite it and build new cities according to new plans in new places? What should those plans be? And who is to decide and to accomplish whatever choice is made? These are structural issues; to confront them and to solve them requires us to consider political and economic issues that affect innumerable milieux.

In so far as an economy is so arranged that slumps occur, the problem of unemployment becomes incapable of personal solution. In so far as war is inherent in the nation-state system and in the uneven industrialization of the world, the ordinary individual in his restricted milieu will be powerless—with or without psychiatric aid—to solve the troubles this system or lack of system imposes upon him. In so far as the family as an institution turns women into darling little slaves and men into their chief providers and unweaned dependents, the problem of a satisfactory marriage remains incapable of purely private solution. In so far as the overdeveloped megalopolis and the overdeveloped automobile are built-in features of the overdeveloped society, the issues of urban living will not be solved by personal ingenuity and private wealth.

What we experience in various and specific milieux, I have noted, is often caused by structural changes. Accordingly, to understand the changes of many personal milieux we are required to look beyond them. And the number and variety of such structural changes increase as the institutions within which we live become more embracing and more intricately connected with one another. To be aware of the idea of social structure and to use it with sensibility is to be capable of tracing such linkages among a great variety of milieux. To be able to do that is to possess the sociological imagination. . . .

DISCUSSION QUESTIONS

1. Using either today's newspaper or some other source of news, identify one example of what C. Wright Mills would call an issue. How is this issue reflected in the personal troubles of people it affects? Why would Mills call it a social issue?

2. What are the major historical events that have influenced the biographies of people in your generation? in your parents' generation? What does this tell you about the influence of society and history on biography?

INFOTRAC COLLEGE EDITION

You can use your access to InfoTrac College Edition to learn more about the subjects covered in this essay. Some suggested search terms include:

divorce	urban development
sociological imagination	war
unemployment	

2

The Forest and the Trees

ALLAN G. JOHNSON

Allan Johnson uses the classic example of the forest and the trees as a metaphor to demon-strate that people in society are participating in something larger than themselves. He also argues that the strong cultural belief in individualism blunts the sociological imagination, because it makes you see only individuals, not the social structures that shape diverse group experiences.

As a form of sociological practice, I work with people in corporations, schools, and universities who are trying to deal with issues of diversity. In the simplest sense, diversity is about the variety of people in the world, the varied mix of gender, race, age, social class, ethnicity, religion, and other social characteristics. In the United States and Europe, for example, the workforce is changing as the percentages who are female or from non-European ethnic and racial backgrounds increase and the percentage who are white and male declines.

If the changing mix was all that diversity amounted to, there wouldn't be a problem since in many ways differences make life interesting and enhance cre-ativity. Compared with homogeneous teams, for example, diverse work teams are usually better with problems that require creative solutions. To be sure, diversity brings with it difficulties to be dealt with such as language barriers and different ways of doing things that can confuse or irritate people. But we're the species with the "big brain," the adaptable ones who learn quickly, so learning to get along with people unlike ourselves shouldn't be a problem we can't handle. Like travelers in a strange land, we'd simply learn about one another and make room for differences and figure out how to make good use of them.

As most people know, however, in the world as it is, difference amounts to more than just variety. It's also used as a basis for including some and excluding others, for rewarding some more and others less, for treating some with respect and dignity and some as if they were less than fully human or not even there. Difference is used as a basis for privilege, from reserving for some the simple human dignities that everyone should have, to the extreme of deciding who lives and who dies. Since the workplace is part of the world, patterns of inequality and oppression that permeate the world also show up at work, even though people may like to think of themselves as "colleagues" or part of "the team." And just as these patterns shape people's lives in often damaging ways, they can eat away at

From: Allan G. Johnson. 1997. *The Forest and the Trees: Sociology as Life, Practice, Promise.* Philadelphia: Temple University Press, pp. 7–27. Reprinted with permission.

the core of a community or an organization, weakening it with internal division and resentment bred and fed by injustice and suffering. . . .

People tend to think of things only in terms of individuals, as if a society or a company or a university were nothing more than a collection of people living in a particular time and place. Many writers have pointed out how individualism affects social life. It isolates us from one another, promotes divisive competition, and makes it harder to sustain a sense of community, of all being "in this together." But individualism does more than affect how we participate in social life. It also affects how we *think* about social life and how we make sense of it. If we think everything begins and ends with individuals—their personalities, biographies, feelings, and behavior—then it's easy to think that social problems must come down to flaws in individual character. If we have a drug problem, it must be because individuals just can't or won't "say no." If there is racism, sexism, heterosexism, classism, and other forms of oppression, it must be because of people who for some reason have the personal "need" to behave in racist, sexist, and other oppressive ways. If evil consequences occur in social life, then it must be because of evil people and their evil ways and motives.

If we think about the world in this way—which is especially common in the United States—then it's easy to see why members of privileged groups get upset when they're asked to look at the benefits that go with belonging to that particular group and the price others pay for it. When women, for example, talk about how sexism affects them, individualistic thinking encourages men to hear this as a personal accusation: "If women are oppressed, then I'm an evil oppressor who wants to oppress them." Since no man wants to see himself as a bad person, and since most men probably don't *feel* oppressive toward women, men may feel unfairly attacked.

In the United States, individualism goes back to the nineteenth century and, beyond that, to the European Enlightenment and the certainties of modernist thinking. It was in this period that the rational mind of the individual person was recognized and elevated to a dominant position in the hierarchy of things, separated from and placed above even religion and God. The roots of individualistic thinking in the United States trace in part to the work of William James who helped pioneer the field of psychology. Later, it was deepened in Europe and the United States by Sigmund Freud's revolutionary insights into the existence of the subconscious and the inner world of individual existence. Over the course of the twentieth century, the individual life has emerged as a dominant framework for understanding the complexities and mysteries of human existence.

You can see this in bookstores and best-seller lists that abound with promises to change the world through "self-help" and individual growth and transformation. Even on the grand scale of societies—from war and politics to international economics—individualism reduces everything to the personalities and behavior of the people we perceive to be "in charge." If ordinary people in capitalist societies feel deprived and insecure, the individualistic answer is that the people who run corporations are "greedy" or the politicians are corrupt and incompetent and otherwise lacking in personal character. The same perspective argues that poverty exists because of the habits, attitudes, and skills of individual poor people, who are blamed for what they supposedly lack as people and told to change if they want anything better for themselves. To make a better world, we think we have to put the "right people" in charge or make better people by liberating human consciousness in a New Age or by changing how children are socialized or by locking up or tossing out or killing people who won't or can't be better than they are. Psychotherapy is increasingly offered as a model for changing not only the inner life of individuals, but also the world they live in. If enough people heal themselves through therapy, then the world will "heal" itself as well. The solution to collective problems such as poverty or deteriorating cities then becomes a matter not of collective solutions but of an accumulation of individual solutions. So, if we want to have less poverty in the world, the answer lies in raising people out of poverty or keeping them from becoming poor, *one person at a time.*

So, individualism is a way of thinking that encourages us to explain the world in terms of what goes on inside individuals and nothing else. We've been able to think this way because we've developed the human ability to be reflexive, which is to say, we've learned to look at ourselves *as selves* with greater awareness and insight than before. We can think about what kind of people we are and how we live in the world, and we can imagine ourselves in new ways. To do this, however, we first have to be able to believe that we exist as distinct individuals apart from the groups and communities and societies that make up our social environment. In other words, the *idea* of the "individual" has to exist before we think about ourselves as individuals, and the idea of the individual has been around for only a few centuries. Today, we've gone far beyond this by thinking of the social environment itself as just a collection of individuals: Society *is* people and people *are* society. To understand social life, all we have to do is understand what makes the individual psyche tick.

If you grow up and live in a society that's dominated by individualism, the idea that society is just people seems obvious. The problem is that this approach ignores the difference between the individual people who participate in social life and the relationships that connect them to one another and to groups and societies. It's true that you can't have a social relationship without people to participate in it and make it happen, but the people and the relationship aren't the same thing. That's why this book's title plays on the old saying about missing the forest for the trees. In one sense, a forest is simply a collection of individual trees; but it's more than that. It's also a collection of trees that exist in *a particular relation* to one another, and you can't tell what that relation is by just looking at each individual tree. Take a thousand trees and scatter them across the Great Plains of North America, and all you have are a thousand trees. But take those same trees and bring them close together and you have a forest. Same individual trees, but in one case a forest and in another case just a lot of trees.

The "empty space" that separates individual trees from one another isn't a characteristic of any one tree or the characteristics of all the individual trees somehow added together. It's something more than that, and it's crucial to understand the *relationships among* trees that make a forest what it is. Paying attention to that "something more"—whether it's a family or a corporation or an entire society—and how people are related to it is at the heart of sociological practice.

THE ONE THING

If sociology could teach everyone just one thing with the best chance to lead toward everything else we could know about social life, it would, I believe, be this: *We are always participating in something larger than ourselves, and if we want to understand social life and what happens to people in it, we have to understand what it is that we're participating in* and *how we participate in it*. In other words, the key to understanding social life isn't just the forest and it isn't just the trees. It's the forest *and* the trees and how they're related to one another. Sociology is the study of how all this happens.

The "larger" things we participate in are called social systems, and they come in all shapes and sizes. In general, the concept of a system refers to any collection of parts or elements that are connected in ways that cohere into some kind of whole. We can think of the engine in a car as a system, for example, a collection of parts arranged in ways that make the car "go." Or we could think of a language as a system, with words and punctuation and rules for how to combine them into sentences that mean something. We can also think of a family as a system—a collection of elements related to one another in a way that leads us to think of it as a unit. These include things such as the positions of mother, father, wife, husband, parent, child, daughter, son, sister, and brother. Elements also include shared ideas that tie those positions together to make relationships, such as how "good mothers" are supposed to act in relation to children or what a "family" is and what makes family members "related" to one another as kin. If we take the positions and the ideas and other elements, then we can think of what results as a whole and call it a social system.

In similar ways, we can think of corporations or societies as social systems. They differ from one another—and from families—in the kinds of elements they include and how those are arranged in relation to one another. Corporations have positions such as CEOs and stockholders, for example; but the position of "mother" isn't part of the corporate system. People who work in corporations can certainly be mothers in families, but that isn't a position that connects them to a corporation. Such differences are a key to seeing how systems work and produce different kinds of consequences. Corporations are sometimes referred to as "families," for example, but if you look at how families and corporations are actually put together as systems, it's easy to see how unrealistic such notions are. Families don't usually "lay off" their members when times are tough or to boost the bottom line, and they usually don't divide the food on the dinner table according to who's the strongest and best able to grab the lion's share for themselves. But corporations dispense with workers all the time as a way to raise dividends and the value of stock, and top managers routinely take a huge share of each year's profits even while putting other members of the corporate "family" out of work.

What social life comes down to, then, is social systems and how people participate in and relate to them. Note that people *participate* in systems without being *parts* of the systems themselves. In this sense, "father" is a position in my family, and I, Allan, am a person who actually occupies that position. It's a crucial distinction that's easy to lose sight of. It's easy to lose sight of because we're so used to thinking solely in terms of individuals. It's crucial because it means that people aren't systems, and systems aren't people, and if we forget that, we're likely to focus on the wrong thing in trying to solve our problems. . . .

INDIVIDUALISTIC MODELS DON'T WORK

Probably the most important basis for sociological practice is to realize that *the individualistic perspective that dominates current thinking about social life doesn't work.* Nothing we do or experience takes place in a vacuum; everything is always related to a context of some kind. When a wife and husband argue about who'll clean the bathroom, for example, or who'll take care of a sick child when they both work outside the home, the issue is never simply about the two of them even though it may seem that way at the time. We have to ask about the larger context in which this takes place. We might ask how this instance is related to living in a society organized in ways that privilege men over women, in part by not making men feel obliged to share equally in domestic work except when they choose to "help out." On an individual level, he may think she's being a nag; she may think he's being a jerk; but it's never as simple as that. What both may miss is that in a different kind of society, they might not be having this argument in the first place because both might feel obliged to take care of the home and children. In similar ways, when we see ourselves as a unique result of the family we came from, we overlook how each family is connected to larger patterns. The emotional problems we struggle with as individuals aren't due simply to what kind of parents we had, for their participation in social systems—at work, in the community, in society as a whole—shaped them as people, including their roles as mothers and fathers.

An individualistic model is misleading because it encourages us to explain human behavior and experience from a perspective that's so narrow it misses most of what's going on. A related problem is that *we can't understand what goes on in social systems simply by looking at individuals.* In one sense, for example, suicide is a solitary act done by an individual, typically while alone. If we ask why people kill themselves, we're likely to think first of how people feel when they do it— hopeless, depressed, guilty, lonely, or perhaps obliged by honor or duty to sacrifice themselves for someone else or some greater social good. That might explain suicides taken one at a time, but what do we have when we add up all the suicides that happen in a society for a given year? What does that number tell us, and, more importantly, about what? The suicide rate for the entire U.S. population in 1994, for example, was twelve suicides per 100,000 people. If we look inside that number, we find that the rate for males was twenty per 100,000, but the rate for females was only five per 100,000. The rate also differs dramatically by race and country and varies over time. The suicide rate for white males, for example, was 71 percent higher than for black males, and the rate for white females was more than twice that for black females. While the rate in the United States was twelve per 100,000, it was thirty-four per 100,000 in Hungary and only seven per 100,000 in Italy. So, in the United States, males and whites are far more likely than females and blacks to kill themselves; and people in the United States are almost twice as likely as Italians to commit suicide but only one third as likely as Hungarians.

If we use an individualistic model to explain such differences, we'll tend to see them as nothing more than a sum of individual suicides. If males are more likely to kill themselves, then it must be because males are more likely to feel suicidally depressed, lonely, worthless, and hopeless. In other words, the psychological factors that cause individuals to kill themselves must be more common among U.S. males than they are among U.S. females, or more common among people in the United States than among Italians. There's nothing wrong with such reasoning; it may be exactly right *as far as it goes*. But that's just the problem: It doesn't go very far because it doesn't answer the question of *why* these differences exist in the first place. Why, for example, would males be more likely to feel suicidally hopeless and depressed than females, or Hungarians more likely than Italians? Or why would Hungarians who feel suicidally depressed be more likely to go ahead and kill themselves than Italians who feel the same way? To answer such questions, we need more than an understanding of individual psychology. Among other things, we need to pay attention to the fact that words like "female," "white," and "Italian" name positions that people occupy in social systems. This draws attention to how those systems work and what it means to occupy those positions in them.

Sociologically, a suicide rate is a number that describes something about a group or a society, not the individuals who belong to it. A suicide rate of twelve per 100,000 tells us nothing about you or me or anyone else. Each of us either commits suicide during a given year or we don't, and the rate can't tell us who does what. In the same way, how individuals feel before they kill themselves isn't by itself enough to explain why some groups or societies have higher suicide rates than others. Individuals can feel depressed or lonely, but groups and societies can't feel a thing. We could consider that Italians might tend to be less depressed than people in the United States, for example, or that in the United States, people might tend to deal with feelings of depression more effectively than Hungarians. It makes no sense at all, however, to say that the United States is more depressed or lonely than Italy.

While it might work to look at what goes on in individuals as a way to explain why one person commits suicide, this can't explain *patterns* of suicide found in social systems. To do this, we have to look at how people feel and behave *in relation* to systems and how these systems work. We need to ask, for example, how societies are organized in ways that encourage people who participate in them to feel more or less depressed or to respond to such feelings in suicidal or nonsuicidal ways. We need to see how belonging to particular groups shapes people's experience as they participate in social life, and how this limits the alternatives they think they can choose from. What is it about being male or being white that can make suicide a path of least resistance? How, in other words, can we go to the heart of sociological practice to ask how people participate in something larger than themselves and see how this affects the choices they make? How can we see the relationship between people and systems that produces variations in suicide rates or, for that matter, just about everything else that we do and experience, from having sex to going to school to working to dying?

Just as we can't tell what's going on in a system just by looking at individuals, we also can't tell what's going on in individuals just by looking at systems. Something may look like one thing in the system as a whole, but something else entirely when we look at the people who participate in it. If we look at the kind of mass destruction and suffering that war typically causes, for example, an individualistic model suggests a direct link with the "kinds" of people who participate in it. If war produces cruelty, bloodshed, aggression, and conquest, then it must be that the people who participate in it are cruel, bloodthirsty, aggressive people who want to conquer and dominate others. Viewing the carnage and destruction that war typically leaves in its wake, we're likely to ask, "What kind of people could do such a thing?" Sociologically, however, this question misleads us by reducing a social phenomenon to a simple matter of "kinds of people" without looking at the systems those people participate in. Since we're always participating in one system or another, when someone drops a bomb that incinerates thousands of people, we can't explain what happened simply by figuring out "what kind of person would do such a thing." In fact, if we look at what's known about people who fight in wars, they appear fairly normal by most standards and anything but bloodthirsty and cruel. Most accounts portray men in combat, for example, as alternating between boredom and feeling scared out of their wits. They worry much less about glory than they do about not being hurt or killed and getting themselves and their friends home in one piece. For most soldiers, killing and the almost constant danger of being killed are traumatic experiences that leave them forever changed as people. They go to war not in response to some inner need to be aggressive and kill, but because they think it's their duty to go, because they'll go to prison if they dodge the draft, because they've seen war portrayed in books and movies as an adventurous way to prove they're "real men," or because they don't want to risk family and friends rejecting them for not measuring up as true patriots.

People aren't systems, and systems aren't people, which means that social life can produce horrible or wonderful consequences without necessarily meaning that the people who participate in them are horrible or wonderful. Good people participate in systems that produce bad consequences all the time. I'm often aware of this in the simplest situations, such as when I go to buy clothes or food. Many of the clothes sold in the United States are made in sweatshops in cities like Los Angeles and New York and in Third World countries, where people work under conditions that resemble slavery in many respects, and for wages that are so low they can barely live on them. A great deal of the fruit and vegetables in stores are harvested by migrant farm workers who work under conditions that aren't much better. If these workers were provided with decent working conditions and paid a living wage, the price of clothing and food would probably be a lot higher than it is. This means that I benefit directly from the daily mistreatment and exploitation of thousands of people. The fact that I benefit doesn't make me a bad person; but my participation in that system does involve me in what happens to them. . . .

DISCUSSION QUESTIONS

1. Johnson argues that there is a tendency in the United States for people to explain everything in individual terms. Using the example of suicide, why are individualistic explanations inadequate? What would sociological explanations emphasize instead?

2. Johnson opens his discussion by noting the diversity that characterizes U.S. society. How does he apply the sociological perspective to his understanding of diversity and its significance?

INFOTRAC COLLEGE EDITION

You can use your access to InfoTrac College Edition to learn more about the subjects covered in this essay. Some suggested search terms include:

diversity
Enlightenment
individualism

suicide
sweatshops

3

Invitation to Sociology

Peter L. Berger

. . . It can be said that the first wisdom of sociology is this—things are not what they seem. This too is a deceptively simple statement. It ceases to be simple after a while. Social reality turns out to have many layers of meaning. The discovery of each new layer changes the perception of the whole.

Anthropologists use the term "culture shock" to describe the impact of a totally new culture upon a newcomer. In an extreme instance such shock will be experienced by the Western explorer who is told, halfway through dinner, that he is eating the nice old lady he had been chatting with the previous day—a shock with predictable physiological if not moral consequences. Most explorers no longer encounter cannibalism in their travels today. However, the first encounters with polygamy or with puberty rites or even with the way some nations drive their automobiles can be quite a shock to an American visitor. With the shock may go not only disapproval or disgust but a sense of excitement that things can really be that different from what they are at home. To some extent, at least, this is the excite-

ment of any first travel abroad. The experience of sociological discovery could be described as "culture shock" minus geographical displacement. In other words, the sociologist travels at home—with shocking results. He is unlikely to find that he is eating a nice old lady for dinner. But the discovery, for instance, that his own church has considerable money invested in the missile industry or that a few blocks from his home there are people who engage in cultic orgies may not be drastically different in emotional impact. Yet we would not want to imply that sociological discoveries are always or even usually outrageous to moral sentiment. Not at all. What they have in common with exploration in distant lands, however, is the sudden illumination of new and unsuspected facets of human existence in society. This is the excitement and, as we shall try to show later, the humanistic justification of sociology.

People who like to avoid shocking discoveries, who prefer to believe that society is just what they were taught in Sunday school, who like the safety of the rules and the maxims of what Alfred Schuetz has called the "world-taken-for-granted," should stay away from sociology. People who feel no temptation before closed doors, who have no curiosity about human beings, who are content to admire scenery without wondering about the people who live in those houses on the other side of that river, should probably also stay away from sociology. They will find it unpleasant or, at any rate, unrewarding. People who are interested in human beings only if they can change, convert, or reform them should also be warned, for they will find sociology much less useful than they hoped. And people whose interest is mainly in their own conceptual constructions will do just as well to turn to the study of little white mice. Sociology will be satisfying, in the long run, only to those who can think of nothing more entrancing than to watch men and to understand things human....

To ask sociological questions, then, presupposes that one is interested in looking some distance beyond the commonly accepted or officially defined goals of human actions. It presupposes a certain awareness that human events have different levels of meaning, some of which are hidden from the consciousness of everyday life. It may even presuppose a measure of suspicion about the way in which human events are officially interpreted by the authorities, be they political, juridical, or religious in character. If one is willing to go as far as that, it would seem evident that not all historical circumstances are equally favorable for the development of sociological perspective.

It would appear plausible, in consequence, that sociological thought would have the best chance to develop in historical circumstances marked by severe jolts to the self-conception, especially the official and authoritative and generally accepted self-conception of a culture. It is only in such circumstances that perceptive men are likely to be motivated to think beyond the assertions of this self-conception and, as a result, question the authorities....

Sociological perspective can then be understood in terms of such phrases as "seeing through," "looking behind," very much as such phrases would be employed in common speech—"seeing through his game," "looking behind the scenes"—in other words, "being up on all the tricks."

...We could think of this in terms of a common experience of people living in large cities. One of the fascinations of a large city is the immense variety of human activities taking place behind the seemingly anonymous and endlessly undifferentiated rows of houses. A person who lives in such a city will time and again experience surprise or even shock as he discovers the strange pursuits that some men engage in quite unobtrusively in houses that, from the outside, look like all the others on a certain street. Having had this experience once or twice, one will repeatedly find oneself walking down a street, perhaps late in the evening, and wondering what may be going on under the bright lights showing through a line of drawn curtains. An ordinary family engaged in pleasant talk with guests? A scene of desperation amid illness or death? Or a scene of debauched pleasures? Perhaps a strange cult or a dangerous conspiracy? The facades of the houses cannot tell us, proclaiming nothing but an architectural conformity to the tastes of some group or class that may not even inhabit the street any longer. The social mysteries lie behind the facades. The wish to penetrate to these mysteries is an analogon to sociological curiosity. In some cities that are suddenly struck by calamity this wish may be abruptly realized. Those who have experienced wartime bombings know of the sudden encounters with unsuspected (and sometimes unimaginable) fellow tenants in the air-raid shelter of one's apartment building. Or they can recollect the startling morning sight of a house hit by a bomb during the night, neatly sliced in half, the facade torn away and the previously hidden interior mercilessly revealed in the daylight. But in most cities that one may normally live in, the facades must be penetrated by one's own inquisitive intrusions. Similarly, there are historical situations in which the facades of society are violently torn apart and all but the most incurious are forced to see that there was a reality behind the facades all along. Usually this does not happen, and the facades continue to confront us with seemingly rocklike permanence. The perception of the reality behind the facades then demands a considerable intellectual effort.

A few examples of the way in which sociology "looks behind" the facades of social structures might serve to make our argument clearer. Take, for instance, the political organization of a community. If one wants to find out how a modern American city is governed, it is very easy to get the official information about this subject. The city will have a charter, operating under the laws of the state. With some advice from informed individuals, one may look up various statues that define the constitution of the city. Thus one may find out that this particular community has a city-manager form of administration, or that party affiliations do not appear on the ballot in municipal elections, or that the city government participates in a regional water district. In similar fashion, with the help of some newspaper reading, one may find out the officially recognized political problems of the community. One may read that the city plans to annex a certain suburban area, or that there has been a change in the zoning ordinances to facilitate industrial development in another area, or even that one of the members of the city council has been accused of using his office for personal gain. All such matters still occur on the, as it were, visible, official, or public level of political life. However, it would be an exceedingly naive person who would believe that this kind of information gives him a rounded picture of the political reality of that community. The sociologist will want to know above all the constituency of the "informal power structure" (as it has been called by Floyd Hunter, an American sociologist interested in such studies), which is a configuration of men and their power that cannot be found in any statutes, and probably cannot be read about in the newspapers. The political scientist or the legal expert might find it very inter-

esting to compare the city charter with the constitutions of other similar communities. The sociologist will be far more concerned with discovering the way in which powerful vested interests influence or even control the actions of officials elected under the charter. These vested interests will not be found in city hall, but rather in the executive suites of corporations that may not even be located in that community, in the private mansions of a handful of powerful men, perhaps in the offices of certain labor unions, or even, in some instances, in the headquarters of criminal organizations. When the sociologist concerns himself with power, he will "look behind" the official mechanisms that are supposed to regulate power in the community. This does not necessarily mean that he will regard the official mechanisms as totally ineffective or their legal definition as totally illusionary. But at the very least he will insist that there is another level of reality to be investigated in the particular system of power. In some cases he might conclude that to look for real power in the publicly recognized places is quite delusional....

Let us take one further example. In Western countries, and especially in America, it is assumed that men and women marry because they are in love. There is a broadly based popular mythology about the character of love as a violent, irresistible emotion that strikes where it will, a mystery that is the goal of most young people and often of the not-so-young as well. As soon as one investigates, however, which people actually marry each other, one finds that the lightning-shaft of Cupid seems to be guided rather strongly within very definite channels of class, income, education, [and] racial and religious background. If one then investigates a little further into the behavior that is engaged in prior to marriage under the rather misleading euphemism of "courtship," one finds channels of interaction that are often rigid to the point of ritual. The suspicion begins to dawn on one that, most of the time, it is not so much the emotion of love that creates a certain kind of relationship, but that carefully predefined and often planned relationships eventually generate the desired emotion. In other words, when certain conditions are met or have been constructed, one allows oneself "to fall in love." The sociologist investigating our patterns of "courtship" and marriage soon discovers a complex web of motives related in many ways to the entire institutional structure within which an individual lives his life—class, career, economic ambition, aspirations of power and prestige. The miracle of love now begins to look somewhat synthetic. Again, this need not mean in any given instance that the sociologist will declare the romantic interpretation to be an illusion. But, once more, he will look beyond the immediately given and publicly approved interpretations....

We would contend, then, that there is a debunking motif inherent in sociological consciousness. The sociologist will be driven time and again, by the very logic of his discipline, to debunk the social systems he is studying. This unmasking tendency need not necessarily be due to the sociologist's temperament or inclinations. Indeed, it may happen that the sociologist, who as an individual may be of a conciliatory disposition and quite disinclined to disturb the comfortable assumptions on which he rests his own social existence, is nevertheless compelled by what he is doing to fly in the face of what those around him take for granted. In other words, we would contend that the roots of the debunking motif in sociology are not psychological but methodological. The sociological frame of reference, with its built-in procedure of looking for levels of reality other than those given in the of-

ficial interpretations of society, carries with it a logical imperative to unmask the pretensions and the propaganda by which men cloak their actions with each other. This unmasking imperative is one of the characteristics of sociology particularly at home in the temper of the modern era...

Credit: Invitation to Sociology by Peter Berger. ©1963. Reprinted by permission of Bantam Doubleday Dell.

Suggested **Web URLs** for further study:
http://sociology.wadsworth.com/
Society for Applied Sociology, founded in 1978, is an international organization for professionals involved in applying sociological knowledge in a wide variety of settings.
http://www.oise.on.ca/~jnorris/qual.html
Resources for qualitative sociologists.

InfoTrac College Edition:
You can find further relevant readings on the World Wide Web at
http://sociology.wadsworth.com

Virtual Society
For further information on this subject including links to relevant web sites, go to the Wadsworth Sociology homepage at
http://sociology.wadsworth.com

4

Body Ritual Among the Nacirema

Horace Miner

The anthropologist has become so familiar with the diversity of ways in which different peoples behave in similar situations that he is not apt to be surprised by even the most exotic customs. In fact, if all of the logically possible combinations of behavior have not been found somewhere in the world, he is apt to suspect that they must be present in some yet undescribed tribe. This point has, in fact, been expressed with respect to clan organization by Murdock (1949: 71). In this light, the magical beliefs and practices of the Nacirema present such unusual aspects that it seems desirable to describe them as an example of the extremes to which human behavior can go.

Professor Linton first brought the ritual of the Nacirema to the attention of anthropologists twenty years ago (1936: 326), but the culture of this people is still very poorly understood. They are a North American group living in the territory between the Canadian Cree, the Yaqui and Tarahumare of Mexico, and the Carib and Arawak of the Antilles. Little is known of their origin, although tradition states that they came from the east. According to Nacirema mythology, their nation was originated by a culture hero, Notgnihsaw, who is otherwise known for two great feats of strength—the throwing of a piece of wampum across the river Pa-To-Mac and the chopping down of a cherry tree in which the Spirit of Truth resided.

Nacirema culture is characterized by a highly developed market economy which has evolved in a rich natural habitat. While much of the people's time is devoted to economic pursuits, a large part of the fruits of these labors and a considerable portion of the day are spent in ritual activity. The focus of this activity is the human body, the appearance and health of which loom as a dominant concern in the ethos of the people. While such concern is certainly not unusual, its ceremonial aspects and associated philosophy are unique.

The fundamental belief underlying the whole system appears to be that the human body is ugly and that its natural tendency is to debility and disease. Incarcerated in such a body, man's only hope is to avert these characteristics through the use of the powerful influences of ritual and ceremony. Every household has one or more shrines devoted to this purpose. The more powerful individuals in this society have several shrines in their houses, and, in fact, the opulence of a house is often referred to in terms of the number of such ritual centers it possesses. Most houses are of wattle and daub construction, but the shrine rooms of the more wealthy are walled with stone. Poorer families imitate the rich by applying pottery plaques to their shrine walls.

While each family has at least one such shrine, the rituals associated with it are not family ceremonies but are private and secret. The rites are normally only discussed with children, and then only during the period when they are being initiated into these mysteries. I was able, however, to establish sufficient rapport with the natives to examine these shrines and to have the rituals described to me.

The focal point of the shrine is a box or chest which is built into the wall. In this chest are kept the many charms and magical potions without which no native believes he could live. These preparations are secured from a variety of specialized practitioners. The most powerful of these are the medicine men, whose assistance must be rewarded with substantial gifts. However, the medicine men do not provide the curative potions for their clients, but decide what the ingredients should be and then write them down in an ancient and secret language. This writing is understood only by the medicine men and by the herbalists who, for another gift, provide the required charm.

The charm is not disposed of after it has served its purpose, but is placed in the charm-box of the household shrine. As these magical materials are specific for certain ills, and the real or imagined maladies of the people are many, the charm-box is usually full to overflowing. The magical packets are so numerous that people forget what their purposes were and fear to use them again. While the natives are very vague on this point, we can only assume that the idea in retaining all the old magical materials is that their presence in the charm-box, before which the body rituals are conducted, will in some way protect the worshipper.

Beneath the charm-box is a small font. Each day every member of the family, in succession, enters the shrine room, bows his head before the charm-box, mingles different sorts of holy water in the font, and proceeds with a brief rite of ablution. The holy waters are secured from the Water Temple of the community, where the priests conduct elaborate ceremonies to make the liquid ritually pure.

In the hierarchy of magical practitioners, and below the medicine men in prestige, are specialists whose designation is best translated "holy-mouth-men." The Nacirema have an almost pathological horror of and fascination with the mouth, the condition of which is believed to have a supernatural influence on all social relationships. Were it not for the rituals of the mouth, they believe that their teeth would fall out, their gums bleed, their jaws shrink, their friends desert them, and their lovers reject them. They also believe that a strong relationship exists between oral and moral characteristics. For example, there is a ritual ablution of the mouth for children which is supposed to improve their moral fiber.

The daily body ritual performed by everyone includes a mouth-rite. Despite the fact that these people are so punctilious about care of the mouth, this rite involves a practice which strikes the uninitiated stranger as revolting. It was reported to me that the ritual consists of inserting a small bundle of hog hairs into the mouth, along with certain magical powders, and then moving the bundle in a highly formalized series of gestures.

In addition to the private mouth-rite, the people seek out a holy-mouth-man once or twice a year. These practitioners have an impressive set of paraphernalia, consisting of a variety of augers, awls, probes, and prods. The use of these objects in the exorcism of the evils of the mouth involves almost unbelievable ritual torture of the client. The holy-mouth-man opens the client's mouth and, using the above-mentioned tools, enlarges any holes which decay may have created in the teeth. Magical materials are put into these holes. If there are no naturally occurring holes in the teeth, large sections of one or more teeth are gouged out so that the supernatural substance can be applied. In the client's view, the purpose of these ministrations is to arrest decay and to draw friends. The extremely sacred and traditional character of the rite is evident in the fact that the natives return to the holy-mouth-man year after year, despite the fact that their teeth continue to decay.

It is to be hoped that, when a thorough study of the Nacirema is made, there will be careful inquiry into the personality structure of these people. One has but to watch the gleam in the eye of a holy-mouth-man, as he jabs an awl into an exposed nerve, to suspect that a certain amount of sadism is involved. If this can be established, a very interesting pattern emerges, for most of the population shows definite masochistic tendencies. It was to these that Professor Linton referred in discussing a distinctive part of the daily body ritual which is performed only by men. This part of the rite involves scraping and lacerating the surface of the face with a sharp instrument. Special women's rites are performed only four times during each lunar month, but what they lack in frequency is made up in barbarity. As part of this ceremony, women bake their heads in small ovens for about an hour. The theoretically interesting point is that what seems to be a preponderantly masochistic people have developed sadistic specialists.

The medicine men have an imposing temple, or *latipso*, in every community of any size. The more elaborate ceremonies required to treat very sick patients can only be performed at this temple. These ceremonies involve not only the thaumaturge but a permanent group of vestal maidens who move sedately about the temple chambers in distinctive costume and headdress.

The *latipso* ceremonies are so harsh that it is phenomenal that a fair proportion of the really sick natives who enter the temple ever recover. Small children whose indoctrination is still incomplete have been known to resist attempts to take them to the temple because "that is where you go to die." Despite this fact, sick adults are not only willing but eager to undergo the protracted ritual purification, if they can afford to do so. No matter how ill the supplicant or how grave the emergency, the guardians of many temples will not admit a client if he cannot give a rich gift to the custodian. Even after one has gained admission and survived the ceremonies, the guardians will not permit the neophyte to leave until he makes still another gift.

The supplicant entering the temple is first stripped of all his or her clothes. In everyday life the Nacirema avoids exposure of his body and its natural functions. Bathing and excretory acts are performed only in the secrecy of the household shrine, where they are ritualized as part of the body-rites. Psychological shock results from the fact that body secrecy is suddenly lost upon entry into the *latipso*. A man, whose own wife has never seen him in an excretory act, suddenly finds himself naked and assisted by a vestal maiden while he performs his natural functions into a sacred vessel. This sort of ceremonial treatment is necessitated by the fact that the excreta are used by a diviner to ascertain the course and nature of the client's sickness. Female clients, on the other hand, find their naked bodies are subjected to the scrutiny, manipulation, and prodding of the medicine men.

Few supplicants in the temple are well enough to do anything but lie on their hard beds. The daily ceremonies, like the rites of the holy-mouth-men, involve discomfort and torture. With ritual precision, the vestals awaken their miserable charges each dawn and roll them about on their beds of pain while performing ablutions, in the formal movements of which the maidens are highly trained. At other times they insert magic wands in the supplicant's mouth or force him to eat substances which are supposed to be healing. From time to time the medicine men come to their clients and jab magically treated needles into their flesh. The fact that these temple ceremonies may not cure, and may kill, the neophyte, in no way decreases the people's faith in the medicine men.

There remains one other kind of practitioner, known as a "listener." This witch-doctor has the power to exorcise the devils that lodge in the heads of people who have been bewitched. The Nacirema believe that parents bewitch their own children. Mothers are particularly suspected of putting a curse on children while teaching them the secret body rituals. The counter-magic of the witch-doctor is unusual in its lack of ritual. The patient simply tells the "listener" all his troubles and fears, beginning with the earliest difficulties he can remember. The memory displayed by the Nacirema in these exorcism sessions is truly remarkable. It is not uncommon for the patient to bemoan the rejection he felt upon being weaned as a babe, and a few individuals even see their troubles going back to the traumatic effects of their own birth.

In conclusion, mention must be made of certain practices which have their base in native esthetics but which depend upon the pervasive aversion to the natural body and its functions. There are ritual fasts to make fat people thin and ceremonial feasts to make thin people fat. Still other rites are used to make women's breasts larger if they are small, and smaller if they are large. General dissatisfaction with breast shape is symbolized in the fact that the ideal form is virtually outside the range of human variation. A few women afflicted with almost inhuman hypermammary development are so idolized that they make a handsome living by simply going from village to village and permitting the natives to stare at them for a fee.

Reference has already been made to the fact that excretory functions are ritualized, routinized, and relegated to secrecy. Natural reproductive functions are similarly distorted. Intercourse is taboo as a topic and scheduled as an act. Efforts are made to avoid pregnancy by the use of magical materials or by limiting intercourse to certain phases of the moon. Conception is actually very infrequent. When pregnant, women dress so as to hide their condition. Parturition takes place in secret, without friends or relatives to assist, and the majority of women do not nurse their infants.

Our review of the ritual life of the Nacirema has certainly shown them to be a magic-ridden people. It is hard to understand how they have managed to exist so long under the burdens which they have imposed upon themselves. But even such exotic customs as these take on real meaning when they are viewed with the insight provided by Malinowski when he wrote (1948: 70):

> Looking from far and above, from our high places of safety in the developed civilization, it is easy to see all the crudity and irrelevance of magic. But without its power and guidance early man could not have mastered his practical difficulties as he has done, nor could man have advanced to the higher stages of civilization.

REFERENCES

Linton, R. 1936. The study of man. New York: Appleton-Century.

Malinowski, B. 1948. Magic, science and religion. Glencoe, IL: Free Press.

Murdock, G. P. 1949. Social structure. New York: Macmillan.

Suggested **Web URLs** for further study:
http://www.beadsland.com/nacirema/#anthro
A web site with further related readings on the Nacirema.
http://ietn.snunit.k12.il/sacred.htm
This site takes the concepts in *Body Ritual* a step further, delving into the Asu society and their worship of Racs.

InfoTrac College Edition:
You can find further relevant readings on the World Wide Web at
http://sociology.wadsworth.com

Virtual Society
For further information on this subject including links to relevant web sites, go to the Wadsworth Sociology homepage at
http://sociology.wadsworth.com

5

India's Sacred Cow

MARVIN HARRIS

Cultures vary dramatically in their beliefs and practices, yet each cultural practice has evolved with some reason behind it. One of these practices is cow worship. In India, the cultural practice among Hindus is to treat cows with great respect, even in the face of human hunger. Harris discusses this practice, which many find curious.

Consider the following as you read:

1. Why are cows sacred? What is sacred in your country that might seem strange to others?

2. What other practices in different cultures do you find strange or unusual, and what purpose might those practices serve for the culture?

GLOSSARY

Untouchables Lowest group in the stratification (caste) system of India.

Hinduism Dominant religious belief system in India.

NEWS PHOTOGRAPHS THAT CAME out of India during the famine of the late 1960s showed starving people stretching out bony hands to beg for food while sacred cattle strolled behind undisturbed. The Hindu, it seems, would rather starve to death than eat his cow or even deprive it of food. The cattle appear to browse unhindered through urban markets eating an orange here, a mango there, competing with people for meager supplies of food.

By Western standards, spiritual values seem more important to Indians than life itself. Specialists in food habits around the world like Fred Simoons at the University of California at Davis consider Hinduism an irrational ideialogy that compels people to overlook abundant, nutritious foods for scarcer, less healthful foods.

What seems to be an absurd devotion to the mother cow pervades Indian life. Indian wall calendars portray beautiful young women with bodies of fat white cows, often with milk jetting from their teats into sacred shrines.

Cow worship even carries over into politics. In 1966 a crowd of 120,000 people, led by holy men, demonstrated in front of the Indian House of Parliament in support of the All-Party Cow Protection Campaign Committee. In Nepal, the only contemporary Hindu kingdom, cow slaughter is severely punished. As one story goes, the car driven by an official of a United States agency struck and killed a cow. In order to avoid the international incident that would have occurred when the official was arrested for murder, the Nepalese magistrate concluded that the cow had committed suicide.

Many Indians agree with Western assessments of the Hindu reverence for their cattle, the zebu, or *Bos indicus*, a large-humped species prevalent in Asia and Africa. M. N. Srinivas, an Indian anthropologist, states: "Orthodox Hindu opinion regards the killing of cattle with abhorrence, even though the refusal to kill vast number of useless cattle which exist in India today is detrimental to the nation." Even the Indian Ministry of Information formerly maintained that "the large animal population is more a liability than an asset in view of our land resources." Accounts from many different sources point to the same conclusion: India, one of the world's great civilizations, is being strangled by its love for the cow.

The easy explanation for India's devotion to the cow, the one most Westerners and Indians

From Human Nature Magazine *1(2), pp. 28, 30–36, February 1978. Copyright © 1978 by Human Nature, Inc.; reprinted by permission of the publisher.*

would offer, is that cow worship is an integral part of Hinduism. Religion is somehow good for the soul, even if it sometimes fails the body. Religion orders the cosmos and explains our place in the universe. Religious beliefs, many would claim, have existed for thousands of years and have a life of their own. They are not understandable in scientific terms.

But all this ignores history. There is more to be said for cow worship than is immediately apparent. The earliest Vedas, the Hindu sacred texts from the second millennium B.C., do not prohibit the slaughter of cattle. Instead, they ordain it as part of sacrificial rites. The early Hindus did not avoid the flesh of cows and bulls; they ate it at ceremonial feasts presided over by Brahman priests. Cow worship is a relatively recent development in India; it evolved as the Hindu religion developed and changed.

This evolution is recorded in royal edicts and religious texts written during the last 3,000 years of Indian history. The Vedas from the first millennium B.C. contain contradictory passages, some referring to ritual slaughter and others to a strict taboo on beef consumption. A. N. Bose, in *Social and Rural Economy of Northern India, 600 B.C.–200 A.D.*, concludes that many of the sacred-cow passages were incorporated into the texts by priests of a later period.

By 200 A.D. the status of Indian cattle had undergone a spiritual transformation. The Brahman priesthood exhorted the population to venerate the cow and forbade them to abuse it or to feed on it. Religious feasts involving the ritual slaughter and the consumption of livestock were eliminated and meat eating was restricted to the nobility.

By 1000 A.D., all Hindus were forbidden to eat beef. Ahimsa, the Hindu belief in the unity of all life, was the spiritual justification for this restriction. But it is difficult to ascertain exactly when this change occurred. An important event that helped to shape the modern complex was the Islamic invasion, which took place in the eighth century A.D. Hindus may have found it politically expedient to set themselves off from the invaders, who were beefeaters, by emphasiz-

ing the need to prevent the slaughter of their sacred animals. Thereafter, the cow taboo assumed its modern form and began to function much as it does today.

The place of the cow in modern India is every place—on posters, in the movies, in brass figures, in stone and wood carvings, on the streets, in the fields. The cow is a symbol of health and abundance. It provides the milk that Indians consume in the form of yogurt and ghee (clarified butter), which contribute subtle flavors to much spicy Indian food.

This, perhaps, is the practical role of the cow, but cows provide less than half the milk produced in India. Most cows in India are not dairy breeds. In most regions, when an Indian farmer wants a steady, high-quality source of milk he usually invests in a female water buffalo. In India the water buffalo is the specialized dairy breed because its milk has a higher butterfat content than zebu milk. Although the farmer milks his zebu cows, the milk is merely a by-product.

More vital than zebu milk to South Asian farmers are zebu calves. Male calves are especially valued because from bulls come oxen, which are the mainstay of the Indian agricultural system.

Small, fast oxen drag wooden plows through late-spring fields when monsoons have dampened the dry, cracked earth. After harvest, the oxen break the grain from the stalk by stomping through mounds of cut wheat and rice. For rice cultivation in irrigated fields, the male water buffalo is preferred (it pulls better in deep mud), but for most other crops, including rainfall rice, wheat, sorghum, and millet, and for transporting goods and people to and from town, a team of oxen is preferred. The ox is the Indian peasant's tractor, thresher, and family car combined; the cow is the factory that produces the ox.

If draft animals instead of cows are counted, India appears to have too few domesticated ruminants, not too many. Since each of the 70 million farms in India requires a draft team, it follows that Indian peasants should use 140 million animals in the fields. But there are only 83 million oxen and male water buffalo on the subcontinent, a shortage of 30 million draft teams.

In other regions of the world, joint ownership of draft animals might overcome a shortage, but Indian agriculture is closely tied to the monsoon rains of late spring and summer. Field preparation and planting must coincide with the rain, and a farmer must have his animals ready to plow when the weather is right. When the farmer without a draft team needs bullocks most, his neighbors are all using theirs. Any delay in turning the soil drastically lowers production.

Because of this dependence on draft animals, loss of the family oxen is devastating. If a beast dies, the farmer must borrow money to buy or rent an ox at interest rates so high that he ultimately loses his land. Every year foreclosures force thousands of poverty-stricken peasants to abandon the countryside for the overcrowded cities.

If a family is fortunate enough to own a fertile cow, it will be able to rear replacements for a lost team and thus survive until life returns to normal. If, as sometimes happens, famine leads a family to sell its cow and ox team, all ties to agriculture are cut. Even if the family survives, it has no way to farm the land, no oxen to work the land, and no cows to produce oxen.

The prohibition against eating meat applies to the flesh of cows, bulls, and oxen, but the cow is the most sacred because it can produce the other two. The peasant whose cow dies is not only crying over a spiritual loss but over the loss of his farm as well.

Religious laws that forbid the slaughter of cattle promote the recovery of the agricultural system from the dry Indian winter and from periods of drought. The monsoon, on which all agriculture depends, is erratic. Sometimes, it arrives early, sometimes late, sometimes not at all. Drought has struck large portions of India time and again in this century, and Indian farmers and the zebus are accustomed to these natural disasters. Zebus can pass weeks on end with little or no food and water. Like camels, they store both in their humps and recuperate quickly with only a little nourishment.

During droughts the cows often stop lactating and become barren. In some cases the condition is permanent but often it is only temporary. If barren animals were summarily eliminated, as Western experts in animal husbandry have suggested, cows capable of recovery would be lost along with those entirely debilitated. By keeping alive the cows that can later produce oxen, religious laws against cow slaughter assure the recovery of the agricultural system from the greatest challenge it faces—the failure of the monsoon.

The local Indian governments aid the process of recovery by maintaining homes for barren cows. Farmers reclaim any animal that calves or begins to lactate. One police station in Madras collects strays and pastures them in a field adjacent to the station. After a small fine is paid, a cow is returned to its rightful owner when the owner thinks the cow shows signs of being able to reproduce.

During the hot, dry spring months most of India is like a desert. Indian farmers often complain they cannot feed their livestock during this period. They maintain the cattle by letting them scavenge on the sparse grass along the roads. In the cities the cattle are encouraged to scavenge near food stalls to supplement their scant diet. These are the wandering cattle tourists report seeing throughout India.

Westerners expect shopkeepers to respond to these intrusions with the deference due a sacred animal; instead, their response is a string of curses and the crack of a long bamboo pole across the beast's back or a poke at its genitals. Mahatma Gandhi was well aware of the treatment sacred cows (and bulls and oxen) received in India. "How we bleed her to take the last drop of milk from her. How we starve her to emaciation, how we ill-treat the calves, how we deprive them of their portion of milk, how cruelly we treat the oxen, how we castrate them, how we beat them, how we overload them" [Gandhi, 1954].

Oxen generally receive better treatment than cows. When food is in short supply, thrifty Indian peasants feed their working bullocks and ignore their cows, but rarely do they abandon the cows to die. When the cows are sick, farmers worry over them as they would over members of the family and nurse them as if they were children. When the rains return and when the fields are harvested, the farmers again feed their cows regularly and reclaim their abandoned animals. The prohibition against beef consumption is a form of disaster insurance for all India.

Western agronomists and economists are quick to protest that all the functions of the zebu cattle can be improved with organized breeding programs, cultivated pastures, and silage. Because stronger oxen would pull the plow faster, they could work multiple plots of land, allowing farmers to share their animals. Fewer healthy, well-fed cows could provide Indians with more milk. But pastures and silage require arable land, land needed to produce wheat and rice.

A look at Western cattle farming makes plain the cost of adopting advanced technology in Indian agriculture. In a study of livestock production in the United States, David Pimentel of the College of Agriculture and Life Sciences at Cornell University, found that 91 percent of the cereal, legume, and vegetable protein suitable for human consumption is consumed by livestock. Approximately three-quarters of the arable land in the United States is devoted to growing food for livestock. In the production of meat and milk, American ranchers use enough fossil fuel to equal more than 82 million barrels of oil annually.

Indian cattle do not drain the system in the same way. In a 1971 study of livestock in West Bengal, Stewart Odend'hal [1972] of the University of Missouri found that Bengalese cattle ate only the inedible remains of subsistence crops—rice straw, rice hulls, the tops of sugar cane, and mustard-oil cake. Cattle graze in the fields after harvest and eat the remains of crops left on the ground; they forage for grass and weeds on the roadsides. The food for zebu cattle costs the human population virtually nothing. "Basically," Odend'hal says, "the cattle convert items of little direct human value into products of immediate utility."

In addition to plowing the fields and producing milk, the zebus produce dung, which fires the hearths and fertilizes the fields of India. Much of the estimated 800 million tons of manure produced annually is collected by the farmers' children as they follow the cows and bullocks from place to place. And when the children see the droppings of another farmer's cattle along the road, they pick those up also. Odend'hal reports that the system operates with such high efficiency that the children of West Bengal recover nearly 100 percent of the dung produced by their livestock.

From 40 to 70 percent of all manure produced by Indian cattle is used as fuel for cooking; the rest is returned to the fields as fertilizer. Dried dung burns slowly, cleanly, and with low heat—characteristics that satisfy the household needs of Indian women. Staples like curry and rice can simmer for hours. While the meal slowly cooks over an unattended fire, the women of the household can do other chores. Cow chips, unlike firewood, do not scorch as they burn.

It is estimated that the dung used for cooking fuel provides the energy-equivalent of 43 million tons of coal. At current prices, it would cost India an extra 1.5 billion dollars in foreign exchange to replace the dung with coal. And if the 350 million tons of manure that are being used as fertilizer were replaced with commercial fertilizers, the expense would be even greater. Roger Revelle of the University of California at San Diego has calculated that 89 percent of the energy used in Indian agriculture (the equivalent of about 140 million tons of coal) is provided by local sources. Even if foreign loans were to provide the money, the capital outlay necessary to replace the Indian cow with tractors and fertilizers for the fields, coal for the fires, and transportation for the family would probably warp international financial institutions for years.

Instead of asking the Indians to learn from the American model of industrial agriculture, American farmers might learn energy conservation from the Indians. Every step in an energy cycle results in a loss of energy to the system. Like a pendulum that slows a bit with each swing, each transfer of energy from sun to plants, plants to animals, and animals to human beings involves energy losses. Some systems are more efficient than others; they provide a higher percentage of the energy inputs in a final, useful form. Seventeen percent of all energy zebus consume is returned in the form of milk, traction, and dung. American cattle raised on Western rangeland return only 4 percent of the energy they consume.

But the American system is improving. Based on techniques pioneered by Indian scientists, as least one commercial firm in the United States is reported to be building plants that will turn manure from cattle feedlots into combustible gas. When organic matter is broken down by anaerobic bacteria, methane gas and carbon dioxide are produced. After the methane is cleansed of the carbon dioxide, it is available for the same purposes as natural gas—cooking, heating, electric generation. The company constructing the biogasification plant plans to sell its product to a gas-supply company, to be piped through the existing distribution system. Schemes similar to this one could make cattle ranches almost independent of utility and gasoline companies, for methane can be used to run trucks, tractors, and cars as well as to supply heat and electricity. The relative energy self-sufficiency that the Indian peasant has achieved is a goal American farmers and industry are now striving for.

Studies like Odend'hal's understate the efficiency of the Indian cow, because dead cows are used for purposes that Hindus prefer not to acknowledge. When a cow dies, an Untouchable, a member of one of the lowest ranking castes in India, is summoned to haul away the carcass. Higher castes consider the body of the dead cow polluting; if they handle it, they must go through a rite of purification.

Untouchables first skin the dead animal and either tan the skin themselves or sell it to a leather factory. In the privacy of their homes, contrary to the teachings of Hinduism, untouchable castes cook the meat and eat it. Indians of all castes rarely acknowledge the existence of these practices to non-Hindus, but most are aware that beefeating takes place. The prohibition against beefeating restricts consumption by the higher castes and helps distribute animal protein to the poorest sectors of the population that otherwise would have no source of these vital nutrients.

Untouchables are not the only Indians who consume beef. Indian Muslims and Christians are under no restriction that forbids them beef, and its consumption is legal in many places. The Indian ban on cow slaughter is state, not national, law and not all states restrict it. In many cities, such as New Delhi, Calcutta, and Bombay, legal slaughterhouses sell beef to retail customers and to restaurants that serve steak.

If the caloric value of beef and the energy costs involved in the manufacture of synthetic leather were included in the estimate of energy, the calculated efficiency of Indian livestock would rise considerably. As well as the system works, experts often claim that its efficiency can be further improved. Alan Heston [et al., 1971], an economist at the University of Pennsylvania, believes that Indians suffer from an overabundance of cows simply because they refuse to slaughter the excess cattle. India could produce at least the same number of oxen and the same quantities of milk and manure with 30 million fewer cows. Heston calculates that only 40 cows are necessary to maintain a population of 100 bulls and oxen. Since India averages 70 cows for every 100 bullocks, the difference, 30 million cows, is expendable.

What Heston fails to note is that sex ratios among cattle in different regions of India vary tremendously, indicating that adjustments in the cow population do take place. Along the Ganges River, one of the holiest shrines of Hinduism, the ratio drops to 47 cows for every 100 male animals. This ratio reflects the preference for dairy buffalo in the irrigated sectors of the Gangetic Plains. In nearby Pakistan, in contrast, where cow slaughter is permitted, the sex ratio is 60 cows to 100 oxen.

Since the sex ratios among cattle differ greatly from region to region and do not even approximate the balance that would be expected if no females were killed, we can assume that some culling of herds does take place; Indians do adjust their religious restrictions to accommodate ecological realities.

They cannot kill a cow but they can tether an old or unhealthy animal until it has starved to death. They cannot slaughter a calf but they can yoke it with a large wooden triangle so that when it nurses it irritates the mother's udder and gets kicked to death. They cannot ship their animals to the slaughterhouse but they can sell them to Muslims, closing their eyes to the fact that the Muslims will take the cattle to the slaughterhouse.

These violations of the prohibition against cattle slaughter strengthen the premise that cow worship is a vital part of Indian culture. The practice arose to prevent the population from consuming the animal on which Indian agriculture depends. During the first millennium B.C., the Ganges Valley became one of the most densely populated regions of the world.

Where previously there had been only scattered villages, many towns and cities arose and peasants farmed every available acre of land. Kingsley Davis, a population expert at the University of California at Berkeley, estimates that by 300 B.C. between 50 million and 100 million people were living in India. The forested Ganges Valley became a windswept semidesert and signs of ecological collapse appeared; droughts and floods became commonplace, erosion took away the rich topsoil, farms shrank as population increased, and domesticated animals became harder and harder to maintain.

It is probable that the elimination of meat eating came about in a slow, practical manner. The farmers who decided not to eat their cows, who saved them for procreation to produce oxen, were the ones who survived the natural disasters. Those who ate beef lost the tools with which to farm. Over a period of centuries, more and more farmers probably avoided beef until an unwritten taboo came into existence.

Only later was the practice codified by the priesthood. While Indian peasants were probably aware of the role of cattle in their society, strong sanctions were necessary to protect zebus from a population faced with starvation. To remove temptation, the flesh of cattle became taboo and the cow became sacred.

The sacredness of the cow is not just an ignorant belief that stands in the way of progress. Like all concepts of the sacred and the profane, this one affects the physical world; it defines the relationships that are important for the maintenance of Indian society.

Indians have the sacred cow, we have the "sacred" car and the "sacred" dog. It would not occur to us to propose the elimination of automobiles and dogs from our society without carefully considering the consequences, and we should not propose the elimination of zebu cattle without first understanding their place in the social order of India.

Human society is neither random nor capricious. The regularities of thought and behavior called culture are the principal mechanisms by which we human beings adapt to the world around us. Practices and beliefs can be rational or irrational, but a society that fails to adapt to its environment is doomed to extinction. Only those societies that draw the necessities of life from their surroundings inherit the earth. The West has much to learn from the great antiquity of Indian civilization, and the sacred cow is an important part of that lesson.

REFERENCES

Gandhi, Mohandas K. 1954. *How to Serve the Cow.* Bombay: Navajivan Publishing House.

Heston, Alan, et al. 1971. "An Approach to the Sacred Cow of India." *Current Anthropology* 12, 191–209.

Odend'hal, Stewart. 1972. "Gross Energetic Efficiency of Indian Cattle in Their Environment." *Journal of Human Ecology* 1, 1–27.

6

Code of the Street

ELIJAH ANDERSON

Elijah Anderson's study of interaction on the street shows the vast array of implicit "codes" of behavior or rules that guide street interaction. His analysis helps explain the complexity of street interaction and provides a sociological explanation of street violence.

In some of the most economically depressed and drug- and crime-ridden pockets of the city, the rules of civil law have been severely weakened, and in their stead a "code of the street" often holds sway. At the heart of this code is a set of prescriptions and proscriptions, or informal rules, of behavior organized around a desperate search for respect that governs public social relations, especially violence, among so many residents, particularly young men and women. Possession of respect—and the credible threat of vengeance—is highly valued for shielding the ordinary person from the interpersonal violence of the street. In this social context of persistent poverty and deprivation, alienation from broader society's institutions, notably that of criminal justice, is widespread. The code of the street emerges where the influence of the police ends and personal responsibility for one's safety is felt to begin, resulting in a kind of "people's law," based on "street justice." This code involves a quite primitive form of social exchange that holds would-be perpetrators accountable by promising an "eye for an eye," or a certain "payback" for transgressions. In service to this ethic, repeated displays of "nerve" and "heart" build or reinforce a credible reputation for vengeance that works to deter aggression and disrespect, which are sources of great anxiety on the inner-city street. . . .

In approaching the goal of painting an ethnographic picture of these phenomena, I engaged in participant-observation, including direct observation, and conducted in-depth interviews. Impressionistic materials were drawn from various social settings around the city, from some of the wealthiest to some of the most economically depressed, including carryouts, "stop and go" establishments, Laundromats, taverns, playgrounds, public schools, the Center City indoor mall known as the Gallery, jails, and public street corners. In these settings I encountered a wide variety of people—adolescent boys and young women (some incarcerated, some not), older men, teenage mothers, grandmothers, and male and female schoolteachers, black and white, drug dealers, and common criminals. To protect the privacy and confidentiality of my subjects, names and certain details have been disguised. . . .

From: Elijah Anderson. 1999. *Code of the Street.* New York: W. W. Norton, pp. 9–11, 32–34, 312–317. Reprinted with permission.

Of all the problems besetting the poor inner-city black community, none is more pressing than that of interpersonal violence and aggression. This phenomenon wreaks havoc daily on the lives of community residents and increasingly spills over into downtown and residential middle-class areas. Muggings, burglaries, carjackings, and drug-related shootings, all of which may leave their victims or innocent bystanders dead, are now common enough to concern all urban and many suburban residents.

The inclination to violence springs from the circumstances of life among the ghetto poor—the lack of jobs that pay a living wage, limited basic public services (police response in emergencies, building maintenance, trash pickup, lighting, and other services that middle-class neighborhoods take for granted), the stigma of race, the fallout from rampant drug use and drug trafficking, and the resulting alienation and absence of hope for the future. Simply living in such an environment places young people at special risk of falling victim to aggressive behavior. Although there are often forces in the community that can counteract the negative influences—by far the most powerful is a strong, loving, "decent" (as inner-city residents put it) family that is committed to middle-class values—the despair is pervasive enough to have spawned an oppositional culture, that of "the street," whose norms are often consciously opposed to those of mainstream society. These two orientations—decent and street—organize the community socially, and the way they coexist and interact has important consequences for its residents, particularly for children growing up in the inner city. Above all, this environment means that even youngsters whose home lives reflect mainstream values—and most of the homes in the community do—must be able to handle themselves in a street-oriented environment.

This is because the street culture has evolved a "code of the street," which amounts to a set of informal rules governing interpersonal public behavior, particularly violence. The rules prescribe both proper comportment and the proper way to respond if challenged. They regulate the use of violence and so supply a rationale allowing those who are inclined to aggression to precipitate violent encounters in an approved way. The rules have been established and are enforced mainly by the street-oriented; but on the streets the distinction between street and decent is often irrelevant. Everybody knows that if the rules are violated, there are penalties. Knowledge of the code is thus largely defensive, and it is literally necessary for operating in public. Therefore, though families with a decency orientation are usually opposed to the values of the code, they often reluctantly encourage their children's familiarity with it in order to enable them to negotiate the inner-city environment.

At the heart of the code is the issue of respect—loosely defined as being treated "right" or being granted one's "props" (or proper due) or the deference one deserves. However, in the troublesome public environment of the inner city, as people increasingly feel buffeted by forces beyond their control, what one deserves in the way of respect becomes ever more problematic and uncertain. This situation in turn further opens up the issue of respect to sometimes intense interpersonal negotiation, at times resulting in altercations. In the street culture, especially among young people, respect is viewed as almost an external entity, one that is hard-won but easily lost—and so must constantly be guarded. The rules of the code in fact provide a framework for negotiating respect. With the right amount of respect, individuals can avoid being bothered in public. This security is important, for if they *are* bothered, not only may they face physical danger, but they will have been disgraced or "dissed" (disrespected). Many of the forms dissing can take may seem petty to middle-class people (maintaining eye contact for too long, for example), but to those invested in the street code, these actions, a virtual slap in the face, become serious indications of the other person's intentions. Consequently, such people become very sensitive to advances and slights, which could well serve as a warning of imminent physical attack or confrontation.

The hard reality of the world of the street can be traced to the profound sense of alienation from mainstream society and its institutions felt by many poor inner-city black people, particularly the young. The code of the street is actually a cultural adaptation to a profound lack of faith in the police and the judicial system—and in others who would champion one's personal security. The police, for instance, are most often viewed as representing the dominant white society and as not caring to protect inner-city residents. When called, they may not respond, which is one reason many residents feel they must be prepared to take extraordinary measures to defend themselves and their loved ones against those who are inclined to aggression. Lack of police accountability has in fact been incorporated into the local status system: the person who is believed capable of "taking care of himself" is accorded a certain deference and regard, which translates into a sense of physical and psychological control. The code of the street thus emerges where the influence of the police ends and where personal responsibility for one's safety is felt to begin. Exacerbated by the proliferation of drugs and easy access to guns, this volatile situation results in the ability of the street-oriented minority (or those who effectively "go for bad") to dominate the public spaces. . . .

The attitudes and actions of the wider society are deeply implicated in the code of the street. Most people residing in inner-city communities are not totally invested in the code; it is the significant minority of hard-core street youth who maintain the code in order to establish reputations that are integral to the extant social order. Because of the grinding poverty of the communities these people inhabit, many have—or feel they have—few other options for expressing themselves. For them the standards and rules of the street code are the only game in town.

And as was indicated above, the decent people may find themselves caught up in problematic situations simply by being at the wrong place at the wrong time, which is why a primary survival strategy of residents here is to "see but don't see." The extent to which some children—particularly those who through upbringing have become most alienated and those who lack strong and conventional social support—experience, feel, and internalize racist rejection and contempt from mainstream society may strongly encourage them to express contempt for the society in turn. In dealing with this contempt and rejection, some youngsters consciously invest themselves and their considerable mental resources in what amounts to an oppositional culture, a part of which is the code of the street. They do so to preserve themselves and their own self-respect. Once they do, any respect they might be able to garner in the wider system pales in comparison with the respect available in the local system; thus they often lose interest in even attempting to negotiate the mainstream system.

At the same time, many less alienated young people have assumed a street-oriented demeanor as way of expressing their blackness while really embracing a much more moderate way of life; they, too, want a nonviolent setting in which to live and one day possibly raise a family. These decent people are trying hard to be part of the mainstream culture, but the racism, real and perceived, that they encounter helps legitimate the oppositional culture and, by extension, the code of the street. On occasion they adopt street behavior; in fact, depending on the demands of the situation, many people attempt to codeswitch, moving back and forth between decent and street behavior. . . .

In addition, the community is composed of working-class and very poor people since those with the means to move away have done so, and there has also been a proliferation of single-parent households in which increasing numbers of kids are being raised on welfare. The result of all this is that the inner-city community has become a kind of urban village, apart from the wider society and limited in terms of resources and human capital. Young people growing up here often receive only the truncated version of mainstream society that comes from television and the perceptions of their peers. . . .

According to the code, the white man is a mysterious entity, a part of an enormous monolithic mass of arbitrary power, in whose view black people are insignificant. In this system and in the local social context, the black man has very little clout; to salvage something of value, he must outwit, deceive, oppose, and ultimately "end-run" the system.

Moreover, he cannot rely on this system to protect him; the responsibility is his, and he is on his own. If someone rolls on him, he has to put his body, and often his life, on the line. The physicality of manhood thus becomes extremely important. And urban brinksmanship is observed and learned as a matter of course. . . .

Urban areas have experienced profound structural economic changes, as deindustrialization—the movement from manufacturing to service and high-tech—and the growth of the global economy have created new economic conditions. Job opportunities increasingly go abroad to Singapore, Taiwan, India, and Mexico, and to nonmetropolitan America, to satellite cities like King of Prussia, Pennsylvania. Over the last fifteen years, for example, Philadelphia has lost 102,500 jobs, and its manufacturing employment has declined by 53 percent. Large numbers of inner-city people, in particular, are not adjusting effectively to the new economic reality. Whereas low-wage jobs—especially unskilled and low-skill factory jobs—used to exist simultaneously with poverty and there was hope for the future, now jobs simply do not exist, the present economic boom notwithstanding. These dislocations have left many inner-city people unable to earn a decent living. More must be done by both government and business to connect inner-city people with jobs.

The condition of these communities was produced not by moral turpitude but by economic forces that have undermined black, urban, working-class life and by a neglect of their consequences on the part of the public. Although it is true that persistent welfare dependency, teenage pregnancy, drug abuse, drug dealing, violence, and crime reinforce economic marginality, many of these behavioral problems originated in frustrations and the inability to thrive under conditions of economic dislocation. This in turn leads to a weakening of social and family structure, so children are increasingly not being socialized into mainstream values and behavior. In this context, people develop profound alienation and may not know what to do about an opportunity even when it presents itself. In other words, the social ills that the companies moving out of these neighborhoods today sometimes use to justify their exodus are the same ones that their corporate predecessors, by leaving, helped to create.

Any effort to place the blame solely on individuals in urban ghettos is seriously misguided. The focus should be on the socioeconomic structure, because it was structural change that caused jobs to decline and joblessness to increase in many of these communities. But the focus also belongs on the public policy that has radically threatened the well-being of many citizens. Moreover, residents of these communities lack good education, job training, and job networks, or connections with those who could help them get jobs. They need enlightened employers able to understand their predicament and willing to give them a chance. Government, which should be assisting people to adjust to the changed economy, is instead cutting what little help it does provide. . . .

The emergence of an underclass isolated in urban ghettos with high rates of joblessness can be traced to the interaction of race prejudice, discrimination, and the effects of the global economy. These factors have contributed to the profound social isolation and impoverishment of broad segments of the inner-city black population. Even though the wider society and economy have been experiencing accelerated prosperity for almost a decade, the fruits of it often miss the truly disadvantaged isolated in urban poverty pockets.

In their social isolation an oppositional culture, a subset of which is the code of the street, has been allowed to emerge, grow, and develop. This culture is essentially one of accommodation with the wider society, but different from past efforts to accommodate the system. A larger segment of people are now not simply isolated but ever more profoundly alienated from the wider society and its institutions. For instance, in conducting the fieldwork for this book, I visited numerous inner-city schools, including elementary, middle, and high schools, located in areas of concentrated poverty. In every one, the so-called oppositional culture was well entrenched. In one elementary school, I learned from interviewing kindergarten, first-grade, second-grade, and fourth-grade teachers that through the first grade, about a fifth of the students were invested in the code of the street; the rest are interested in the subject matter and eager to take instruction from the teachers—in effect, well disciplined. By the fourth grade, though, about three-quarters of the students have bought into the code of the street or the oppositional culture.

As I have indicated throughout this work, the code emerges from the school's impoverished neighborhood, including overwhelming numbers of single-parent homes, where the fathers, uncles, and older brothers are frequently incarcerated—so frequently, in fact, that the word "incarcerated" is a prominent part of the young child's spoken vocabulary. In such communities there is not only a high rate of crime but also a generalized diminution of respect for law. As the residents go about meeting the exigencies of public life, a kind of people's law results, . . . Typically, the local streets are, as was we saw, tough and dangerous places where people often feel very much on their own, where they themselves must be personally responsible for their own security, and where in order to be safe and to travel the public spaces unmolested, they must be able to show others that they are familiar with the code—that physical transgressions will be met in kind.

In these circumstances the dominant legal codes are not the first thing on one's mind; rather, personal security for self, family, and loved ones is. Adults, dividing themselves into categories of street and decent, often encourage their children in this adaptation to their situation, but at what price to the children and at what price to wider values of civility and decency? As the fortunes of the inner city continue to decline, the situation becomes ever more dismal and intractable. . . .

DISCUSSION QUESTIONS

1. List several ways that subtle or nonverbal behavior becomes important "on the street."
2. What specific ways does Anderson see street behavior as stemming from social structural conditions for African Americans?

INFOTRAC COLLEGE EDITION

You can use your access to InfoTrac College Edition to learn more about the subjects covered in this essay. Some suggested search terms include:

inner-city violence
oppositional culture
police harassment

street violence
streetwise

7

Upper-Class Power

HAROLD R. KERBO

In class-based stratification systems the upper classes or elites of society dominate the corporate structure and the political structure. Kerbo analyzes the means by which the upper class dominates the corporate structure and the political structure.

As you read, ask yourself the following questions:

1. *What tactics do members of the upper class use in order to dominate?*
2. *What changes would you make to adjust the power of the upper class?*

UPPER-CLASS ECONOMIC POWER

If we have an upper class in this country that, because of its power, can be described as a governing class, by what means does it govern or dominate? . . . We will examine first how the upper class is said to have extensive influence over the economy through stock ownership, then turn to the question of economic power through extensive representation in major corporate offices.

Stock Ownership As some argue, the most important means of upper-class economic power lies in its ownership of the primary means of production. The upper class has power over our economy because of its control of the biggest corporations through stock ownership. . . .

Legally, the ultimate control of corporations is found not with top corporate executives, but with major stockholders. In a sense, top corporate executives and boards of directors are charged with managing these corporations for the real owners—the stockholders. Stockholders have the authority to elect corporate directors

who are to represent stockholder interests. These directors are then responsible for general corporate policy, including the task of filling top executive positions. The day-to-day management of the corporation is in turn the responsibility of the executive officers, who must generally answer to stockholders and their representatives on the board of directors.

Assuming for now that corporate authority actually operates this way . . . the largest stockholder or stockholders in a corporation should be in control. Thus, if we find that upper-class families have extensive stock ownership and that this stock is in major corporations, we can say that upper-class families dominate the American economy.

It is clear . . . that wealth is very unequally distributed in this country—more so even than family or personal income. One of the most important categories of wealth . . . is corporate stock. . . . 1 percent of the people in this country owned *56.5 percent* of the privately held corporate stock, and only 0.5 percent of the people owned *49.3 percent* of the privately held corporate stock in the United States. Thus, from 1 to 0.5 percent of the people in this country . . . hold most of the privately owned corporate stock.

This concentration of private stock ownership is even more striking when we find that most of the remaining stock is controlled by large financial corporations (see U.S. Senate Committee on Governmental Affairs 1978a, 1980; Kerbo and Della Fave 1983, 1984). To the degree that the upper class also has a lot of influence over these financial corporations (such as banks with large amounts of stock control in other big corporations), the actual stock control of the upper class is much greater. . . .

In the early stages of industrialization in this country the control of corporations was fairly easy to estimate. Most corporations were owned, and thus controlled, by specific families. We knew, for example, that the Rockefeller family controlled Standard Oil, the McCormick family controlled International Harvester, the Mellon family controlled the Aluminum Company of America, and the Morgan family controlled Morgan Bank by virtue of their extensive stock ownership of these companies. But this concentration of stock ownership by specific families in one or a few corporations has changed greatly in recent decades. Few clearly family-controlled corporations such as the Ford Motor Company (with the Ford family owning 40 percent of the stock) are found today.

Because of the wide distribution of stockholders in most corporations, government agencies and researchers agree that 5 to 10 percent ownership in a particular company by a family will often result in control of that company by the family.

A government study, however, found only 13 of the top 122 corporations in this country to be clearly controlled by one family (see U.S. Senate Committee on Governmental Affairs 1978a:252). But we must emphasize clearly controlled. One of the problems in determining control is that the ownership of stock in specific corporations is often hidden. For example, the owner of stock may be listed under meaningless names (such as street names) or under trusts and foundations (Zeitlin, 1974). To make the situation even more complex, corporations (especially banks) control stock in other corporations.

Consider the following situation: A family owns about 2 percent of the stock in corporation A, with other families also owning about 2 percent each. In turn, this original family owns, say, 5 percent of the stock in corporation B (a bank) and 6 percent in corporation C (an insurance company). We find upon further investigation that company B (the bank) controls 4 per-cent of the stock in corporation A, and corporation C (the insurance company) controls 7 percent of the stock in corporation A. Who controls corporation A?

It *may* be that our original family does, through its stock in corporation A, as well as B and C. But other families own stock in A who in addition have much stock in corporations D and E. And (you are probably ahead of me), corporations D and E also control stock in corporation A! This example is not an exaggeration, as anyone will see in examining the data on stock ownership published in a Senate study (U.S. Senate Committee on Governmental Affairs 1978a, 1980). In the face of this complexity of wide stockholdings, many researchers simply conclude that top managers of a corporation control by default (for example, Berle 1959; Galbraith 1971; Bell 1976). But, as we will see in the following, this generalization also has many drawbacks.

Upper-Class Backgrounds of Economic Elites
Aside from actual stock ownership, there is another possible means of upper-class leverage over the economy. After the authority of stockholders in a corporation, we find the board of directors and top executive officers. We will call these people *economic elites*. The family backgrounds of these economic elites may be important in how they think, whom they trust, and what group interests they serve while making decisions in their positions of authority in the corporate world. Ruling-class theorists such as Domhoff believe that these economic elites often come from, or have backgrounds in, upper-class families. Thus, even if upper-class families may not own enough stock to control many corporations, their people are there in important positions of authority. . . .

Domhoff's (1967) examined the directors from many top corporations. He found . . . that of the top twenty industrial corporations, 54 percent of the board members were from the upper class; of the top fifteen banks, 62 percent were upper-class members; of the top fifteen insurance companies, 44 percent were upper-class members; of the top fifteen transportation companies, 53 percent were upper-class members; and of the top fifteen utility corporations, 30 percent were upper-class members. Clearly we find much overrepresentation by the upper class on these boards of directors when it is noted that the upper class accounts for only about 0.5 percent of the population. . . .

In another study Soref (1976) took a random sample of board members from the top 121 corporations in the United States. Using Domhoff's definition of upper class, he found upper-class board members had more board positions in other companies (average of 3.49 for upper-class directors, 2.0 for others), and were more often members of board subcommittees that made important long-range decisions in the company. . . .

In conclusion, we find some evidence supporting the argument that the upper class is able to dominate the economy through positions of authority in major corporations. But this evidence is far from conclusive. . . .

There is also the question of whether upper-class members act exclusively to protect the interests of the upper class when in positions of corporate authority. In part, this second reservation pertains to the strength of upper-class unity and consciousness discussed earlier. It is clear that corporate elite membership in social clubs and interlocking directorates through multiple board memberships help unify the structure of large corporations today. However, the question of whose interests (an upper class or corporate elites themselves) are served by this unified corporate structure remains inadequately answered.

UPPER-CLASS POLITICAL POWER

The next questions of importance for ruling-class or governing-class theorists are the degree and means of political power exercised by the upper class. The significance of the state, and especially the federal government, on domestic affairs in this nation has increased rapidly since the 1930s. We find today a federal government with an annual budget well over $1.5 trillion, with programs designed for such purposes as regulating the economy as well as its traditional job of managing foreign affairs.

The potential impact of the federal government upon upper-class interests is clear. If the upper class is to maintain a position of dominance in the nation, it is imperative that it have influence over the state as well as the economy. In this section we will consider evidence suggesting upper class influence over the government through (1) direct participation by the upper class in politics, (2) the selection of government leaders, (3) the activities of lobby organizations, and (4) organizations established to shape the development of government policy.

Upper-Class Participation in Government
Research on direct participation by the upper class in government is focused heavily on the president's cabinet. Cabinet members are under the direction of the president, but because of the president's many concerns and lack of time in gathering all the needed information in making policy, the president must rely heavily upon cabinet members for advice and information. If these cabinet members represent the interests of the upper class, they can provide the president with information to guide his policy decisions in a way that will ensure that upper-class interests are maintained. . . .

Using his definition of upper-class membership outlined earlier, Domhoff (1967:97–99; see also Kerbo and Della Fave 1979:7) examined the backgrounds of secretaries of state, the treasury, and defense between 1932 and 1964. He found that 63 percent of the secretaries of state, 62 percent of the secretaries of defense, and 63 percent of the secretaries of the treasury could be classified as members of the upper class before assuming office. . . . As Domhoff admits, the preceding represents only a small part of the cabinet for a period of little more than thirty years. But with these positions we find the upper class represented in proportions far greater than their 0.5 percent of the population would suggest.

Since Domhoff's earlier work, an extensive study of cabinet members has been conducted by

Beth Mintz (1975). Using Domhoff's indicators of upper-class membership, Mintz (1975, along with Peter Freitag, 1975) undertook the massive job of examining the backgrounds of all cabinet members (205 people) serving between 1897 and 1973. Her most interesting finding at this point is that *66 percent* of these cabinet members could be classified as members of the upper class before obtaining their cabinet positions. . . . Also interesting is that the number of cabinet members coming from the upper class was fairly consistent between 1897 and 1973. . . . And in case anyone believes that the wealthy and upper class strongly favor Republicans over Democrats, Mintz's data show that Republican presidents chose over 71 percent of their cabinet members from the upper class, while Democratic presidents chose over 60 percent from the upper class.

In her background research on these cabinet members, Mintz also included information pertaining to the previous occupations of these people. Along with Freitag (1975), she reports that over 76 percent of the cabinet members were associated with big corporations before or after their cabinet position, 54 percent were from *both* the upper class and top corporate positions, and *90 percent* either came from the upper class or were associated with big corporations. Focusing on corporate ties of cabinet members, Freitag (1975) shows that these ties have not changed much over the years, and vary only slightly by particular cabinet position. In fact, even most secretaries of labor have been associated with big corporations in the capacity of top executives, board members, or corporate lawyers.

Most ruling-class or governing-class theorists consider the cabinet to be the most important position for direct government participation by the upper class. The cabinet allows easy movement into government and then back to top corporate positions. As might be expected, Mintz (1975) found most cabinet members between 1897 and 1973 coming from outside of government, rather than working their way up within government bureaucracies. The United States and England are unique in this aspect of top government elite recruitment. Put-

nam (1976:48–49) has found that in most other Western industrial societies the top political elites (with positions comparable to those in the U.S. cabinet) are more likely to come from within government bureaucracies, working their way to the top in a line of career promotions. In the United States and England, this atypical method of political elite recruitment affords the upper class and corporate elite opportunities for political influence lacking in these other industrial nations.

In a massive three-volume work by Burch (1981) examining elites throughout American history, we find that the rich and corporate elite have always dominated the top federal government positions. From 1789 to 1861, 96 percent of the cabinet and diplomatic appointees "were members of the economic elite, with a great many landowners, lawyers, and merchants in the group" (Domhoff 1983:142). Then from 1861 to 1933 the proportion was 84 percent, with more of these people now coming from major corporations that did not exist before 1861. . . .

Political Campaign Contributions Today it costs money, lots of money, to obtain a major elective office. In 1972, for example, Richard Nixon spent $60 million to win reelection, while his opponent spent $30 million. Since this time limits have been placed on presidential campaigns, but House and Senate campaigns have not been so restricted. In the 1978 U.S. congressional elections, special-interest groups alone contributed $35 million to candidates. This figure increased to $55 million in 1980, and to $150 million in 1988! The average Senate campaign in 1988 cost $4 million.

In his famous work on the power elite just a little over thirty years ago, C. Wright Mills had relatively little to say about campaign contributions. But the subject can no longer be neglected. Especially in an age when political campaigns are won more through presenting images than through issues, the image-creating mass media are extremely important and costly. Most presidents and congressional officeholders are wealthy, but they are not superrich. With a few rare exceptions, they cannot afford to finance their own political campaigns. Who, then, pays for these campaigns? Thousands of contributors send $25 or $50 to favored candidates. For the most part, however, the money comes from corporations and the wealthy.

With the nationwide reaction against Watergate and the many illegal campaign contributions to Nixon's reelection committee in 1972, some election reforms were undertaken by Congress in 1974. Among these reforms was the creation of a voluntary $1-per-person campaign contribution from individual income tax reports. A Presidential Election Campaign Fund was established to distribute this money to the major parties and candidates during an election year. In addition, a Federal Election Commission was established to watch over campaign spending, and people were limited to a $1000 contribution in any single presidential election, with organizations limited to $5000. Perhaps these reforms contributed to less spending in the 1976 presidential election (Dye 1979:90); Carter and Ford spent a combined total of about $50 million in 1976, compared with Nixon and McGovern's $90 million in 1972. But $50 million continues to be a substantial investment, and requires large contributors.

An interesting outcome of the campaign reform law of 1974 is that much of the illegal activity in Nixon's 1972 campaign was *made legal* as long as correct procedures are followed. For example, organizations are limited to $5000 in political contributions per election. However, if there are more organizations, more money can be contributed. And this is precisely what happened by 1976. There was an explosion in the number of political action committees (PACs) established by large corporations and their executives, an increase far outnumbering those established by any other group, such as labor unions (Domhoff 1983:125). By the 1980 congressional elections, 1585 corporate, health industry, and other business PACs contributed $36 million to candidates, while $13 million was contributed by 240 labor union PACs.

Campaign contributions, therefore, continue to be an important means of political influence.

The wealthy are not assured that their interests will be protected by those they help place in office, but they obviously consider the gamble worth taking. Usually, it is hoped that these campaign contributions are placing people in office who hold political views that lead to the defense of privilege when unforeseen challenges to upper-class interests occur along the way.

For example, it seems that campaign contributions by oil companies to congressional candidates paid off in 1979 when 95 percent of the people receiving this campaign money voted for the bill sponsored by the oil industry challenging President Carter's windfall profits tax on oil companies. The oil industry investments in campaign contributions will bring a sizable return in increased profits over the years.

Since the early 1970s, a number of studies have been done on this subject (Mintz 1989). For example, Allen and Broyles (1989) examined data pertaining to the campaign contributions of 100 of the most wealthy families (629 individuals) in the United States. They found that about one-half of these individuals made large contributions. And it was the more "visible" and active rich who made these large contributions. By this they mean that the rich were more likely to make contributions if they were corporate directors or executives, were listed in *"Who's Who,"* and/or were directors of nonprofit foundations. These people were more likely to contribute to Republicans, and this was especially so with the new rich, non-Jews, and people with extensive oil stocks. In a similar manner, Burris (1987) found a split between the old rich (Yankees) and the new rich in who they supported with their money (the new rich were more likely to support Republicans). Burris also found that the rich were more likely to make large campaign contributions if their company did business with the federal government (such as a defense contractor) or was in some way regulated by the government.

In another study, Boies (1989) examined the top 500 companies in the United States between 1976 and 1980 to determine what explains the varied amount of money they contribute through PACs. As we might expect from what has already been discussed, he found that companies with more material interests in the outcomes of government policy were most likely to contribute huge amounts through PACs. Specifically, they were more likely to contribute large amounts if the company was a top defense contractor, if they were trying to get the government to approve a new corporate merger, or if they were the subject of some kind of criminal investigation by the government. And in another study of PAC contributions by big corporations, Clawson, Newstadtl, and Bearden (1986) found extensive consensus by big corporations on the "best" business candidates to support: When looking at individual campaigns, they found that in 75 percent of the cases one candidate received nine times more of the corporate PAC money compared with the political opponent. And in a large study of corporate campaign contributions, Mizruchi (1992) found that corporations grouped together through various ties (such as interlocking directors . . .) are more likely to support the same politicians and political issues even if many corporations in the group have no individual interests in doing so.

Congressional Lobbying If the interests of the wealthy are not ensured by their direct participation in government, and if those the wealthy helped put in office seem to be forgetting their debtors, a third force can be brought into action. The basic job of a lobbyist is to make friends among congressional leaders, provide them with favors such as trips, small gifts, and parties, and, most importantly, provide these leaders with information and arguments favoring their employers' interests and needs. All of this requires a large staff and lots of money.

In one of the first empirical studies of the effects of certain characteristics of corporations on government policies toward these corporations (such as tax policies), Salamon and Siegfried (1977) found that the size of the corporation showed a strong inverse relation to the amount of taxes paid by the corporation. And this inverse relation between size of the corpo-

ration and the corporation's tax rate was especially upheld when examining the oil companies and including their state as well as federal taxes paid (Salamon and Siegfried 1977:1039). Thus, the bigger the corporation, the less it tends to pay in corporate taxes.

Later studies have confirmed this relationship between size (and power) and corporate tax rates. Jacobs (1988), however, measured the concentration of powerful corporations within each type of industry. The findings were similar: The more corporate concentration (meaning the size of the firms in the industry and their dominance in the industry), the lower the taxes for the corporations in that industry. In examining how this is done in the oil industry and health-care industry, Laumann, Knoke, and Kim (1985) studied 166 government policy decisions relating to these industries and interviewed 458 lobbyists for these industries. They found that there are leading corporations in these industries that have a reputation for being most politically active in influencing government for the overall industry, and that this reputation is very accurate when measuring their lobbying activity. . . .

Lobby organizations, therefore, can be of major importance in ensuring that the special interests of a wealthy upper-class and corporate elite are served. If special favors are not completely ensured through direct participation in the cabinet and campaign contributions, the powerful lobby organizations may then move into action. The upper class and big business are not the only groups that maintain lobby organizations in Washington. The American Medical Association, the National Rifle Association, the Milk Producers Association, and many others have maintained successful lobby organizations. But when considering the big issues such as how to deal with inflation, tax policy, unemployment, foreign affairs, and many others that broadly affect the lives of people in this country, the corporate and upper-class lobbies are most important. . . .

Shaping Government Policy Of the various means of upper-class and corporate political influence, the type least recognized by the general public is referred to as the *policy-forming process* (see Domhoff 1979:61–128; 1983:98–112; 1990; Dye 1990:250–270). As scholars believe, in the long run this means of political influence is perhaps one of the most important. The basic argument is this: The federal government is faced with many national problems for which there are many possible alternative solutions. For example, consider the problem of unemployment. The possible government means of dealing with this problem are varied, and a key is that different solutions to the problem may favor different class interests. Some possible solutions (such as stimulating the economy with low interest rates and restricting imports) are believed to favor the working class and help create new jobs, and thus are pushed by labor unions. Other possible solutions (such as the "Reagonomics" idea of cutting taxes for the rich and corporations) favor the interests of corporations and the upper class. . . . One important means of ensuring that the federal government follows a policy that is favorable to your class interests is to convince the government through various types of research data that one line of policy is the overall best policy. Generating the needed information and spelling out the exact policy required take a lot of planning, organization, personnel, and resources. And there must be avenues for getting this policy information to the attention of government leaders. It is no surprise, ruling-class theorists argue, that the upper class and its corporations are able to achieve this and guide government policy in their interests. . . .

At the heart of this process are (1) upper-class and corporate *money and personnel* (2) that fund and guide *research* on important questions through foundations and universities, (3) then process the information through *policy-planning groups* sponsored by the upper class (4) that make direct recommendations to government, and (5) influence the opinion-making centers, such as the media and government commissions, which in turn influence the population and government leaders in favoring specific policy alternatives. . . .

Many writers in sociology, political science, and economics have come to stress the increased importance of information and ideas generated through research in guiding the economy and government in advanced or postindustrial societies (see Galbraith 1971; Bell 1976). As a consequence, some writers have argued that an upper-class or wealthy elite is no longer in control of the economy or political system because the ideas and specialized knowledge are in the hands of a new group of elites—strategic elites or technocrats (see Galbraith 1971; Keller 1963).

Others, especially ruling-class theorists, counter by charging that the knowledge and information behind the operation of the economy and government today are not always neutral. Much of this knowledge is generated through upper-class sponsorship, and thus favors its class interests. Increasingly, knowledge needed by corporations and government is generated through research conducted at major universities. Scientific research requires a lot of time, money, and personnel. The upper class and corporations, it is argued, influence the research process through funding and authority positions in major research-oriented universities.

A major source of funds for research is large foundations. These foundations possess extensive wealth that is given to fund research projects (see Lundberg 1968:498–505) that the foundation directors judge to be important in generating information needed in guiding political and economic decisions. In most cases, these large foundations were established by wealthy people as a means of reducing taxes. But these families often maintain control of the foundations, influencing their funding policies. . . .

In a study of top foundations (those with over half the assets held by all foundations), Dye (1983:143) found that 50 percent of the directors were members of upper-class social clubs.

Also important in the research process are the major universities in which much of this research is conducted. . . . In these universities faculty are often released from their teaching responsibilities to devote most of their time to conducting research sponsored by large corporations and foundations, as well as the federal government. One means of upper-class and corporate influence, therefore, is through guiding what type of research is conducted by the faculty.

We have only a few studies of the exact impact of funding sources on this research, but what we do have is enlightening. For example, Useem, Hoops, and Moore . . . have found that there is a relationship between members from the upper class on a university's board of trustees and obtaining more funds from corporations and foundations. . . . A majority of these professors admitted that their research plans (what type of research they could do) were influenced by the policies of funding agencies (in this case, the federal government). In other words, they were doing the research the funding agency thought was most important, not what they or their scientific disciplines thought most important. . . .

Finally, there is the more general influence over university policy that may be exercised by corporations and the upper class. Most universities are governed much like a corporation. Above the executive officers (such as presidents and vice presidents) is the board of trustees (resembling a board of directors in a corporation). This board of trustees has broad authority in governing the university and its general policies. Thus, it is often deemed important to understand the outside interests of the university board of trustees.

In Dye's (1995) study of elites he examined the backgrounds of presidents and trustees of the top twelve private universities. . . . He found that *62 percent* of these university trustees were members of just 37 exclusive upper-class clubs. Much of the research sponsored by corporations and the upper class is in state-sponsored universities not included in Dye's sample. But other research indicates that the trustees of these universities are also dominated by corporations and the upper class (Domhoff 1967:77–79; Dye 1983:157–160).

In this policy-forming process the next important link is through what has been called *policy-planning groups*. The corporate elites and upper class come together in these groups, dis-

cuss policy, publish and disseminate research, and, according to Dye and Domhoff, arrive at some consensus about what should be done in the nation. The most important of the policy groups are sponsored directly by the upper class for the purpose of linking the research information discussed earlier to specific policy alternatives and making certain these policy alternatives find their way to government circles.

Perhaps the most has been written about the Council on Foreign Relations (CFR) and the Committee on Economic Development (CED). Both groups are clearly upper-class institutions (as defined by Domhoff), the former specializing in foreign policy and the latter specializing in domestic issues. The CFR was established shortly after World War I by upper-class members with the direct intent of influencing the U.S. government with respect to their business interests overseas (see Shoup 1975). Among the CFR's early successes were to have the government define Japan as an economic threat by 1940, to establish some of the ideas behind the development of the World Bank and the United Nations, and to motivate the government to define certain parts of the world as important areas of economic interest (multinational corporation interests). Membership in the CFR is limited to 1400 people, half of whom are members of the upper class. (Domhoff 1983). The CED emerged out of the Business Advisory Council in 1942 to continue the input into government by the upper class that began with this earlier organization in the 1930s (Domhoff 1970:123–128; 1979:67–69; Collins 1977).

We do not have studies of the overall membership of the CED, as we do with the CFR; Dye . . . , however, has traced the backgrounds of directors of both the CED ($n = 61$) and the CFR ($n = 22$), finding them to be strongly upper-class. There were an average of 4.1 corporate directorships among CED directors (3.2 for the CFR) and an average of 1.0 government offices held (such as cabinet, 3.0 for the CFR); 72 percent belonged to upper-class clubs (64 percent for the CFR), and 62 percent went to elite universities (. . . 82 percent for the CFR). With respect to research on major universities, 67 percent of CED directors and 68 percent of CFR directors were also trustees of major universities. . . .

Various government commissions are established from time to time to make recommendations on such issues as civil disorders, the conduct of the CIA, and energy. . . . These commissions make public the recommendations of these upper-class policy groups and provide their members with a semiofficial position in the government.

As for the national news media, they are often said to have a liberal slant in their views and to possess much power in shaping public and government opinion. . . . But the moderate conservative wing of the upper class and corporate leaders most influences the media. The major television networks, magazines, and newspapers are highly concentrated and tied to corporations. In terms of the backgrounds of top leaders in the national media, Dye (1995) found 33 percent had previous careers in big corporations and 44 percent were members of upper-class clubs. Their upper-class backgrounds are not as extensive as those of corporate leaders, but neither are the top media leaders from humble origins.

The backgrounds of media directors, the extensive corporate influence through ownership, and the huge funding from advertising all contribute to making mass media organizations cautious in presenting views that may be overly critical of the upper class and corporate interests. Information critical of these interests is not ignored by the mass media. The upper class might not even want this information to be ignored, for corrective action is often needed to prevent economic problems and corporate abuse from getting out of hand and requiring more drastic solutions that may harm more general corporate interests. The news media are in part a policing agency involved in calling attention to problems that need correction. It is not what is criticized as much as how it is criticized, where blame is placed, and what possible solutions are offered.

One final point requires emphasis. Few theorists writing in this area (on the upper class or, more specifically, on upper-class influence in the mass media) suggest that the upper-class or corporate elites completely control the mass media in the country. Neither do most writers in this area believe that there is some kind of upper-class secret conspiracy to control the mass media—or anything else in the country, for that matter. Rather, they are trying to call attention to an economic structure that allows more influence (in the many ways outlined previously) to fall into the hands of groups like the upper-class and corporate elites. Each class or economic interest group tends to have a worldview or way of perceiving reality that has been shaped by its own economic and political interests. When one group has more influence over the major means of conveying information, its view of reality often comes to be accepted by more people.

In summarizing the total policy-forming process, we find an underground network in this country that is highly influenced by corporate and upper-class institutions. The federal government and Congress have the authority to adopt or reject the policy recommendations flowing from this process, but most often they accept them, leaving the government to decide exactly how the policy will be carried out (Dye 1995).

The Upper Class: A Conclusion

. . . We have found some support for the existence of upper-class unity through interaction patterns in prep schools, social clubs, policy-formation organizations, and multiple corporate board positions. We have also found evidence of upper-class influence in the economy through stock ownership and membership on corporate boards. And we have found evidence of upper-class political influence through direct participation in government, campaign contributions, lobby organizations, and a policy-formation process. Upper-class interests are said to be maintained through these means of influence in the economy and the political system. . . .

Editors' Note: For documentation, see article source on page 135.

8

Welfare Reform in America: A Clash of Politics and Research

DIANA M. ZUCKERMAN

All institutions are interrelated. Zuckerman deals with the impact of politics on welfare reform, illustrating the close relationship of the political and economic institutions.

As you read this article, ask yourself the following questions:

1. Many people see welfare as "something for nothing." Do you agree that welfare is necessary? Why?

2. If welfare is "something for nothing," would not subsidies to various industries also fit this claim? Why?

THE 1996 PERSONAL RESPONSIBILITY and Work Opportunity Reconciliation Act (PRWORA) radically changed welfare as we knew it, and data on its impact on the most vulnerable Americans are just becoming available. . . .

The controversial passage of PRWORA was the culmination of many years of debate as well as concerns expressed across the political spectrum about the extent to which the welfare system should be considered a failure or an essential safety net. On the right, there were many years of anecdotes about "welfare queens" driving fancy cars, buying steaks with their food stamps, and teaching their children that welfare made working unnecessary. . . . On the left, there was an assumption that welfare saved innocent lives but also a growing concern about the deteriorating conditions in the inner city, where welfare dependence was sometimes a way

of life being handed down from generation to generation, often accompanied by drug abuse, violence, teen pregnancy, and other social ills.

Research should have provided essential information to help determine how the welfare system should be changed, but instead, research was used as an ideological weapon to support conflicting points of view. . . . They could be used to prove both that most families on welfare were on it for short periods of time and that there was a hard-core group of families that stay on welfare for many years (Pavetti, 1996). Similarly, the statistics could be used to show that teen pregnancies were statistically significant predictors of long-term welfare and poverty (GAO, 1994, pp. 94–115) or that many welfare recipients were the victims of a crisis and just needed help for a few months before they were able to support themselves (Greenberg, 1993). . . .

This article describes how political and public pressures and compelling anecdotes overpowered the efforts of progressive public policy organizations and researchers, resulting in legislation focused on getting families off welfare rather than getting families out of poverty. . . .

Welfare Reform as a Presidential Issue

As a presidential candidate, Bill Clinton made it clear that he would not defend the welfare system but instead would work to change it. . . . As President, he quickly appointed experts to work on welfare reform, with particular focus on

A longer version of this article was published in the Journal of Social Issues, *Winter 2000, Vol. 56, No. 4. Dr. Zuckerheim is president of the National Center for Policy Research (CPR) for Women & Families and can be reached at dz@center4policy.org.*

toughening child support laws and requiring welfare recipients to prepare for self-sufficiency (Koppelman, 1993). Although the public and policymakers were ready for major changes in the welfare system, many did not realize that a law passed in 1988, the Family Support Act, already had strengthened child support collection and ordered states to require able-bodied recipients to enter remedial education or job training projects. President Clinton had been instrumental in negotiating that legislation as an officer of the National Governors' Association, and the bill was expected to help single mothers and to encourage more women to move from welfare to work. However, the weakened economy of the late 1980s led to a surge in the welfare rolls instead, with the size of those rolls increasing 25% from 1989 to 1992. As a result of the recession, states were unable to provide matching funds to claim their full share of the federal funding for Job Opportunities and Basic Skills (JOBS), a training program. The law did not seem to be working, and the pressure to "do something about welfare" grew.

As a candidate, Clinton had promised to reform health care as well as welfare, and as President, he decided to focus on health care reform legislation first. This was a logical choice, because the lack of affordable health care was a major disincentive for single mothers who wanted to move from welfare to work. The Clinton administration strategy was to first pass a law that would make health care affordable for the working poor, so that it would be easier to make the other legislative changes necessary to reduce the welfare rolls. Improving access to health care would help those families that would lose Medicaid when they left welfare for low-level jobs that did not offer health insurance as a benefit.

While health care reform took center stage in the public eye, a welfare reform plan was being quietly developed by Clinton administration officials. As Assistant Secretary for Children and Families at HHS, Mary Jo Bane wanted to refocus the welfare system on work and to give states more flexibility regarding welfare policies (Bane, 1997). States were already submitting welfare reform proposals to the federal government to request waivers from the federal requirements. . . .

Meanwhile, polls were showing tremendous public support for requiring all "able-bodied" welfare recipients, including mothers with young children, to get education or training for up to 2 years and then to work (Ellwood, 1996). Assistant HHS Secretaries Bane and David Ellwood wanted the federal law to set consistent national criteria and restrictions, in order to avoid a race to the bottom by the states. According to Ellwood, their proposal to reform welfare had four major goals:

1. *Make work pay.* Low-income workers need a living wage, health care, and child care to make working make sense instead of welfare.
2. *Two-year limits.* Transform the welfare system from a handout to a hand up, with clear requirements to work after 2 years of training or education.
3. *Child support enforcement.* Require absent parents to pay, whether or not they were married.
4. *Fight teen pregnancy.* The plan offered grants to high-risk schools that proposed innovative initiatives to lower rates of teen pregnancy and also supported a national clearinghouse and a few intensive demonstration projects.

The public seemed ready for these kinds of changes, but the Clinton administration was concerned about the cost. In order to move single mothers from welfare to work, it would be necessary to provide job training, child care, and other services for many of them. The cost of those programs and services would initially be high, and it was expected that the savings as families moved off welfare would not be great enough to make up for those extra costs. Since President Clinton had also promised to cut the country's enormous budget deficit, and since a major goal of welfare reform was to save money and make the federal government smaller, it did not seem politically feasible to expect taxpayers to pay more for welfare reform than they were paying for the existing welfare system, even in the short term. To save money, the Clinton plan included a slow phase-in of the program, which caused some conservative critics to accuse the administration of not being serious about reform (Ellwood, 1996).

Congress and Welfare Reform

For a variety of reasons, President Clinton had difficulty obtaining the support of his own party on welfare, health care, and other issues. As a moderate "New Democrat," his positions often seemed too conservative for the more liberal Democrats and too liberal for the more conservative ones, most of whom were southern and concerned about reelection as the Republican Party gained support in the South. Conservative Democrats developed their own welfare reform plan with a faster phase-in. In addition, conservatives from both parties were concerned that the Clinton plan did not sufficiently address out-of-wedlock childbearing and provided too many federal requirements instead of giving the states the autonomy to decide about welfare reform (Ellwood, 1996).

Why did the Clinton plan fail? Ellwood (1996) speculates that they should have tried to pass welfare reform before health care reform instead of afterward. . . . As someone involved in health care reform legislation in the Senate at the time, I believe that the problem with the timing was not lack of attention but rather the weakened credibility of the Clinton administration because of the barrage of criticism aimed at its health care proposal. Ellwood also speculates that the President's promise to "end welfare as we know it" was a potent sound bite but did not address the concerns of many Democrats about whether the new system would be better than the old. Ellwood believes that the phrase "2 years and you're off" was even more destructive, because it implied no help at all after 2 years, which he says is "never what was intended." I agree that these were problems, and in addition, the tension and lack of trust between the congressional Democrats and the Clinton administration contributed to the view of many Democrats that the Clinton welfare plan was too controversial and would make them politically vulnerable. . . .

The 1994 election, which resulted in the Republican takeover of the House and Senate, changed the political dynamics. The result was that every congressional committee was chaired by a Republican instead of a Democrat and composed primarily of Republicans rather than Democrats. Instead of being chaired by the most liberal Democrats, the committees that would vote on welfare reform were now chaired by conservative Republicans. Although the Republicans had only a small majority in the House, they had the control of committee chairmanships and disproportionate membership on the committees. This meant that the Republican leadership had tremendous power to control the welfare reform bill.

Even more important than the leadership of the congressional committees was the leadership of the House of Representatives, which changed from a liberal Democrat to Newt Gingrich, an outspoken critic of "big government," especially for social programs. Gingrich had been a major architect of the Contract With America, which specified that welfare should be available for only 2 years and that benefits should not be available to minor mothers or for children born to mothers on welfare. The shellacking that the Democrats experienced in the election was perceived as a mandate for the Contract With America (Merida, 1994), including a more punitive welfare reform plan than the one the Clinton administration had proposed.

Meanwhile, state governors demanded more say about how money in the new welfare program would be spent, resulting in a bill that looked more like a block grant than a social program. This had the political benefit of getting Congress off the hook: It would not have to make the difficult political decisions about restrictions and instead could put those decisions in the hands of the state governments.

The media were also influential and tended to focus on the shortcomings of the welfare program that was in place, Aid for Families with Dependent Children (AFDC). . . .

As the ideological battle continued around it, Congress was under tremendous pressure to pass a welfare reform bill. . . .

Throughout 1995 and 1996, the Republican majority controlled the policy agenda and welfare reform was their cause. In that political climate, it would have been very difficult for progressive organizations to succeed in their public education and lobbying efforts, regardless of research results. It was especially difficult for liberal legislators to suggest that welfare mothers should be able to stay home and care for their children when nationwide 55% of mothers with children under the age of 3 were employed, most of them full time (Pavetti, 1997). To make matters worse, the progressive advocates did not have solid research findings to support their opposition to the Republican leadership's welfare reform bill, other than frightening but questionable statistics describing the number of children who would fall into poverty if their mothers were thrown off welfare. This left the most progressive members of Congress with little ammunition to use against the most conservative proposals. The slim Republican majority in Congress was joined by enough Democrats to create a substantial majority for the welfare reform bill that passed in 1996.

The bill that Congress eventually passed is lengthy and complicated, but the introductory section includes "findings" that explicitly show the ideology behind the legislation. There are 10 findings, and the first three set the tone:

1. Marriage is the foundation of a successful society.
2. Marriage is an essential institution of a successful society which promotes the interests of children.
3. Promotion of responsible fatherhood and motherhood is integral to successful child rearing and the well-being of children. (U.S. Congress, 1996, p. 6)

The bill's focus on marriage and responsible parenthood reflects the Republican Party's ties to the Christian right as well as the growing disenchantment with government programs throughout the country in the early and mid-1990s. The rest of the findings, however, use research data to support this focus, and many of the statistics are ones that have been employed by experts across the ideological spectrum to support public policies aimed at reducing teen pregnancy, reducing poverty, and other goals that are as popular among liberal Democrats as conservative Republicans, as well as everything in between. For example, the next finding pointed out that "only 54 percent of single-parent families with children had a child support order established and, of that 54 percent, only about one-half received the full amount due" (U.S. Congress, 1996, p. 6).

Another major concern was the growth of welfare. The fifth finding points out that the number of individuals on welfare had more than tripled since 1965 and that more than two-thirds were children. The number of children on welfare every month increased from 3.3 million in 1965 to 9.3 million in 1992, although the number of children in the United States declined during those years. The legislation also points out that 89% of the children receiving AFDC were living in homes without fathers and that the percentage of unmarried women nearly tripled between 1970 and 1991.

The next finding includes details regarding pregnancies among unmarried teens and concludes "if the current trend continues, 50 percent of all births by the year 2015 will be out-of-wedlock" (U.S. Congress, 1996, p. 7). The findings recommended that strategies to combat teenage pregnancy "must address the issue of male responsibility, including statutory rape culpability and prevention" and points out that most teen mothers "have histories of sexual and physical abuse, primarily with older adult men."

Despite the clear ideological underpinnings of the bill, some of the findings could be embraced by both political parties. For example, the bill correctly points out that unmarried teenage mothers are more likely to go on welfare and to spend more years on welfare. It also points out that babies of unwed mothers are at risk for very low or moderately low bith weight, for growing up to have lower cognitive attainment and lower educational aspirations, and for child abuse and neglect. They are more likely to grow up to be teen parents and to go on welfare and less likely to have an intact marriage.

The problems of single parenting were also described, showing how they set in motion a cycle of welfare and poverty:

■ Mothers under 20 years of age are at the greatest risk of bearing low birth weight babies.
■ The younger the single-parent mother, the less likely she is to finish high school.
■ Young women who have children before finishing high school are more likely to receive welfare assistance for a longer period of time.
■ Children of teenage single parents have lower cognitive scores, lower educational aspirations, and a greater likelihood of becoming teenage parents themselves.
■ Children of single-parent homes are three times more likely to fail and repeat a year in grade school and almost four times more likely to be expelled or suspended from school than are children from intact two-parent families.
■ Of those youth held for criminal offenses within the State juvenile justice system, only 30% lived primarily in a home with both parents, compared to 74% of the general population of children.

The costs of teen parenting were delineated, with an estimate that "between 1985 and 1990, the public cost of births to teenage mothers under the Aid to Families with Dependent Children program, the food stamp program, and the Medicaid program" (U.S. Congress, 1996, p. 8) was $120 billion. In a climate of deficit reduction and support for smaller government, that estimate was extremely compelling.

The welfare reform bill includes nine sections, referred to as "titles," and several are more generous than would have been expected given the Republican control of Congress and the Republicans' opposition to "big government." For example, Title VI on child care authorizes increased federal money so that child care is more available and affordable. President Clinton, however, expressed considerable concerns about Title IV, which banned most legal immigrants from most federal benefit programs, and Title VIII, which cut the food stamp program across the board and

also restricted food stamps to unemployed adults without disabilities or dependents to 3 months out of every 36.

The welfare reform law had a great deal of support from governors around the country, because it gave them enormous flexibility regarding the spending of federal funds. The rationale was that states could experiment with new approaches, under the assumption that what works in a rural state, for example, might not work in a more urban environment. Heavy subsidies for day care or job training might be useful in some areas, for example, but unnecessary in others.

Why Not Wait for Data?

Although data were quoted in the welfare reform bill, there were no convincing data to predict what would actually happen if the bill passed. A "natural experiment" was taking place, however, that could have answered those questions. Between January 1987 and August 1996, 46 states had received approval for waivers to experiment with AFDC and welfare-to-work programs (GAO, 1997). Since welfare reform represented such a dramatic change in policies, with many lives at stake, it would have been logical to delay a federal welfare reform law until the data were analyzed from those programs. For example, by May 1997, the General Accounting Office, which is a research branch of Congress, had published a report entiled *Welfare Reform: States' Early Experiences with Benefits Termination,* based on a study conducted at the request of Senator Pat Moynihan. The study found that the benefits of 18,000 families were terminated under waivers through December 1996, most of them in Iowa, Massachusetts, and Wisconsin. More than 99% of these families failed to comply with program requirements; for example, some wanted to stay home with their children or were unwilling to do community service or work for low wages (GAO, 1997). These findings could have been used to design a welfare reform process that protected some of these families, but the bill was passed before the data were available.

Instead, the little research that was already completed was used to push welfare reform forward. For example, Vermont had applied for waivers to the welfare requirements, and its welfare restructuring project was the nation's first statewide demonstration of time-limited welfare (Zengerle, 1997). In 2 years, Vermont raised the number of welfare parents with jobs from 20% to 26% and increased their average monthly earnings from $373 to $437. Of course, it was also important to note that Vermont increased its social services budget by 50%, in part to create new jobs. Welfare recipients who were unable to find jobs in the private sector were eligible for 10 months' employment in public jobs or working for nonprofit organizations. It also would have been logical to note that Vermont has relatively few welfare recipients and that its experience is likely to be different from that of most other states. Nevertheless, this study was used to show the success of welfare reform. . . .

The Reality of Welfare Reform

Although the welfare reform bill that passed in 1996 was radical and potentially devastating to poor families, the booming economy during the next four years and political compromises resulted in a law that no longer seemed as extreme or partisan as it once did. For example, in the short term, almost every state received more federal funds under welfare reform that it did prior to reform (Nightingale & Brennan, 1998). Perhaps most important, the Clinton administration was able to influence the bill through regulations. The final regulations, announced in April 1999, contain exceptions to the rules that make the bill less rigid. For example, states may continue to provide welfare benefits for longer than 60 months to up to 20% of the welfare caseload based on hardship or domestic violence, and the 20% limit can be exceeded if there are federally recognized "good cause domestic violence waivers" (Schott, Lazere, Goldberg, & Sweeney, 1999). In addition, states will be penalized if they sanction a single parent caring for a child under age 6 if the parent can demonstrate his or her inability to obtain child care.

Research results are finally coming in from across the country. The Urban Institute (Loprest, 1999) reports that most adults leaving welfare between 1995 and 1997 got a new job or increased earnings. They also report that former welfare recipients work more hours than employed near-poor mothers who were not previously receiving welfare. Nevertheless, many families are doing poorly since welfare reform was implemented, and the number of children in extreme poverty (less than half the poverty level) has increased (Sherman, 1999). Between 1995 and 1997, the average income of the poorest 20% of female-headed households fell an average of $580 per family, primarily due to the loss of food stamps and other government benefits (Primus, Rawlings, Larin, & Porter, 1999).

Research had little impact on the passage of welfare reform in 1996, although statistics were used by both sides in the national debate. Is it possible that new research on the impact of welfare reform will influence welfare policies in the future? The studies in this issue provide very useful information about the barriers to success for welfare mothers who attempt to move into the workforce on a permanent basis, with important implications for how policies can maximize success and minimize tragedy for vulnerable families. Now that the costs of the welfare program have been drastically reduced and the national annual budget deficit has turned into a surplus, these studies may manage to attract the attention of policymakers. Unfortunately, welfare reform has made national policy changes in this area even more difficult, because decisions are now made in 50 different states, rather than by the federal government.

REFERENCES

Elwood, D.T. (1996). Welfare reform as I knew it: When bad things happen to good policies. *American Prospect, 26,* 22–29.

General Accounting Office (GAO). (1994). *Teenage mothers least likely to become self-sufficient.* GAO/HEHS-94-115. Washington, DC: GAO.

General Accounting Office (GAO). (1997). *Welfare reform: States' early experience with benefit termination.* GAO/HEHS-97-74. Washington, DC: GAO.

9

Money and the World We Want

ANDREW HACKER

Two issues are covered in this reading: First, is there a class structure, and what is its breakdown? Second, what are the consequences of this class structure?

As you read, ask yourself the following questions:

1. What problems result from the way the United States distributes income?

2. What changes would you make to help all people to be fully Americans?

GLOSSARY

Corollary A natural result or easily drawn conclusion.
Esoteric Understood by those with special knowledge.
Skepticism Doubt, unbelief.

THE THREE DECADES SPANNING 1940 to 1970 were the nation's most prosperous years. Indeed, so far as can happen in America's kind of economy, a semblance of redistribution was taking place. During this generation, the share of national income that went to the bottom fifth of families rose by some fractions of a point to an all-time high, while that received by the richest fifth fell to its lowest level. This is the very period of shared well-being that many people would like to re-create in this country.

Yet in no way is this possible. It was an atypical era, in which America won an adventitious primacy because of a war it delayed entering and its geographic isolation which spared it the ravages that the other combatants suffered.

America's postwar upsurge lasted barely three decades. The tide began to turn in the early 1970s. Between 1970 and 1980, family income

rose less than 7 percent. And that small increase resulted entirely from the fact that additional family members were joining the workforce. Indeed, the most vivid evidence of decline is found in the unremitting drop in men's earnings since 1970. Averages and medians, however, conceal important variations, such as that some American households have done quite well for themselves during the closing decades of the century. Those with incomes of $1 million or more have reached an all-time high, as are families and individuals making over $100,000. By all outward appearances, there is still plenty of money around, but it is landing in fewer hands. Yet it is by no means apparent that people are being paid these generous salaries and options and fees because their work is adding much of substance to the nation's output. Indeed, the coming century will test whether an economy can flourish by exporting most notably action movies and flavored water.

The term *upper class* is not commonly used to describe the people in America's top income tier since it connotes a hereditary echelon that passes on its holdings from generation to generation. Only a few American families have remained at the very top for more than two or three generations, and even when they do, as have the du Ponts and Rockefellers, successive descendants slice the original pie into smaller and smaller pieces. So if America does not have a "class" at its apex, what should we call the people who have the most money? The answer is to refer to them as we usually do, as being "wealthy" or "rich."

Reprinted with permission of Scribner, a division of Simon & Schuster, Inc., from Money: Who Has How Much and Why, *by Andrew Hacker. Copyright 1997 by Andrew Hacker.*

How Families Fare: Three Tiers

Tier	Income Range	Number of Families/Percentage	
Comfortable	Over $75,000	12,961,000	18.6%
Coping	$25,000–$75,000	36,872,000	53.0%
Deprived	Under $25,000	19,764,000	28.4%

The rich, members of the 68,064 households who in 1995 filed federal tax returns that declared a 1994 income of $1 million or more, have varied sources of income. . . . For present purposes, wealth may be considered holdings that would yield you an income of $1 million a year without your having to put in a day's work. Assuming a 7 percent return, it would take income-producing assets of some $15 million to ensure that comfort level.

Unfortunately, we have no official count of how many Americans possess that kind of wealth. It is measurably less than 68,064, since those households report that the largest segment of their incomes come from salaries. Indeed, among the chairmen of the one hundred largest firms, the median stock holding is only $8.4 million. A liberal estimate of the number of wealthy Americans would be about thirty thousand households, one-thirtieth of one percent of the national total.

This still puts almost 90 percent of all Americans between the very poor and the wealthy and the rich. One way to begin to define this majority is by creating a more realistic bottom tier than merely those people who fall below the official poverty line. Since Americans deserve more than subsistence, we may set $25,000 a year for a family of three as a minimum for necessities without frills. And even this is a pretty bare floor. Indeed, only about 45 percent of the people questioned in the Roper-Starch poll felt that their households could "get by" on $25,000 a year. In 1995, almost 20 million families—28.4 percent of the total—were living below that spartan standard. This stratum is a varied group. . . . For over a third, all of their income comes from sources other than employment, most typically Social Security and public assistance. Over 43.3 percent of the house-

holds have only one earner, who at that income level is usually a woman and the family's sole source of support. The remainder consists of families where two or more members have had jobs of some kind, which suggests sporadic employment at close to the minimum wage. Whatever designation we give to these households—poor or just getting by—their incomes leave them deprived of even the more modest acquisitions and enjoyments available to the great majority of Americans.

The question of who belongs to America's middle class requires deciding where to place its upper and lower boundaries. While it is difficult to set precise boundaries for this stratum, it is accurate to say that, by one measure or another, most Americans fit into a middle class.

While it is meaningless to classify the households in the middle of America's income distribution because this stratum is so substantial and it encompasses such a wide range of incomes, meaningful divisions can be drawn in our country's overall income distribution.

This book has sought to make clear that the prominent place of the rich tells us a great deal about the kind of country we are, as does the growing group of men and women with $100,000 salaries and households with $100,000 incomes. The same stricture applies to the poor, who, while not necessarily increasing in number, are too often permanently mired at the bottom. This noted, a three-tier division can be proposed, with the caveat that how you fare on a given income can depend on local costs and social expectations.

. . .

That the rich have become richer would seem to bear out Karl Marx's well-known prediction. The nation's greatest fortunes are substantially larger than those of a generation ago. House-holds with incomes exceeding $1 million a year are also netting more in real purchasing power. At a more mundane level, the top 5 percent of all households in 1975 averaged $122,651 a year; by 1995, in inflation-adjusted dollars, their average annual income had ascended to $188,962.

But Marx did not foresee that the number of rich families and individuals would actually increase over time. Between 1979 and 1994, the number of households declaring incomes of $1 million or more rose from 13,505 to 68,064, again adjusting for inflation. In 1996, *Forbes*'s 400 richest Americans were all worth at least $400 million. In 1982, the year of the magazine's first list, only 110 people in the 400 had holdings equivalent to the 1996 cutoff figure. In other words, almost three-quarters of 1982's wealthiest Americans would not have made the 1996 list. And families with incomes over $100,000—once more, in constant purchasing power—increased almost threefold between 1970 and 1995, rising from 3.4 percent to 9 percent of the total. During the same period, the group of men making more than $50,000 rose from 12 percent of the total to 17 percent.

It is one thing for the rich to get richer when everyone is sharing in overall economic growth, and it is quite another for the better off to prosper while others are losing ground or standing still. But this is what has been happening. Thus 1995 found fewer men earning enough to place them in the $25,000 to $50,000 tier compared with twenty-five years earlier. And the proportion in the bottom bracket has remained essentially unchanged. But this is not necessarily a cause for cheer. In more halcyon times, it was assumed that each year would bring a measure of upward movement for people at the bottom of the income ladder and a diminution of poverty.

The wage gap of our time reflects both the declining fortunes of many Americans and the rise of individuals and households who have profited from recent trends. Economists generally agree on what brought about static wages and lowered living standards. In part, well-paying

jobs are scarcer because goods that were once produced here, at American wage scales, are now made abroad and then shipped here for sale. A corollary cause has been the erosion of labor unions, which once safeguarded generous wages for their members. Between 1970 and 1996, the portion of the workforce represented by unions fell from 27 percent to 15 percent. Today, the most highly organized occupations are on public payrolls, notably teachers and postal employees. Only 11 percent of workers in the private sector belong to unions. For most of the other 89 percent this means that their current paychecks are smaller than they were in the past.

Analysts tend to differ on the extent to which the paltriness of the minimum wage has lowered living standards. Despite the 1996 increase, the minimum wage produces an income that is still below the poverty line. Even more contentious is the issue of to what degree immigrants and aliens have undercut wages and taken jobs once held by people who were born here. We can all cite chores that Americans are unwilling to do, at least at the wages customarily paid for those jobs. Scouring pots, laundering clothes, herding cattle, and caring for other people's children are examples of such tasks. At the same time, employers frequently use immigrants to replace better-paid workers, albeit by an indirect route. The most common practice is to remove certain jobs from the firm's payroll and then to hire outside contractors, who bring in their own staffs, which are almost always lower paid and often recently arrived in this country.

Most economists agree that the primary cause of diverging earnings among American workers has been the introduction of new technologies. These new machines and processes are so esoteric and complex that they require sophisticated skills that call for premium pay. In this view, the expanded stratum of Americans earning over $50,000 is made up largely of men and women who are adept at current techniques for producing goods, organizing information, and administering personnel. New technologies have reduced the number of people who are needed as telephone operators, tool and die makers, and aircraft mechanics. Between 1992 and 1996, Delta Airlines was scheduling the same number of flights each year, even though it was discharging a quarter of its employees. Closer to the top, there is a strong demand for individuals who are skilled at pruning payrolls. And this cadre has been doing its work well. . . . [I]n 1973, the five hundred largest industrial firms employed some 15.5 million men and women. By 1993, these firms employed only 11.5 million people. But this reduction in the industrial workforce amounted to more than a loss of 4 million positions. Given the increase in production that took place over this twenty-year period, it meant a comparable output could be achieved in 1993 with half as many American workers as were needed in 1973. In fact, American workers account for an even smaller share of the output, since many of the top five hundred industrial firms are having more of their production performed by overseas contractors and subsidiaries.

So what special skills do more highly educated workers have that make them eligible for rising salaries? In fact, such talents as they may display have only marginal ties to technological expertise. The years at college and graduate school pay off because they burnish students' personalities. The time spent on a campus imparts cues and clues on how to conduct oneself in corporate cultures and professional settings. This demeanor makes for successful interviews and enables a person to sense what is expected of him during the initial months on a job.

Does America's way of allocating money make any sense at all? Any answer to this question requires establishing a rationale. The most common explanation posits that the amounts people get are set in an open market. Thus, in 1995, employers offered some 14.3 million jobs that paid between $20,000 and $25,000, and were able to find 14.3 million men and women who were willing to take them. The same principle applied to the 1.7 million positions pegged at $75,000 to $85,000, and to the dozen or so corporate chairmen who asked for or were given more than $10 million. By the same token, it

can be argued that market forces operate at the low end of the scale. Wal-Mart and Pepsico's Pizza Hut cannot force people to work for $6.50 an hour, but those companies and others like them seem to attract the workers they need by paying that wage.

The last half century gave many groups a chance to shield themselves from the labor auction.

But many, if not most, of these protections are no longer being renewed. The up-and-coming generations of physicians, professors, and automobile workers are already finding that they must settle for lower pay and fewer safeguards and benefits. The most graphic exception to this new rule has been in the corporate world, where boards of directors still award huge salaries to executives, without determining whether such compensation is needed to keep their top people from leaving or for any other reason. They simply act as members of an inbred club who look after one another. Only rarely do outside pressures upset these arrangements, which is why they persist.

A market rationale also presumes that those receiving higher offers will have superior talents or some other qualities that put them in demand. Some of the reasons why one person makes more than another make sense by this standard. Of course, a law firm will pay some of its members more if they bring in new business or satisfy existing clients. Two roommates have just received master's degrees with distinction, one in education and the other in business administration. The former's first job is teaching second-graders and will pay $23,000. The latter, at an investment firm, will start at $93,000. About all that can be said with certainty is that we are unlikely to arrive at a consensus on which roommate will be contributing more to the commonweal.

Would America be a better place to live, and would Americans be a happier people, if incomes were more evenly distributed? Even as the question is being posed, the answers can be anticipated.

One side will respond with a resounding "Yes!" After which will come a discourse on how poverty subverts the promise of democracy, while allowing wealth in so few hands attests to our rewarding greed and selfishness. There would be far less guilt and fear if the rich were not so rich and no Americans were poor. But the goal, we will be told, is not simply to take money from some people and give it to others. Rather, our goal should be to create a moral culture where citizens feel it is right to have no serious disparities in living standards. Other countries that also have capitalist economies have shown that this is possible.

Those who exclaim "No way!" in response to the same question will be just as vehement. To exact taxes and redistribute the proceeds is an immoral use of official power since it punishes the productive and rewards the indolent. And do we want the government telling private enterprises what wages they can offer? The dream of economic equality has always been a radical's fantasy. Apart from some primitive societies, such a system has never worked. If you want efficiency and prosperity, and almost everyone does, then variations in incomes are part of the equation.

These different responses arise in part from disparate theories of human nature. Since the earliest days of recorded history, philosophers have disagreed over whether our species is inherently competitive or cooperative.

Also at issue is whether greater economic equality can only be achieved by giving oppressive powers to the state, either to limit incomes through heavy taxes or by setting levels of earnings.

Of course, the price that America pays for economic inequality is its persisting poverty.

In one way or another all Americans will pay the high costs of poverty. California now spends more on its prison system than it does on higher education, and other states will soon be following suit. Bolstering police forces is hardly cheap: upward of $75,000 per officer, when overtime and benefits are added in. Being poor means a higher chance of being sick or being shot, or bearing low-birth-weight babies, all of which

consume medical resources and have helped to make Medicaid one of the costliest public programs. In addition, poor Americans now represent the fastest-growing group of AIDS victims: mainly drug users and the women and children they infect. Generally, $100,000 worth of medical treatment is spent on each person dying of AIDS. The poor also have more of their children consigned to "special education" classes, which most never leave and where the tab can reach three times the figure for regular pupils.

Additional expenses are incurred by families who put as much distance as possible between themselves and the poor. Doing so often entails the upkeep of gated communities, security systems, and privately supplied guards. Yet these are expenses better-off Americans readily bear. They are willing to foot the bills for more prisons and police, as well as the guns they keep in their bedrooms and the alarms for their cars. Indeed, their chief objection is to money given to non-married mothers who want to be at home with their pre-school-age children. Virtually every such penny is begrudged, followed by the demand that these mothers take jobs even before their children go to kindergarten. While the imposition of work may make some taxpayers cheerier, it will not do much to close the income gap.

How disparities in income affect the nation's well-being has long been debated by economists. Much of the argument centers on what people do with their money. The poor and those just trying to cope devote virtually all of what they have to necessities plus the few extras they can afford. If their incomes were raised, they would obviously spend more, which would create more demand and generate more jobs. It should not be forgotten that the year 1929, which was noted for a severe imbalance in incomes, gave us a devastating economic depression that lasted a decade.

The traditional reply to critics of economic inequality has been that we need not only the rich, but also a comfortably off class, who are able to put some of their incomes into investments. In other words, disparities give some people more than they "need," which allows them to underwrite the new enterprises that benefit everyone. While there is obvious validity to this argument, it should be added that much of this outlay now goes to paper contrivances, which have only a remote connection with anything productive, if any at all. Nor are the rich as necessary as they may once have been, since institutions now supply most invested capital. Metropolitan Life, Merrill Lynch, Bank of America, and the California Public Employees Pension Fund put substantially more into new production than do the 68,064 families with $1 million incomes.

In one sphere, the income gap comes closer to home. Most young Americans will not live as well as their parents did. Indeed, in many instances this is already occurring. A generation ago, many men had well-paid blue-collar jobs; now their sons are finding that those jobs are no longer available. In that earlier era, college graduates could enter a growing managerial stratum; today, firms view their payrolls as bloated and are ending the security of corporate careers. . . .

The patterns of decline prevail if the entire nation is viewed as the equivalent of family. Federal programs now award nine times as much to retirees as they do to the nation's children, so senior citizens as a group fare better than younger Americans. Twice as many children as Americans over the age of sixty live in households below the poverty line. (And as death approaches, the government is more generous: almost 30 percent of the total Medicare budget is spent on the terminal year of elderly patients' lives.) Many retired persons have come to view a comfortable life as their entitlement, and have concluded that they no longer have obligations to repay. Grandparents tend to support campaigns for the rights of the elderly, not for school bonds and bigger education budgets.

In the end, the issue may be simply stated: what would be required for all Americans—or at least as many as possible—to make the most of their lives? . . .

Poverty takes its greatest toll in the raising of children. With a few exceptions, being poor con-

signs them to schools and surroundings that do little to widen their horizons. The stark fact is that we have in our midst millions of bright and talented children whose lives are fated to be a fraction of what they might be. And by any moderate standard, deprivation extends above the official poverty line. In most of the United States, families with incomes of less than $25,000 face real limits to the opportunities open to their children. Less than one child in ten from these households now enters and graduates from college. The statistics are apparent to outside observers, and to the children themselves, who very early on become aware of the barriers they face. And from this realization results much of the behavior that the rest of the society deplores. The principal response from solvent Americans has been to lecture the poor on improving their ways.

No one defends poverty, but ideologies differ on what can or should be done to alleviate it. Conservatives generally feel it is up to the individual: those at the bottom should take any jobs they can find and work hard to pull themselves up. Hence the opposition to public assistance, which is seen as eroding character and moral fiber. Indeed, conservatives suggest that people will display character and moral fiber if they are made to manage on their own.

Not many voting Americans favor public disbursements for the poor or even for single working mothers who cannot make ends meet. Most American voters have grown weary of hearing about the problems of low-income people. Yet even those who are unsettled by the persistence of income imbalances no longer feel that government officials and experts know how to reduce the disparities.

Of course, huge redistributions occur everyday. Funds for Social Security are supplied by Americans who are currently employed, providing their elders with pensions that now end up averaging $250,000 above what their own contributions would have warranted. Agricultural subsidies give farmers enough extra cash to ensure that they will have middle-class comforts. The same subventions furnish farms owned by corporations with generous profit margins. . . .

In contrast, there is scant evidence that public programs have done much for the bottom tiers of American society. Despite the New Deal and the Great Society, including public works and public assistance, since 1935, share of income going to the poorest fifth of America's households has remained between 3.3 percent and 4.3 percent. Thus, if many elderly Americans have been raised from poverty, it is clear that younger people are now taking their places. . . .

All parts of the population except the richest fifth have smaller shares of the nation's income than they did twenty years ago. The gulf between the best-off and the rest shows no signs of diminishing, and by some political readings this should mean increased tensions between the favored fifth and everyone else. But declines in living standards have not been so severe or precipitous as to lead many people to question the equity of the economic system. The economy has ensured that a majority of Americans remain in moderate comfort and feel able to count their lives a reasonable success. Airline reservationists making $14,000 do not consider themselves "poor," and no one tells them that they are. Thus a majority of Americans still see themselves as middle class, and feel few ties or obligations to the minority with incomes less than their own.

Given this purview, why should the way America distributes its income be considered a problem? At this moment, certainly, there is scant sentiment for imposing further taxes on the well-to-do and doing more for the poor. As has been observed, there is little resentment felt toward the rich; if anything, greater animus is directed toward families receiving public assistance. Nor is it regarded as untoward if the well-off use their money to accumulate luxuries while public schools must cope with outdated textbooks and leaking roofs. Although this book is about money, about why some have more and others less, it should not be read as a plea for income redistribution. The reason is straightforward: if people are disinclined to share what they have, they will not be persuaded by a reproachful tone. Rather, its aim is to enhance our understanding of ourselves, of the forces that propel us, and the shape we are giving to the nation of which we are a part.

How a nation allocates its resources tells us how it wishes to be judged in the ledgers of history and morality. America's chosen emphasis has been on offering opportunities to the ambitious, to those with the desire and the drive to surpass. America has more self-made millionaires and more men and women who have attained $100,000 than any other country.

But because of the upward flow of funds, which has accelerated in recent years, less is left for those who lack the opportunities or the temperament to succeed in the competition. The United States now has a greater percentage of its citizens in prison or on the streets, and more neglected children, than any of the nations with which it is appropriately compared. Severe disparities—excess alongside deprivation—sunder the society and subvert common aims. With the legacy we are now creating, millions of men, women, children are prevented from being fully American, while others pride themselves on how much they can amass.

10

The Garment Industry in the Restructuring Global Economy

EDNA BONACICH, LUCIE CHENG, NORMA CHINCHILLA, NORA HAMILTON, AND PAUL ONG

These authors describe the consequences of the new processes in the global economy, particularly as they affect different classes of people in different international locales. The authors note the different interpretations that various scholars have given to the process of globalization—some seeing its positive effects, others being more critical of the impact of globalization on women workers, immigrants, and the working class.

Global integration, a long-standing feature of the world economy, is currently undergoing a restructuring. Generally, until after World War II, the advanced industrial countries of western Europe and the United States dominated the world economy and controlled most of its industrial production. The less-developed countries tended to concentrate in the production of raw materials. Since the late 1950s, and accelerating rapidly in the 1980s, however, industrial production has shifted out of the West, initially to Japan, then to the Asian NICs (newly industrializing countries—namely, Hong Kong, Taiwan, South Korea, and Singapore), and now to almost every country of the world. Less-developed countries are not manufacturing mainly for the domestic market or following a model of "import substitution"; rather, they are manufacturing for export, primarily to developed countries, and pursuing a development strategy of export-led industrialization. What we are witnessing has been termed by some a "new international division of labor" [Fröbel, Heinrichs, and Kreye 1980).

The developed countries are faced with the problem of "deindustrialization" in terms of traditional manufacturing, as their manufacturing base is shifted to other, less-developed countries (Bluestone and Harrison 1982). At the same time, they are faced with a massive rise in imports that compete with local industries' products, moving to displace them. This shift is accompanied by the rise of a new kind of transnational corporation (TNC). Of course, TNCs have existed since the beginning of the European expansion, but they concentrated mainly on the production of agricultural goods and raw materials and, in the postwar period, on manufacturing for the host country market. The new TNCs are global firms that are able to use advanced communications and transportation technology to coordinate manufacturing in multiple locations simultaneously. They engage in "off-

From: Edna Bonacich, Lucie Cheng, Norma Chinchilla, Nora Hamilton and Paul Ong, (eds.). 1994. *Global Production: The Apparel Industry in the Pacific Rim*. Philadelphia: Temple University Press, pp. 3–18. Reprinted with permission.

shore sourcing" to produce primarily for the home market (Grunwald and Flamm 1985; Sklair 1989).

TNCs sometimes engage in direct foreign investment, but globalized production does not depend on it. They can arrange for production in numerous locations through other, looser connections, such as subcontracting and licensing. In other words, TNCs can set up complex networks of global production without owning or directly controlling their various branches.

The nation-state has increasingly declined as an economic unit, with the result that states are often unable to control the actions of powerful TNCs. The TNCs are supragovernmental actors that make decisions on the basis of profit-making criteria without input from representative governments. Of course, strong states are still able to exercise considerable influence over trade policies and over the policies of the governments of developing countries.

Some scholars have used the concept of "commodity chains" to describe the new spatial arrangements of production (Gereffi and Korzeniewicz 1994). The concept shows how design, production, and distribution are broken down and geographically dispersed, with certain places serving as centers within the chain. Power is differentially allocated along the chain, and countries and firms vie to improve their position in the chain.

Focusing on the geographic aspects of global production also has led to the concept of "global cities" (Sassen 1991). These are coordination centers for the global economy, where planning takes place. They house the corporate headquarters of TNCs, as well as international financial services and a host of related business services. These cities have become the "capitals" of the new global economy.

Another way to view the restructuring is to see it as the proletarianization of most of the world. People who had been engaged primarily in peasant agriculture or in other forms of noncapitalist production are now being incorporated into the industrial labor force. Many of these people are first-generation wage-workers, and a disproportionate number of them are women. These "new" workers sometimes retain ties to noncapitalist sectors and migrate between them and capitalist employment, making their labor cheaper than that of fully proletarianized workers. But even if they are not attached to noncapitalist sectors, first-generation workers tend to be especially vulnerable to exploitative conditions. Thus, an important feature of the new globalization is that TNCs are searching the world for the cheapest available labor and are finding it in developing countries.

Countries pursuing export-led industrialization typically follow strategies that encourage the involvement of foreign capital. They offer incentives, including tax holidays and the setting up of export processing zones (EPZs), where the bureaucracy surrounding importing and exporting is curtailed; sometimes they also promise cheap and controllable labor. Countries using this development strategy do not plan to remain the providers of cheap labor for TNCs, however: they hope to move up the production ladder, gaining more economic power and control. They want to shift from labor-intensive manufactures to capital-intensive, high-technology goods. They hope to follow the path of Japan and the Asian NICs and become major economic players in the global economy.

Sometimes participation in global capitalist production is foisted on nations by advanced-industrial countries and/or suprastate organizations such as the World Bank and the International Monetary Fund (IMF), where advanced countries wield a great deal of influence. The United States, in particular, has backed regimes that support globalized production and has pushed for austerity programs that help to make labor cheap. At the same time, developed countries, including the United States, have been affected by the restructured global economy. Accompanying the rise in imports and deindustrialization has been a growth in unemployment and a polarization between the rich and the poor (Harrison and Bluestone 1988). This trend has coincided with increased racial polarization, as people of color have faced a disproportionate impact from these developments.

A rise in immigration from less-developed to more-developed countries has also accompanied globalization. The United States, for example, has experienced large-scale immigration from the Caribbean region and from Asia, two areas pursuing a manufacturing-for-export development strategy. At least part of this immigration is a product of globalization, as people are dislocated by the new economic order and are forced to emigrate for survival (Sassen 1988). Dislocations occur not only because global industries displace local ones (as in the case of agribusiness displacing peasants), but also because austerity programs exacerbate the wage gap between rich and poor countries (making the former ever more desirable). Political refugees, often from countries where the United States has supported repressive regimes, have added to the rise in immigration as well. Finally, some immigration results when people move to service global enterprise as managers, trade representatives, or technicians.

In the advanced countries, the immigration of workers has created a "Third World within." In this case, the newly created proletariat is shifting location. These immigrants play a part in the efforts of the advanced countries to hold on to their industries, by providing a local source of cheap labor to counter the low labor standards in competing countries.

In sum, we are seeing a shakeup of the old world economic order. Some countries have used manufacturing for export as a way to become major economic powers (Appelbaum and Henderson 1992; Gereffi and Wyman 1990). These countries now threaten U.S. dominance. Other countries are trying to pursue this same path, but it is not clear whether they will succeed. Meanwhile, despite the fact that the United States is suffering some negative consequences from the global restructuring, certain U.S.-based TNCs are deeply implicated in the process and benefit from it.

CONTRASTING VIEWS OF RESTRUCTURING

The new globalization receives different interpretations and different evaluations (Gondolf, Marcus, and Dougherty 1986). Some focus on the positive side; they see global production as increasing efficiency by allowing each country to specialize in its strengths. Less-developed countries are able to provide low-cost, unskilled labor while developed countries provide management, technical, and financial resources. Together they are able to maximize the efficient use of resources. The result is that more goods and services are produced more cheaply, to the benefit of all. Consumers, in particular, are seen as the great beneficiaries of globalized production, because of the abundance of low-cost, higher-quality goods from which to choose.

Globalization can be seen as part of the new system of flexible specialization (Piore and Sabel 1984). Consumer markets have become more differentiated, making the old, industrial system of mass production in huge factories obsolete. To be competitive today, a firm must be able to produce small batches of differentiated goods for diverse customers. Globalization contributes to this process by enabling firms to produce a vast range of products in multiple countries simultaneously.

Another aspect of the positive view is to see the entrance of less-developed countries into manufacturing for export as a step toward their industrialization and economic development. Although countries may enter the global economy at a tremendous disadvantage, by participating in exports they are able to accumulate capital and gradually increase their power and wealth. Japan and the Asian NICs have demonstrated the possibilities; now other countries can follow a similar path.

Although workers in the advanced countries may suffer some dislocation by the movement of industry abroad, in the long run they are seen to be beneficiaries of this process. While lower-skilled, more labor-intensive jobs will move to the developing countries, the advanced countries will gain higher-technology jobs, as well as jobs in coordinating and managing the global economy. Thus workers in the advanced countries will be "pushed up" to more middle-class positions, servicing and directing the workers in the rest of the world. Moreover, as other countries develop, their purchasing power will increase, leading to larger markets for the products of the developed countries. Growth in exports means growth in domestic production, and thus growth in domestic employment.

Those who favor globalization also note its inevitability. The economic logic that is propelling global production is immensely powerful. Technology allows globalization, and competition forges it; there is really no stopping the process, so the best one can do is adapt on the most favorable terms possible. Nations feel they must get into the game quickly so as not to be left behind.

A favorable standpoint on globalization is typically coupled with an optimistic view of the effects of immigration. Like new nations entering the global economy, immigrant workers are seen as having to suffer in the short run in order to make advances in the future. Instead of being viewed as exploited, the immigrants are seen as being granted an opportunity—one that they freely choose—to better their life circumstances. They may start off being paid low wages because they lack marketable skills, but with time, they or their children will acquire such skills and will experience upward mobility.

In general, a positive view of globalization is accompanied by a belief in the benefits of markets and free trade. The market, rather than political decision making, should, it is felt, be the arbiter of economic decision making. This favorable and inevitable view of globalization is by far the most predominant approach. It is promoted by the U.S. government, by the TNCs, by many governments in developing countries, and by various international agencies. This position receives considerable support from academics, especially economists, who provide governmental agencies with advice. It is the dominant world policy.

There is, however, a less sanguine interpretation of globalization voiced by U.S. trade unionists and many academics who study development, labor, women, inequality, and social class (Castells and Henderson 1987; Kamel 1990; Kolko 1988; Peet 1987; Ross and Trachte 1990; Sklair 1989). In general, their view is that globalization has a differential class impact: globalization is in the interests of capitalists, especially capitalists connected with TNCs, and of sectors of the capitalist class in developing nations. But the working class in both sets of countries is hurt, especially young women workers, who have become the chief employees of the TNCs (Fernandez-Kelly 1983; Fuentes and Ehrenreich 1983; Mies 1986; Nash and Fernandez-Kelly 1983).

Some argue that globalization is part of a response to a major crisis that has emerged in the advanced capitalist countries. In particular, after the post-World War II boom, the economies of these countries stagnated and profits declined; stagnation was blamed on the advances made by workers under the welfare state. Capital's movement abroad, which was preceded in the United States by regional relocation, is an effort to cut labor costs, weaken unions, and restore profitability. Put generally, globalization can be seen, in part, as an effort to discipline labor.

Globalization enables employers to pit workers from different countries against one another. Regions and nations must compete to attract investment and businesses. Competitors seek to undercut one another by offering the most favorable conditions to capital. Part of what they seek to offer is quality, efficiency, and timeliness, but they also compete in terms of providing the lowest possible labor standards: they promise a low-cost, disciplined, and unorganized work force. Governments pledge to ensure these conditions by engaging in the political repression of workers' movements (Deyo 1989).

The disciplining of the working class that accompanies globalization is not limited to conditions in the workplace. It also involves a cutback in state social programs. For example, in the United States, under the Reagan-Bush administrations, efforts were made to curtail multiple programs protecting workers' standard of living; these tax-based programs were seen as hindering capital accumulation. The argument was made that if these funds were invested by the private sector, everyone would benefit, including workers. This same logic has been imposed on developing countries; they have been granted aid and loans on the condition that they engage in austerity programs that cut back on social spending. The impact of such cutbacks is that workers are less protected from engaging in bargains of desperation when they enter the work force.

This view of globalization is accompanied by a pessimism about the policy of export-led development. Rather than believing that performing assembly for TNCs will lead to development, critics fear that it is another form of dependency, with the advanced capitalist countries and their corporations retaining economic (and political) control over the global economy (Bello and Rosenfeld 1990).

Critics also note a negative side to immigrants' experiences (Mitter 1986; Sassen 1988). They see the immigration of workers as, in part, a product of globalization and TNC activity, as workers in less-developed countries find their means of livelihood disrupted by capitalist penetration. Immigrants are thus not just people seeking a better life for themselves, but often those "forced" into moving because thet have lost the means to survive. On arrival in the more-advanced economies, they are faced with forms of coercion, including immigration regulations, racism, and sexism, that keep them an especially disadvantaged work force. Especially coercive is the condition of being an undocumented immigrant. Critics point out that those who favor globalization promote the free movement of commodities and capital, but not the free movement of labor, in the form of open borders. Political restrictions on workers add to the weakening of the working class.

In sum, the critical perspective sees globalization as an effort to strengthen the hand of capital and weaken that of labor. The favorable view argues that the interests of capital and labor are not antagonistic and that everyone benefits from capital accumulation, investment, economic growth, and the creation of jobs. Critics, on the other hand, contend that certain classes benefit at the expense of others, and that, even if workers in poor countries do get jobs, these jobs benefit the capitalists much more than they do the workers, and also hurt the workers in the advanced capitalist countries through deindustrialization.

Where does the truth lie? . . .

To a certain extent, one's point of view depends on geographic location. Generally, Asian countries, especially the NICs, appear to be transforming themselves from dependencies into major actors and competitors in the global economy, leading to an optimism about the effects of globalization. This optimism, however, blots out the suffering and labor repression that is still occurring for some workers in these countries, despite the rise in standard of living for the majority.

On the other hand, the Caribbean region generally faces a harsher reality, in part because the closeness and dominance of the United States pose special problems for these countries. They are more likely to get caught in simple assembly for the TNCs, raising questions about whether manufacturing for export will be transformable into broader economic development. Of course, some in these countries are firm believers in this policy and are pursuing it avidly, but there are clear signs that many workers are severely exploited in the process. . . .

Other confusing issues remain. For example, do women benefit from their movement into the wage sector (proletarianization) as a result of globalization? A case can be made that working outside the home and earning money gives women new-found power in their relations with men. It can also be argued, however, that these women remain under patriarchal control, but that now, in addition to their fathers and husbands, they are under the control of male bosses. They have double and even triple workloads, as they engage in wage labor, domestic labor, and often industrial homework and other forms of informalized labor (Ward 1990).

The two points of view lead to different politics. Those who hold the favorable outlook advocate working for the breakdown of all trade and investment barriers and to pushing rapidly ahead toward global integration. Critics are not trying to stem these forces completely, but rather, are attempting to set conditions on them. For example, globalization should be allowed only if labor and environmental standards are protected in the process. Similarly, the rights of workers to form unions should be safeguarded, so that business cannot wantonly pit groups of workers against one another. . . .

NOTES

Appelbaum, Richard P., and Jeffrey Henderson, eds. 1992. *States and Development in the Asian Pacific Rim.* Newbury Park, CA.: Sage.

Bello, Walden, and Stephanie Rosenfeld. 1990. *Dragons in Distress: Asia's Miracle Economies in Crisis.* San Francisco: Institute for Food and Development Policy.

Castells, Manuel, and Jeffrey Henderson. 1987. "Technoeconomic Restructuring, Sociopolitical Processes, and Spatial Transformation: A Global Perspective." In *Global Restructuring and Territorial Development,* edited by Jeffrey Henderson and Manuel Castells, 1–17. London: Sage.

Deyo, Frederic C. 1989. Beneath the Miracle: *Labor Subordination in the New Asian Industrialism.* Berkeley: University of California Press.

Fernandez-Kelly, M. Patricia. 1983. *For We Are Sold, I and My People: Women and Industry in Mexico's Frontier.* Albany: State University of New York Press.

Fröbel, Folker, Jürgen Heinrichs, and Otto Kreye. 1980. *The New International Division of Labour: Structural Unemployment in Industrialised Countries and Industrialisation in Developing Countries.* Cambridge: Cambridge University Press.

Fuentes, Annette, and Barbara Ehrenreich. 1983. *Women in the Global Factory.* Boston: South End Press.

Gereffi, Gary, and Miguel Korzeniewicz, eds. 1994. *Commodity Chains and Global Capitalism.* Westport, CT.: Greenwood Press.

Gereffi, Gary, and Donald L. Wyman, eds. 1990. *Manufacturing Miracles: Paths of Industrialization in Latin America and East Asia.* Princeton: Princeton University Press.

Gondolf, Edward W., Irwin M. Marcus, and James P. Daugherty. 1986. *The Global Economy: Divergent Perspectives on Economic Change.* Boulder, CO: Westview Press.

Grunwald, Joseph, and Kenneth Flamm. 1985. *The Global Factory: Foreign Assembly in International Trade.* Washington, D.C.: Brookings Institution.

Harrison, Bennett, and Barry Bluestone, 1988. *The Great U-Turn: Corporate Restructuring and the Polarizing of America.* New York: Basic Books.

Kamel, Rachael. 1990. *The Global Factory: Analysis and Action for a New Economic Era.* Philadelphia: American Friends Service Committee.

Kolko, Joyce. 1988. *Restructuring the World Economy.* New York: Pantheon.

Mies, Maria. 1986. *Patriarchy and Accumulation on a World Scale: Women in the International Division of Labor.* London: Zed Books.

Mitter, Swasti. 1986. *Common Fate, Common Bond: Women in the Global Economy.* London: Pluto Press.

Nash, June, and M. Patricia Fernandez-Kelly, eds. 1983. *Women, Men, and the International Division of Labor.* Albany: State University of New York Press.

Peet, Richard, ed. 1987. *International Capitalism and Industrial Restructuring.* Boston: Allen and Unwin.

Piore, Michael J., and Charles F. Sabel. 1984. *The Second Industrial Divide: Possibilities for Prosperity.* New York: Basic Books.

Ross, Robert J. S., and Kent C. Trachte. 1990. *Global Capitalism: The New Leviathan.* Albany: State University of New York Press.

Sassen, Saskia. 1988. *The Mobility of Labor and Capital: A Study in International*

Investment and Labor Flow. Cambridge: Cambridge University Press.

———. 1991. *The Global City: New York, London, Tokyo.* Princeton: Princeton University Press.

Sklair, Leslie. 1989. *Assembling for Development: The Maquila Industry in Mexico and the United States.* London: Unwin Hyman.

DISCUSSION QUESTIONS

1. What is a *commodity chain?* What evidence do you see of commodity chains in the wardrobe that you wear?

2. Compare and contrast the two perspectives on the new globalization that the authors describe. How do proponents of the positive and critical views of globalization view immigration?

INFOTRAC COLLEGE EDITION

You can use your access to InfoTrac College Edition to learn more about the subjects covered in this essay. Some suggested search term include:

commodity chains
guest workers
immigration

international (or global) division of labor
newly industrializing countries
transnational corporation

11

Modernization's Challenge to Traditional Values: Who's Afraid of Ronald McDonald?

RONALD INGLEHART AND WAYNE E. BAKER

Is there such a thing as world *values? We turn to a discussion of the "World Values Survey" to find that world values break down into rich and poor societies' values. These values create stress on all countries—pressure toward change and resistance to change, as seen in the next article on terrorism. Understanding challenges to traditional values helps shed light on terrorism in the world.*

Think about the following questions as you read this article:

1. How do values shape culture?

2. When does modernization lead to change, and when is there resistance to change?

Originally published in the March/April 2001 issue of The Futurist. *Used with permission from the World Future Society, 7910 Woodmont Avenue, Suite 450, Bethesda, Maryland 20814. Telephone: 301/656-8274; Fax: 301/951-0394; http://www.wfs.org*

GLOSSARY

Values A culture's collective ideas about right and wrong, good or bad, desirable or undesirable.
Economic globalization Influence of dominant economic systems spreading around the world.

THE WORLD VALUES SURVEY—a two-decade-long examination of the values of 65 societies coordinated by the University of Michigan's Institute for Social Research—is the largest investigation ever conducted of attitudes, values, and beliefs around the world. This study has carried out three waves of representative national surveys: the first in 1981–1982, the second in 1990–1991, and the third in 1995–1998. The fourth wave is being completed in 1999–2001. The study now represents some 80% of the world's population. These societies have per capita GNPs ranging from $300 to more than $30,000. Their political systems range from long-established stable democracies to authoritarian states.

The World Values Survey data have been used by researchers around the world for hundreds of publications in more than a dozen languages. Studies that have been based on the data cover a wide range of topics, including volunteerism in Europe, political partisanship and social class in Ireland, democratization in Korea, liberalization in Mexico, future values in Japan, and the religious vote in Western Europe.

This article examines the relationship between cultural values and economic globalization and modernization: What impact does economic development have on the values of a culture, and vice versa? Is a future "McWorld" inevitable?

Rich Values, Poor Values

The World Values Survey data show us that the world views of the people of rich societies differ systematically from those of low-income societies across a wide range of political, social, and religious norms and beliefs. The two most significant dimensions that emerged reflected, first, a polarization between *traditional* and *secular-rational* orientations toward authority and, sec-

ond, a polarization between *survival* and *self-expression* values. By *traditional* we mean those societies that are relatively authoritarian, place strong emphasis on religion, and exhibit a mainstream version of preindustrial values such as an emphasis on male dominance in economic and political life, respect for authority, and relatively low levels of tolerance for abortion and divorce. Advanced societies, or *secular-rational,* tend to have the opposite characteristics.

A central component of the survival vs. self-expression dimension involves the polarization between materialist and postmaterialist values. Massive evidence indicates that a cultural shift throughout advanced industrial society is emerging among generations who have grown up taking survival for granted. Values among this group emphasize environmental protection, the women's movement, and rising demand for participation in decision making in economic and political life. During the past 25 years, these values have become increasingly widespread in almost all advanced industrial societies for which extensive time-series evidence is available.

Economic development brings with it sweeping cultural change, some modernization theorists tell us. Others argue that cultural values are enduring and exert more influence on society than does economic change. Who's right?

One goal of the World Values Survey is to study links between economic development and changes in values. A key question that we ask is whether the globalization of the economy will necessarily produce a homogenization (or, more specifically, an Americanization) of culture—a so-called "McWorld."

In the nineteenth century, modernization theorists such as Karl Marx and Friedrich Nietzsche made bold predictions about the future of industrial society, such as the rise of labor and the decline of religion. In the twentieth century, non-Western societies were expected to abandon their traditional cultures and assimilate the technologically and morally "superior" ways of the West.

Clearly now, at the start of the twenty-first century, we need to re-think "modernization." Few people today anticipate a proletarian revolution, and non-Western societies such as East Asia have surpassed their Western role models in key aspects of modernization, such as rates of economic growth. And few observers today attribute moral superiority to the West.

On the other hand, one core concept of modernization theory still seems valid: Industrialization produces pervasive social and cultural consequences, such as rising educational levels, shifting attitudes toward authority, broader political participation, declining fertility rates, and changing gender roles. On the basis of the World Values Surveys, we believe that economic development has systematic and, to some extent, predictable cultural and political consequences. Once a society has embarked on industrialization—the central element of the modernization process—certain changes are highly likely to occur. But economic development is not the *only* force at work.

In the past few decades, modernization has become associated with *post*-industrialization: the rise of the knowledge and service-oriented economy. These changes in the nature of work had major political and cultural consequences, too. Rather than growing more materialistic with increased prosperity, postindustrial societies are experiencing an increasing emphasis on quality-of-life issues, environmental protection, and self-expression.

While industrialization increased human dominance over the environment—and consequently created a dwindling role for religious belief—the emergence of postindustrial society is stimulating further evolution of prevailing world views in a different direction. Life in postindustrial societies centers on services rather than material objects, and more effort is focused on communicating and processing information. Most people spend their productive hours dealing with other people and symbols.

Thus, the rise of postindustrial society leads to a growing emphasis on self-expression. Today's unprecedented wealth in advanced societies means an increasing share of the population grows up taking survival for granted. Their value priorities shift from an overwhelming emphasis on economic and physical security toward an increas-

ing emphasis on subjective well-being and quality of life. "Modernization," thus, is not linear—it moves in new directions.

How Values Shape Culture

Different societies follow different trajectories even when they are subjected to the same forces of economic development, in part because situation-specific factors, such as a society's cultural heritage, also shape how a particular society develops. Recently, Samuel Huntington, author of *The Clash of Civilizations* (Simon & Schuster, 1996), has focused on the role of religion in shaping the world's eight major civilizations or "cultural zones": Western Christianity, Orthodox, Islam, Confucian, Japanese, Hindu, African, and Latin American. These zones were shaped by religious traditions that are still powerful today, despite the forces of modernization.

Other scholars observe other distinctive cultural traits that endure over long periods of time and continue to shape a society's political and economic performance. For example, the regions of Italy in which democratic institutions function most successfully today are those in which civil society was relatively well developed in the nineteenth century and even earlier, as Robert Putnam notes in *Making Democracy Work* (Princeton University Press, 1993). And a cultural heritage of "low trust" puts a society at a competitive disadvantage in global markets because it is less able to develop large and complex social institutions, Francis Fukuyama argues in *Trust: The Social Virtues and the Creation of Prosperity* (Free Press, 1995).

The impression that we are moving toward a uniform "McWorld" is partly an illusion. The seemingly identical McDonald's restaurants that have spread throughout the world actually have different social meanings and fulfill different social functions in different cultural zones. Eating in a McDonald's restaurant in Japan is a different social experience from eating in one in the United States, Europe, or China.

Likewise, the globalization of communication is unmistakable, but its effects may be overesti-

Two Dimensions of Cross-Cultural Variation

1. Traditional vs. Secular-Rational Values	2. Survival vs. Self-Expression Values
Traditional values emphasize the following:	**Survival** values emphasize the following:
• God is very important in respondent's life.	• Respondent gives priority to economic and physical security over self-expression and quality of life.
• Respondent believes it is more important for a child to learn obedience and religious faith than independence and determination.	• Respondent describes self as not very happy.
• Respondent believes abortion is never justifiable.	• Respondent has not signed and would not sign a petition.
• Respondent has strong sense of national pride.	• Respondent believes homosexuality is never justifiable.
• Respondent favors more respect for authority.	• Respondent believes you have to be very careful about trusting people.
Secular-Rational values emphasize the opposite.	**Self-Expression** values emphasize the opposite.

Source: World Values Survey (http://wvs.isr.umich.edu)

mated. It is certainly apparent that young people around the world are wearing jeans and listening to U.S. pop music; what is less apparent is the persistence of underlying value differences.

. . . *Predicting Values*

. . . Cross-cultural variation is highly constrained. That is, if the people of a given society place a strong emphasis on religion, that society's relative position on many other variables can be predicted—such as attitudes toward abortion, national pride, respect for authority, and childrearing. Similarly, survival vs. self-expression values reflect wide-ranging but tightly correlated clusters of values: Materialistic (survival-oriented) societies can be predicted to value maintaining order and fighting inflation, while postmaterialistic (self-expression-oriented) societies can be predicted to value freedom, interpersonal trust, and tolerance of outgroups.

Economic development seems to have a powerful impact on cultural values: The value systems of rich countries differ systematically from those of poor countries. If we superimpose an income "map" over the values map, we see that all 19 societies with an annual per capita GNP of over $15,000 rank relatively high on both dimensions. . . . This economic zone cuts

across the boundaries of the Protestant, ex-Communist, Confucian, Catholic, and English-speaking cultural zones.

On the other hand, all societies with per capita GNPs below $2,000 fall into a cluster . . . in an economic zone that cuts across the African, South Asian, ex-Communist, and Orthodox cultural zones. The remaining societies fall into two intermediate cultural-economic zones. Economic development seems to move societies in a common direction, regardless of their cultural heritage. Nevertheless, distinctive cultural zones persist two centuries after the industrial revolution began.

Of course, per capita GNP is only one indicator of a society's level of economic development. Another might be the percentage of the labor force engaged in the agricultural sector, the industrial sector, or the service sector. The shift from an agrarian mode of production to industrial production seems to bring with it a shift from traditional values toward increasing rationalization and secularization.

But a society's cultural heritage also plays a role: All four of the Confucian-influenced societies (China, Taiwan, South Korea, and Japan) have relatively secular values, regardless of the proportion of their labor forces in the industrial sector. Conversely, the historically Roman Catholic societies (e.g., Italy, Portugal, and Spain) display relatively traditional values when compared with Confucian or ex-Communist societies with the same proportion of industrial workers. And virtually all of the historically Protestant societies (e.g., West Germany, Denmark, Norway, and Sweden) rank higher on the survival/self-expression dimension than do all of the historically Roman Catholic societies, regardless of the extent to which their labor forces are engaged in the service sector.

We can conclude from this that changes in GNP and occupational structure have important influences on prevailing world views, but traditional cultural influences persist.

Religious traditions appear to have had an enduring impact on the contemporary value systems of the 65 societies. But a society's culture reflects its entire historical heritage. A central historical event of the twentieth century was the rise and fall of a Communist empire that once ruled one-third of the world's population. Communism left a clear imprint on the value systems of those who lived under it. East Germany remains culturally close to West Germany despite four decades of Communist rule, but its value system has been drawn toward the Communist zone. And although China is a member of the Confucian zone, it also falls within a broad Communist-influenced zone. Similarly, Azerbaijan, though part of the Islamic cluster, also falls within the Communist superzone that dominated it for decades.

The Deviant U.S.

The World Value Map clearly shows that the United States is a deviant case. We do not believe it is a prototype of cultural modernization for other societies to follow, as some postwar modernization theorists have naively assumed. The United States has a much more traditional value system than any other advanced industrial society.

On the traditional/secular-rational dimension, the United States ranks far below other rich societies, with levels of religiosity and national pride comparable to those found in developing soci-

eties. The United States does rank among the most advanced societies along the survival/self-expression dimension, but even here it does not lead the world. The Swedes and the Dutch seem closer to the cutting edge of cultural change than do the Americans.

Modernization theory implies that as societies develop economically their cultures tend to shift in a predictable direction. Our data supports this prediction. Economic differences are linked with large and pervasive cultural differences. But we find clear evidence of the influence of long-established cultural zones.

Do these cultural clusters simply reflect economic differences? For example, do the societies of Protestant Europe have similar values simply because they are rich? No. The impact of a society's historical-cultural heritage persists when we control for GDP per capita and the structure of the labor force. On a value such as *interpersonal trust* (a variable on the surival/self-expression dimension), even rich Catholic societies rank lower than rich Protestant ones.

Within a given society, however, Catholics rank about as high on interpersonal trust as do Protestants. The shared historical experience of given nations, not individual personality, is crucial. Once established, the cross-cultural differences linked with religion have become part of a national culture that is transmitted by the educational institutions and mass media of given societies to the people of that nation. Despite globalization, the nation remains a key unit of shared experience, and its educational and cultural institutions shape the values of almost everyone in that society.

The Persistence of Religious and Spiritual Beliefs

As a society shifts from an agrarian to an industrial economy and survival comes to be taken for granted, traditional religious beliefs tend to decline. Nevertheless, as the twenty-first century opens, cleavages along religious lines remain strong. Why has religion been so slow to disappear?

History has taken an ironic turn: Communist-style industrialization was especially favorable to secularization, but the collapse of Communism has given rise to pervasive insecurity—and a return to religious beliefs. Five of the seven ex-Communist societies for which we have time-series data show rising church attendance.

Throughout advanced industrial societies we see two contrasting trends: the decline of attendance at religious services on the one hand, and on the other the persistence of religious beliefs and the rise of spirituality. The need for answers to spiritual questions such as why we are here and where we are going does not die out in postindustrial society. Spiritual concerns will probably always be part of the human outlook. In fact, in the three successive waves of the World Values Survey, concern for the meaning and purpose of life became *stronger* in most advanced industrial societies.

Conclusion: Whither Modernization?

Economic development is associated with pervasive, and to an extent predictable, cultural changes. Industrialization promotes a shift from traditional to secular-rational values; postindustrialization promotes a shift toward more trust, tolerance, and emphasis on well-being. Economic collapse propels societies in the opposite direction.

Economic development tends to push societies in a common direction, but rather than converging they seem to move along paths shaped by their cultural heritages. Therefore, we doubt that the forces of modernization will produce a homogenized world culture in the foreseeable future.

Certainly it is misleading to view cultural change as "Americanization." Industrializing societies in general are *not* becoming like the United States. In fact, the United States seems to be a deviant case: Its people hold much more traditional values and beliefs than do those in any other equally prosperous society. If any societies exemplify the cutting edge of cultural change, it would be the Nordic countries.

Finally, modernization is probabilistic, not deterministic. Economic development tends to transform a given society in a predictable direction, but the process and path are not inevitable. Many factors are involved, so any prediction must be contingent on the historical and cultural context of the society in question.

Nevertheless, the central prediction of modernization theory finds broad support: Economic development is associated with major changes in prevailing values and beliefs. The world views of rich societies differ markedly from those of poor societies. This does not necessarily imply cultural convergence, but it does predict the general direction of cultural change and (insofar as the process is based on intergenerational population replacement) even gives some idea of the rate at which such change is likely to occur.

In short, economic development will cause shifts in the values of people in developing nations, but it will not produce a uniform global culture. The future may *look* like McWorld, but it won't feel like one.

12

In the Barrios: Latinos and the Underclass Debate

JOAN MOORE AND RAQUEL PINDERHUGHES

In an important work by sociologist William Julius Wilson called The Truly Disadvantaged, *the term* underclass *was introduced to mean persistent poverty due largely to economic restructuring. The use of this term has been debated by scholars. Some see it blaming the victim, the poor, for their condition because of their values and behaviors. Others see it as a debate over who is responsible for the poor—the individuals themselves or society? Behavioral pathology or economic structure?*

In this discussion by Moore and Pinderhughes, the concept of underclass is considered as it applies to Latinos.

As you read, consider the following:

1. *Does the term* underclass *apply to the Latino population?*
2. *What makes the Latino population unique as a minority group in the United States?*

Joan Moore and Raquel Pinderhughes, eds., In the Barrios: Latinos and the Underclass Debate. *New York: Russell Sage Foundation, 1993. Excerpts from pp. xi to xxxix.*

GLOSSARY

Underclass   Meaning is debated, but it often refers to the poorest of the poor in the United States.
Polarization of the labor market   High- and low-level jobs but few in the middle.
Rustbelt   Area of the country (Midwest) where jobs are being lost.
Sunbelt   Area of the country (mostly south) where jobs are increasing.
Informal economic activities   Outside government control, small-scale.

IN THE PUBLICATION *THE Truly Disadvantaged,* William Julius Wilson's seminal work on persistent, concentrated poverty in Chicago's black neighborhoods, Wilson used the term "underclass" to refer to the new face of poverty, and traced its origins to economic restructuring. He emphasized the impact of persistent, concentrated poverty not only on individuals but on communities.

. . . The term "Hispanic" is used particularly by state bureaucracies to refer to individuals who reside in the United States who were born in, or trace their ancestry back to, one of twenty-three Spanish-speaking nations. Many of these individuals prefer to use the term "Latino.". . .

No matter what the details, when one examines the history of the term underclass among sociologists, it is clear that Wilson's 1987 work seriously jolted the somewhat chaotic and unfocused study of poverty in the United States. He described sharply increasing rates of what he called "pathology" in Chicago's black ghettos. By this, Wilson referred specifically to female headship, declining marriage rates, illegitimate births, welfare dependency, school dropouts, and youth crime. The changes in the communities he examined were so dramatic that he considered them something quite new.

Two of the causes of this new poverty were particularly important, and his work shifted the terms of the debate in two respects. First, Wilson argued effectively that dramatic increases in joblessness and long-term poverty in the inner city were a result of major economic shifts—eco-nomic restructuring. "Restructuring" referred to changes in the global economy that led to deindustrialization, loss and relocation of jobs, and a decline in the number of middle-level jobs—a polarization of the labor market. Second, he further fueled the debate about the causes and consequences of persistent poverty by introducing two neighborhood-level factors into the discussion. He argued that the outmigration of middle- and working-class people from the urban ghetto contributed to the concentration of poverty. These "concentration effects" meant that ghetto neighborhoods showed sharply increased proportions of very poor people. This, in turn, meant that residents in neighborhoods of concentrated poverty were isolated from "mainstream" institutions and role models. As a result, Wilson postulates, the likelihood of their engaging in "underclass behavior" was increased. Thus the social life of poor communities deteriorated because poverty intensified. . . .

The Latino Population— Some Background

American minorities have been incorporated into the general social fabric in a variety of ways. Just as Chicago's black ghettos reflect a history of slavery, Jim Crow legislation, and struggles for civil and economic rights, so the nation's Latino barrios reflect a history of conquest, immigration, and a struggle to maintain cultural identity.

In 1990 there were some 22 million Latinos residing in the United States, approximately 9 percent of the total population. Of these, 61 percent were Mexican in origin, 12 percent Puerto Rican, and 5 percent Cuban. These three groups were the largest, yet 13 percent of Latinos were of Central and South American origin and another 9 percent were classified as "other Hispanics."[1] Latinos were among the fastest-growing segments of the American population, increasing by 7.6 million, or 53 percent, between 1980 and 1990. There are predictions that Latinos will outnumber blacks by the twenty-first century. If Latino immigration and fertility continue at their current rate, there will be over 54 million Latinos in the United States by the year 2020.

This is an old population: as early as the sixteenth century, Spanish explorers settled what is now the American Southwest. In 1848, Spanish and Mexican settlers who lived in that region became United States citizens as a result of the Mexican-American War. Although the aftermath of conquest left a small elite population, the precarious position of the masses combined with the peculiarities of southwestern economic development to lay the foundation for poverty in the current period (see Barrera 1979; Moore and Pachon 1985).

In addition to those Mexicans who were incorporated into the United States after the Treaty of Guadalupe Hidalgo, Mexicans have continually crossed the border into the United States, where they have been used as a source of cheap labor by U.S. employers. The volume of immigration from Mexico has been highly dependent on fluctuations in certain segments of the U.S. economy. This dependence became glaringly obvious earlier in this century. During the Great Depression of the 1930s state and local governments "repatriated" hundreds of thousands of unemployed Mexicans, and just a few years later World War II labor shortages reversed the process as Mexican contract-laborers (braceros) were eagerly sought. A little later, in the 1950s, massive deportations recurred when "operation Wetback" repatriated hundreds of thousands of Mexicans. Once again, in the 1980s, hundreds of thousands crossed the border to work in the United States, despite increasingly restrictive legislation.

High levels of immigration and high fertility mean that the Mexican-origin population is quite young—on the average, 9.5 years younger than the non-Latino population—and the typical household is large, with 3.8 persons, as compared with 2.6 persons in non-Latino households (U.S. Bureau of the Census 1991b). Heavy immigration, problems in schooling, and industrial changes in the Southwest combine to constrain advancement. The occupational structure remains relatively steady, and though there

is a growing middle class, there is also a growing number of very poor people. . . .

Over the past three decades the economic status of Puerto Ricans dropped precipitously. By 1990, 38 percent of all Puerto Rican families were below the poverty line. A growing proportion of these families were concentrated in poor urban neighborhoods located in declining industrial centers in the Northeast and Midwest, which experienced massive economic restructuring and diminished employment opportunities for those with less education and weaker skills. The rising poverty rate has also been linked to a dramatic increase in female-headed households. Recent studies show that the majority of recent migrants were not previously employed on the island. Many were single women who migrated with their young children (Falcon and Gurak 1991). Currently, Puerto Ricans are the most economically disadvantaged group of all Latinos. As a group they are poorer than African Americans.

Unlike other Latino migrants, who entered the United States as subordinate workers and were viewed as sources of cheap labor, the first large waves of Cuban refugees were educated middle- and upper-class professionals. Arriving in large numbers after Castro's 1959 revolution, Cubans were welcomed by the federal government as bona fide political refugees fleeing communism and were assisted in ways that significantly contributed to their economic well-being. Cubans had access to job-training programs and placement services, housing subsidies, English-language programs, and small-business loans. Federal and state assistance contributed to the growth of a vigorous enclave economy (with Cubans owning many of the businesses and hiring fellow Cubans) and also to the emergence of Miami as a center for Latin American trade. Cubans have the highest family income of all Latino groups. Nevertheless, in 1990, 16.9 percent of the Cuban population lived below the poverty line.

In recent years large numbers of Salvadorans and Guatemalans have come to the United States in search of refuge from political repression. But unlike Cubans, few have been recognized by the U.S. government as bona fide refugees. Their settlement and position in the labor market have been influenced by their undocumented (illegal) status. Dominicans have also come in large numbers to East Coast cities, many also arriving as undocumented workers. Working for the lowest wages and minimum job security, undocumented workers are among the poorest in the nation.

Despite their long history and large numbers, Latinos have been an "invisible minority" in the United States. Until recently, few social scientists and policy analysts concerned with understanding stratification and social problems in the United States have noticed them. Because they were almost exclusively concerned with relations between blacks and whites, social scientists were primarily concerned with generating demographic information on the nation's black and white populations, providing almost no information on other groups.[2] Consequently, it has been difficult, sometimes impossible, to obtain accurate data about Latinos.

Latinos began to be considered an important minority group when census figures showed a huge increase in the population. By 1980 there were significant Latino communities in almost every metropolitan area in the nation. As a group, Latinos have low education, low family incomes, and are more clustered in low-paid, less-skilled occupations. Most Latinos live in cities, and poverty has become an increasing problem. On the whole, Latinos are more likely to live in poverty than the general U.S. population: poverty is widespread for all Latino subgroups except Cubans. They were affected by structural factors that influenced the socioeconomic status of all U.S. workers. In 1990, 28 percent were poor as compared with 13 percent of all Americans and 32 percent of African Americans (U.S. Bureau of the Census 1991b). Puerto Ricans were particularly likely to be poor. . . .

The Importance of Economic Restructuring

The meaning of economic restructuring has shaped the debate about the urban underclass. . . .

First, there is the "Rustbelt in the Sunbelt" phenomenon. Some researchers have argued that deindustrialization has been limited to the Rustbelt, and that the causal chain adduced by Wilson therefore does not apply outside that region. But the fact is that many Sunbelt cities developed manufacturing industries, particularly during and after World War II. Thus Rustbelt-style economic restructuring—deindustrialization, in particular—has also affected them deeply. In the late 1970s and early 1980s cities like Los Angeles experienced a major wave of plant closings that put a fair number of Latinos out of work (Morales 1985).

Second, there has been significant reindustrialization and many new jobs in many of these cities, a trend that is easily overlooked. Most of the expanding low-wage service and manufacturing industries, like electronics and garment manufacturing, employ Latinos (McCarthy and Valdez 1986; Muller and Espenshade 1986), and some depend almost completely on immigrant labor working at minimum wage (Fernandez-Kelly and Sassen 1991). In short, neither the Rustbelt nor the Sunbelt has seen uniform economic restructuring.

Third, Latinos are affected by the "global cities" phenomenon, particularly evident in New York and Chicago. This term refers to a particular mix of new jobs and populations and an expansion of both high- and low-paid service jobs (see Sassen-Koob 1984). When large multinational corporations centralize their service functions, upper-level service jobs expand. The growing corporate elite want more restaurants, more entertainment, more clothing, and more care for their homes and children, but these new consumer services usually pay low wages and offer only temporary and part-time work. The new service workers in turn generate their own demand for low-cost goods and services. Many of them are Latino immigrants and they create what Sassen calls a "Third World city . . . located in dense groupings spread all over the city": this new "city" also provides new jobs (1989, p. 70).

Los Angeles . . . has experienced many of these patterns.[3] The loss of manufacturing jobs has been far less visible than in New York or Chicago, for although traditional manufacturing declined, until the 1990s high-tech manufacturing did not. Moreover, Los Angeles' international financial and trade functions flourished (Soja 1987). The real difference between Los Angeles on the one hand and New York and Chicago on the other was that more poor people in Los Angeles seemed to be working.[4] In all three cities internationalization had similar consequences for the *structure* of jobs for the poor. More of the immigrants pouring into Los Angeles were finding jobs, while the poor residents of New York and Chicago were not.

Fourth, even though the deindustrialization framework remains of overarching importance in understanding variations in the urban context of Latino poverty, we must also understand that economic restructuring shows many different faces. It is different in economically specialized cities. Houston, for example, has been called "the oil capital of the world," and most of the devastating economic shifts in that city were due to "crisis and reorganization in the world oil-gas industry" (Hill and Feagin 1987, p. 174). Miami is another special case. The economic changes that have swept Miami have little to do with deindustrialization, or with Europe or the Pacific Rim, and much to do with the overpowering influence of its Cuban population, its important "enclave economy," and its "Latino Rim" functions (see Portes and Stepick 1993).

Finally, economic change has a different effect in peripheral areas. Both Albuquerque and Tucson are regional centers in an economically peripheral area. Historically, these two cities served the ranches, farms, and mines of their desert hinterlands. Since World War II, both became military centers, with substantial high-tech defense industrialization.[5] Both cities are accustomed to having a large, poor Latino population, whose poverty is rarely viewed as a crisis. In Tucson, for example, unemployment for Mexican Americans has been low, and there is stable year-round income. But both cities remain marginal to the national economy, and this means that the fate of their poor depends more on local factors.

Laredo has many features in common with other cities along the Texas border, with its substantial military installations, and agricultural and tourist functions. All of these cities have been affected by general swings in the American and Texan economy. These border communities have long been the poorest in the nation, and their largely Mexican American populations have suffered even more from recent economic downturns. They are peripheral to the U.S. economy, but the important point is that their economic well-being is intimately tied to the Mexican economy. They were devastated by the collapse of the peso in the 1980s. They are also more involved than most American cities in international trade in illicit goods, and poverty in Laredo has been deeply affected by smuggling. Though Texas has a long history of discrimination against Mexican Americans, race is not an issue within Laredo itself, where most of the population—elite as well as poor—is of Mexican descent. . . .

The Informal and Illicit Economies

The growth of an informal economy is part and parcel of late twentieth-century economic restructuring. Particularly in global cities, a variety of "informal" economic activities proliferates— activities that are small-scale, informally organized, and largely outside government regulations (cf. Portes, Castells, and Benton 1989). Some low-wage reindustrialization, for example, makes use of new arrangements in well-established industries (like home work in the garment industry, as seamstresses take their work home with them). Small-scale individual activities such as street vending and "handyman" house repairs and alterations affect communities in peripheral as well as global cities. . . . These money-generating activities are easily ignored by researchers who rely exclusively on aggregate data sources: they never make their way into the statistics on labor-market participation, because they are "off the books." But they play a significant role in the everyday life of many African American neighborhoods as well as in the barrios.

And, finally, there are illicit activities—most notoriously, a burgeoning drug market. There is not much doubt that the new poverty in the United States has often been accompanied by a resurgence of illicit economic activities (see Fagan, forthcoming, for details on five cities). It is important to note that most of the Latino communities . . . have been able to contain or encapsulate such activities so that they do not dominate neighborhood life. But in most of them there is also little doubt that illicit economic activities form an "expanded industry." They rarely provide more than a pittance for the average worker: but for a very small fraction of barrio households they are part of the battery of survival strategies.

Researchers often neglect this aspect of the underclass debate because it is regarded as stigmatizing. However, some . . . make it clear that the neglect of significant income-generating activities curtails our understanding of the full range of survival strategies in poor communities. At the worst (as in Laredo) it means that we ignore a significant aspect of community life, including its ramifications in producing yet more overpolicing of the barrios. Even more important, many of these communities have been able to encapsulate illicit economic activities so that they are less disruptive. This capacity warrants further analysis.

Immigration

Immigration—both international and from Puerto Rico—is of major significance for poor Latino communities in almost every city in every region of the country. Further, there is every reason to believe that immigration will continue to be important.[6]

First, it has important economic consequences. Immigration is a central feature of the economic life of global cities: for example, Los Angeles has been called the "capital of the Third World" because of its huge Latino and Asian immigration (Rieff 1991). In our sample, those cities most bound to world trends (New York, Los Angeles, Chicago, Houston, and Miami) experienced massive Latino immigration in the 1980s. In the Los Angeles, Houston, and Miami communities . . . immigration is a major factor in the labor market, and the residents of the "second settlement" Puerto Rican communities described in New York and Chicago operate within a context of both racial and ethnic change and of increased Latino immigration. The restructured economy provides marginal jobs for immigrant workers, and wage scales seem to drop for native-born Latinos in areas where immigration is high.[7] This is a more complicated scenario than the simple loss of jobs accompanying Rustbelt deindustrialization. Immigrants are ineligible for most government benefits, are usually highly motivated, and are driven to take even the poorest-paying jobs. They are also more vulnerable to labor-market swings.

These may be construed as rather negative consequences, but in addition, immigrants have been a constructive force in many cities. For example, these authors point to the economic vitality of immigrant-serving businesses. Socially and culturally, there are references . . . to the revival of language and of traditional social controls, the strengthening of networks, and the emergence of new community institutions. Recent research in Chicago focuses on the "hard work" ethos of many Mexican immigrants and the extensive resource base provided by kinship networks, a pattern that is echoed and amplified. . . . Most of Tucson's Chicano poor—not just immigrants—are involved in such helping networks.

Though immigrants have been less important in the peripheral cities of Albuquerque, Laredo, and Tucson, each of these cities is special in some way. Albuquerque has attracted few Mexican immigrants, but it draws on a historical Latino labor pool—English-speaking rural *Manitos*—who are as economically exploitable as are Spanish-speaking immigrants from Mexico. Until recently Tucson was also largely bypassed by most Mexican immigrants. Instead, there is an old, relatively self-contained set of cross-border networks, with well-established pathways of family movement and mutual aid.

Similar networks also exist in Laredo. Laredo's location on the border means that many of its workers are commuters—people who work in Laredo but live in Mexico.

In recent years, immigration has not been very significant in most African American communities, and as a consequence it is underemphasized in the underclass debate. It is also often interpreted as wholly negative. This is partly because the positive effects can be understood only by researchers who study immigrant communities themselves, partly because in some places large numbers of immigrants have strained public resources, and partly because immigrants have occasionally become a source of tension among poor minority populations. Though the specific contouring of immigration effects varies from place to place, in each city . . . immigration is a highly significant dimension of Latino poverty, both at the citywide level and also in the neighborhoods. It is an issue of overriding importance for the understanding of Latino poverty, and thus for the understanding of American urban poverty in general. . . .

The concentration of poverty comes about not only because of market forces or the departure of the middle classes for better housing; in Houston, Rodriguez shows that restructuring in real estate had the effect of concentrating poverty. Concentrated poverty can also result from government planning. Chicago's decision decades ago to build a concentration of high-rise housing projects right next to one another is a clear case in point. Another is in New York's largely Latino South Bronx, where the city's ten-year-plan created neighborhoods in which the least enterprising of the poor are concentrated, and in which a set of undesirable "Not-In-My-Back-Yard" institutions, such as drug-treatment clinics and permanent shelters for the homeless, were located. These neighborhoods are likely to remain as pockets of unrelieved poverty for many generations to come (Vergara 1991). It was not industrial decline and the exodus of stable working people that created these pockets: the cities of Chicago and New York chose to segregate their problem populations in permanent buildings in those neighborhoods. . . .

In addition, studies demonstrate that it is not just poverty that gets concentrated. Most immigrants are poor, and most settle in poor communities, thus further concentrating poverty. But, as Rodriguez shows, immigrant communities may be economically, culturally, and socially vital. Social isolation early in the immigration process, he argues, can strengthen group cohesion and lead to community development, rather than to deterioration. Los Angeles portrays institution-building among immigrants in poor communities, and institutional "resilience" characterizes many of the communities . . . especially New York and Chicago. Analysis of poverty in Tucson points to the overwhelming importance of "funds of knowledge" shared in interdependent household clusters. Although a priori it makes sociological sense that concentrated poverty should destroy communities, these studies offer evidence that a different pattern emerges under certain circumstances. To use Grenier and Stepick's term, "social capital" also becomes concentrated.

In short, the concentration of poverty need not plunge a neighborhood into disarray. . . . This line of reasoning raises other issues. If it isn't just demographic shifts that weaken neighborhoods, then what is it? These questions strike at the heart of the underclass debate. The old, rancorous controversy about the usefulness of the "culture of poverty" concept questioned whether the poor adhered to a special set of self-defeating values, and if so, whether those values were powerful enough to make poverty self-perpetuating. That argument faded as research focused more effectively on the situational and structural sources of poverty. We do not intend to revive this controversy. It is all too easy to attribute the differences between Latino and black poverty to "the culture." This line can be invidious, pitting one poor population against another in its insinuation that Latino poverty is somehow "better" than black poverty. (Ironically, this would reverse another outdated contention—i.e., that Latinos are poor *because* of their culture.) . . .

Other Aspects of Urban Space . . .

Where a poor neighborhood is located makes a difference.

First, some are targets for "gentrification." This is traditionally viewed as a market process by which old neighborhoods are revitalized and unfortunate poor people displaced. But there is a different perspective. Sassen (1989) argues that gentrification is best understood in the context of restructuring, globalization, and politics. It doesn't happen everywhere . . . gentrification, along with downtown revitalization and expansion, affects Latino neighborhoods in Chicago, Albuquerque, New York, and west side Los Angeles. In Houston, a variant of "gentrification" is documented. Apartment owners who were eager to rent to Latino immigrants when a recession raised their vacancy rates were equally eager to "upgrade" their tenants when the economy recovered and the demand for housing rose once again. Latinos were "gentrified" out of the buildings.

Second, Latinos are an expanding population in many cities, and they rub up against other populations. Most of the allusions to living space center on ethnic frictions accompanying the expansion of Latino areas of residence. Ethnic succession is explicit in Albuquerque and in Chicago. . . . It is implicit in East Los Angeles, with the Mexicanization of Chicano communities, and in Houston, with the immigration of Central Americans to Mexican American neighborhoods and the manipulated succession of Anglos and Latinos. In Albuquerque and East Los Angeles, Latinos are "filling-in" areas of the city, in a late phase of ethnic succession. Ethnic succession is *not* an issue in Laredo because the city's population is primarily of Mexican origin. It is crucial in Miami, where new groups of immigrants are establishing themselves within the Latino community: newer immigrants tend to move into areas vacated by earlier Cuban arrivals, who leave for the suburbs. In Brooklyn, a different kind of urban ecological function is filled by the Puerto Rican barrio—that of an ethnic buffer between African American and Anglo communities. Los Angeles' Westlake area is most strongly affected by its location near downtown: it is intensely involved in both gentrification and problems of ethnic succession. Here the Central Americans displaced a prior population, and, in turn, their nascent communities are pressured by an expanding Koreatown to the west and by gentrification from the north and from downtown.

These details are important in themselves, but they also have implications for existing theories of how cities grow and how ethnic groups become segregated (and segregation is closely allied to poverty). Most such theories take the late nineteenth-century industrial city as a point of departure—a city with a strong central business district and clearly demarcated suburbs. In these models, immigrants initially settle in deteriorating neighborhoods near downtown. Meanwhile, earlier generations of immigrants, their predecessors in those neighborhoods, leapfrog out to "areas of second settlement," often on the edge of the city. . . .

Thus it is no surprise that the "traditional" Rustbelt pattern of ethnic location and ethnic succession fails to appear in most cities discussed in this volume. New Latino immigrants are as likely to settle initially in communities on the edge of town (near the new jobs) as they are to move near downtown; or their initial settlement may be steered by housing entrepreneurs, as in Houston. The new ecology of jobs, housing, and shopping malls has made even the old Rustbelt cities like Chicago less clearly focused on a central downtown business district.

Housing for the Latino poor is equally distinctive. Poor communities in which one-third to one-half of the homes are owner-occupied would seem on the face of it to provide a different ambience from public housing—like the infamous phalanx of projects on Chicago's South Side that form part of Wilson's focus. . . .

Finally, space is especially important when we consider Mexican American communities on the border. Mexican Americans in most border communities have important relationships with kin living across the border in Mexico, and this is certainly the case in Tucson and Laredo. But space is also important in economic matters. Shopping, working, and recreation are conditioned by the proximity of alternative opportunities on both sides of the border. And in Laredo the opportunities for illicit economic transactions also depend on location. The Laredo barrios in which illicit activities are most concentrated are located right on the Rio Grande River, where cross-border transactions are easier.

In sum, when we consider poor minority neighborhoods, we are drawn into a variety of issues that go well beyond the question of how poverty gets concentrated because middle-class families move out. We must look at the role of urban policy in addition to the role of the market. We must look at the factors that promote and sustain segregation. We must look at how housing is allocated, and where neighborhoods are located within cities. And, finally, we must look at how the location of a neighborhood facilitates its residents' activity in licit and illicit market activities.

REFERENCES

Editors' Note: Complete notes can be found in the original article under title.

AFL-CIO Industrial Union Department 1986. *The Polarization of America.* Washington, DC: AFL-CIO Industrial Union Department.

Auletta, Ken, 1982. *The Underclass.* New York: Random House.

Barrera, Mario, 1979. *Race and Class in the Southwest.* Notre Dame, IN: University of Notre Dame Press.

Bluestone, Barry, and Bennett Harrison, 1982. *The Deindustrialization of America.* New York: Basic Books.

Chenault, Lawrence Royce, 1938. *The Puerto Rican Migrant in New York.* New York: Columbia University Press.

Clark, Margaret, 1959. *Health in the Mexican American Culture.* Berkeley: University of California Press.

Crawford, Fred, 1961. *The Forgotten Egg.* San Antonio, TX: Good Samaritan Center.

Edmundson, Munro S., 1957. *Los Manitos: A Study of Institutional Values.* New Orleans: Tulane University, Middle American Research Institute.

Ellwood, David T., 1988. *Poor Support: Poverty in the American Family.* New York: Basic Books.

Falcon, Luis, and Douglas Gurak, 1991. "Features of the Hispanic Underclass: Puerto Ricans and Dominicans in New York." Unpublished manuscript.

Fernandez-Kelly, Patricia, and Saskia Sassen, 1991. "A Collaborative Study of Hispanic Women in the Garment and Electronics Industries: Executive Summary." New York: New York University, Center for Latin American and Caribbean Studies.

Galarza, Ernesto, 1965. Merchants of Labor. San Jose, CA: The Rosicrucian Press, Ltd.

Goldschmidt, Walter, 1947. *As You Sow.* New York: Harcourt, Brace.

Gosnell, Patricia Aran, 1949. *Puerto Ricans in New York City.* New York: New York University Press.

Handlin, Oscar, 1959. *The Newcomers: Negroes and Puerto Ricans.* Cambridge, MA: Harvard University Press.

Hill, Richard Child, and Joe R. Feagin, 1987. "Detroit and Houston: Two Cities in Global Perspective." In Michael Peter Smith and Joe R. Feagin, eds. In *The Capitalist City,* pp. 155–177. New York: Basil Blackwell.

Kluckhohn, Florence, and Fred Strodtbeck, 1961. *Variations in Value Orientations.* Evanston, IL: Row, Peterson.

Leonard, Olen, and Charles Loomis, 1938. *Culture of a Contemporary Rural Community: El Cerito, NM.* Washington, DC: U.S. Department of Agriculture.

Levy, Frank, 1977. "How Big Is the Underclass?" Working Paper 0090-1. Washington, DC: Urban Institute.

Maldonado-Denis, Manuel, 1972. *Puerto Rico: A Sociohistoric Interpretation.* New York: Random House.

Massey, Douglas, and Mitchell Eggers, 1990. "The Ecology of Inequality: Minorities and the Concentration of Poverty." *American Journal of Sociology* 95:1153–1188.

Matza, David, 1966. "The Disreputable Poor." In Reinhardt Bendix and Seymour Martin Lipset, eds. *Class, Status and Power,* pp. 289–302. New York: Free Press.

McCarthy, Kevin, and R. B. Valdez, 1986. *Current and Future Effects of Mexican Immigration in California.* Santa Monica, CA: Rand Corporation.

McWilliams, Carey, 1949. *North From Mexico.* New York: J. B. Lippincott.

Menefee, Seldon, and Orin Cassmore, 1940. *The Pecan Shellers of San Antonio.* Washington: WPA, Division of Research.

Mills, C. Wright, Clarence Senior, and Rose K. Goldsen, 1950. *The Puerto Rican Journey.* New York: Harper.

Montiel, Miguel, 1970. "The Social Science Myth of the Mexican American Family." *El Grito* 3:56–63.

Moore, Joan, 1989. "Is There a Hispanic Underclass?" *Social Science Quarterly* 70:265–283.

Moore, Joan, and Harry Pachon, 1985. *Hispanics in the United States*. Englewood Cliffs, NJ: Prentice Hall.

Morales, Julio, 1986. *Puerto Rican Poverty and Migration: We Just Had to Try Elsewhere*. New York: Praeger.

Morales, Rebecca, 1985. "Transitional Labor: Undocumented Workers in the Los Angeles Automobile Industry." *International Migration Review* 17:570–96.

Morris, Michael, 1989. "From the Culture of Poverty to the Underclass: An Analysis of a Shift in Public Language." *The American Sociologist* 20: 123–133.

Muller, Thomas, and Thomas J. Espenshade, 1986. *The Fourth Wave*. Washington, DC: Urban Institute Press.

Murray, Charles, 1984. *Losing Ground*. New York: Basic Books.

Padilla, Elena, 1958. *Up From Puerto Rico*. New York: Columbia University Press.

Perry, David, and Alfred Watkins, 1977. *The Rise of the Sunbelt Cities*. Beverly Hills, CA: Sage.

Portes, Alejandro, Manuel Castells, and Lauren A. Benton, 1989. *The Informal Economy*. Baltimore: Johns Hopkins University Press.

Portes, Alejandro, and Alex Stepick, 1993. *City on the Edge: The Transformation of Miami*. Berkeley: University of California Press.

Rand, Christopher, 1958. *The Puerto Ricans*. New York: Oxford University Press.

Ricketts, Erol, and Isabel V. Sawhill, 1988. "Defining and Measuring the Underclass." *Journal of Policy Analysis and Management* 7:316–325.

Rieff, David, 1991. *Los Angeles: Capital of the Third World*. New York: Simon and Schuster.

Rodriguez, Clara, 1989. *Puerto Ricans: Born in the U.S.A.* Boston: Unwin Hyman.

Romano-V, Octavio I, 1968. "The Anthropology and Sociology of the Mexican Americans." *El Grito* 2:13–26.

Russell, George, 1977. "The American Underclass." *Time Magazine* 110 (August 28):14–27.

Sanchez, George, 1940. *Forgotten People: A Study of New Mexicans*. Albuquerque: University of New Mexico Press.

Sassen, Saskia, 1989. "New Trends in the Sociospatial Organization of the New York City Economy." In Robert Beauregard, ed. *Economic Restructuring and Political Response*. Newberry Park, CA.

Sassen-Koob, Saskia, 1984. "The New Labor Demand in Global Cities." In Michael Smith, ed. *Cities in Transformation*. Beverly Hills, CA: Sage.

Saunders, Lyle, 1954. *Cultural Differences and Medical Care*. New York: Russell Sage Foundation.

Senior, Clarence Ollson, 1965. *Our Citizens from the Caribbean*. New York: McGraw Hill.

Soja, Edward, 1987. "Economic Restructuring and the Internationalization of the Los Angeles Region." In Michael Peter Smith and Joe R. Feagin, eds. *The Capitalist City*, pp. 178–198. New York: Basil Blackwell.

Stevens Arroyo, Antonio M., 1974. *The Political Philosophy of Pedro Abizu Campos: Its Theory and Practice*. Ibero American Language and Area Center. New York: New York University Press.

Sullivan, Mercer L., 1989a. *Getting Paid: Youth Crime and Work in the Inner City*. Ithaca: Cornell University Press.

Taylor, Paul, 1928. *Mexican Labor in the U.S.: Imperial Valley*. Berkeley: University of California Publications in Economics.

———, 1930. *Mexican Labor in the U.S.: Dimit County, Winter Garden District, South Texas*. Berkeley: University of California Publications in Economics.

———, 1934. *An American-Mexican Frontier*. Chapel Hill, NC: University of North Carolina Press.

U.S. Bureau of the Census, 1991b. *The Hispanic Population in the United States: March 1991*. Current Population Reports, Series P-20, No. 455. Washington, DC: U.S. Government Printing Office.

Vaca, Nick, 1970. "The Mexican American in the Social Sciences." *El Grito* 3:17–52.

Vergara, Camilo Jose, 1991. "Lessons Learned: Lessons Forgotten: Rebuilding New York City's Poor Communities." *The Livable City* 15:3–9.

Wagenheim, Kal, 1975. *A Survey of Puerto Ricans on the U.S. Mainland*. New York: Praeger.

Wakefield, Dan, 1959. *Island in the City*. New York: Corinth Books.

Wilson, William Julius, 1987. *The Truly Disadvantaged: The Inner City, the Underclass, and Public Policy*. Chicago: The University of Chicago Press.

———, 1990. "Social Theory and Public Agenda Research: The Challenge of Studying Inner-city Social Dislocations." Paper presented at Annual Meeting of the American Sociological Association.

13

Koreans in Small Entrepreneurial Businesses

ILSOO KIM

In contrast to Mexican Americans, Koreans represent a new immigrant group that has achieved significant success and is heading toward upward mobility in American society. Kim's article shows us some of the contrasts separating the conditions of this group from Garza's population, not the least of which is their immigration to America in complete family groups, enabling them to marshall all their attention and resources on their members and life in the new country. Like the Mexican Americans, the Koreans are willing to self-sacrifice and defer gratification so that their children can enjoy a better life, but unlike them, they are usually legal immigrants who do not have to worry about being arrested and deported, enabling them to pool the resources of their extended kinship networks into small business enterprises where they all work. Highly capitalistic and raised in middle-class backgrounds, the Koreans save their money and reinvest it, operating small shops and participating in international trade between America and Asia. Unlike earlier groups of Asian immigrants, these Koreans move beyond their strictly ethnic group affiliations to strongly involve themselves with community institutions in their new urban neighborhoods. Compare and contrast the experiences of Mexican Americans and Korean Americans. Why do you think these two groups have experienced such different histories in American society? Based on these experiences, what do you think is the future of these groups in the United States?

A high proportion of Korean immigrants across the nation have chosen small business as the means for pursuing the American dream in postindustrial America. As in the case of Jewish immigrants at the turn of the century, post–1965 Korean immigrants have developed small businesses as an economic beachhead for their own and their children's further advancement in American society. In fact, Korean immigrants have earned a new racial epithet—"Kew" or "Korean Jew." In the New York metropolitan area alone, Korean immigrants, as of 1985, ran some 9,000 small business enterprises, certainly contributing to the recent vitality of the New York economy.

Given the structural changes in the American, and especially the New York, economy in which small businesses have declined in number (Freedman 1983:103), why have Korean immigrants "inundated" small businesses and reacti-

From New Immigrants in New York, Nancy Foner (ed.). ©1987 Columbia University Press. Reprinted by permission.

vated a traditional immigrant path to the American dream? The massive Korean entry into small businesses may be welcomed as a revival of old patterns by those who lament the loss of "rugged individualism" and entrepreneurship in the United States and the dominant trend toward business concentration, centralization, and bureaucratization. But Korean involvement in small business is not a duplication of patterns found among "old" European immigrants earlier in the century. Rather, it must be understood on its own terms—a product of Korean immigrants' homeland-derived socioeconomic and cultural characteristics or resources as well as broader socioeconomic conditions in their new land. . . .

This essay focuses on three modern, structural factors that have supported or been conducive to the proliferation of Korean small businesses in New York. The first factor is the utilization of modern "ethnic class resources" which Koreans brought with them from their home country. These ethnic class resources include advanced education, economic motivation or "success ideology," and money. The second factor is the economic opportunities available in New York where limited employment possibilities in the mainstream economy coincided with opportunities that opened up in New York's economic structure due to demographic, residential, and ethnic changes in the city. Finally, the third factor is the role of such "modern" ethnic institutions as the mass media, churches, and businessmen's associations in the New York Korean community. . . .

THE BACKGROUND OF NEW KOREAN IMMIGRANTS

Migration and Settlement Patterns

The Korean community in the New York metropolitan area is the result of the 1965 Immigration and Nationality Act which ended the severe numerical limits on immigration from Asian countries. According to the 1980 census, 94 percent of the Korean-born population in the New York metropolitan area arrived since 1965.

The reason most Koreans give for emigrating to America is basically "to find a better life." Behind this rather simple answer are a number of complex push factors, including Korean population pressure and political instability. The political uncertainty in South Korea, caused mainly by the military tension between South and North Korea since the Korean War (1950–53), led many middle- and upper-middle-class Koreans to leave for the United States in fear of another Korean war, especially in the 1970s (see Illsoo Kim 1984). Population pressures have also driven South Koreans from their homeland. In a nation roughly the size of the state of Maine, the number of people has grown from 25 million in 1960 to 40 million in 1984. The population density of South Korea is the third highest in the world. This population explosion, along with rapid industrialization and urbanization, has led to typical Third World urban problems—severe crowding, pollution, and intense economic competition for limited resources and opportunities.

South Korea has also witnessed a revolution of rising expectations, a result of the country's rapid economic development through increasing international trade as well as the population's encounters with Western, especially American, mass culture. Koreans are now fascinated by American life-styles, which the vast majority cannot hope to obtain in South Korea. The disparity between their desires and their limited resources and opportunities has tended to make urban, especially college-educated, Koreans restless and dissatisfied and to intensify their conviction that South Korea is not a good place to live. As I will discuss later, the majority of Korean immigrants are drawn from this urban middle class in South Korea. . . .

Korean immigrants have predominantly settled in large metropolitan areas in the United States. The largest Korean community is in the Los Angeles metropolitan area, followed by New York, and then Chicago. Within the New York metropolitan area, Koreans have not formed one single territorial community, although there are heavy concentrations in the white lower-middle-class sections of Flushing, Jackson Heights, Corona, and Elmhurst in Queens. Even in these neighborhoods, Korean immigrants have not established single-block residential enclaves and they live among members of the second or third generation of old European immigrants as well as such new immigrants as Cubans and other Asians (see Illsoo Kim 1981:181–86 for characteristics of the Korean nonterritorial community). Once Koreans make it in New York City—as doctors, engineers, or successful businessmen—they nearly always move to the suburbs.

Socioeconomic Characteristics

The recent Korean immigration is selective and includes a high proportion of well-educated urban middle-class people. A majority of Korean immigrants are drawn from the upper middle or middle classes in the major cities of South Korea such as Seoul, Pusan, and Taegue (Illsoo Kim 1981:38) and thus had experience of living in large modern urban centers before moving to the United States.

Despite the fact that so many Korean immigrants come to New York with high levels of education, professional experience, and an urban middle-class background, most are not able to obtain well-paid professional, white-collar work in the mainstream American occupational structure. Such work requires proficiency in English and a long period of training in large-scale American organizations— insuperable barriers to most Korean immigrants. In urban America, especially in New York, the center of economic activities has shifted to white-collar, service industries; lacking professional service skills, Koreans are handicapped.

Under these circumstances, Korean immigrants, who generally had little propensity for commercial activity in South Korea, often turn to small business in New York. In so doing, they utilize the very ethnic class resources they bring with them—money, advanced education, high economic motivation, a work ethic, and professional or sometimes business skills. I refer to these resources as "ethnic class resources" since they are mainly derived from the social class circumstances of the immigrants in South Korea, a homogeneous ethnic state. Many Korean immigrants in New York come with money they can use to set up small businesses. Their educational background means they have skills relevant to running businesses. And the fact that large numbers held high-level and prestigious jobs in South Korea gives them the confidence and motivation to work hard to succeed.

The Immigrant Family

Koreans have generally come to New York with members of their nuclear family, their basic social unit, although frequently a family is temporarily separated so that a pioneer member can establish an economic base or because of a bureaucratic delay under United States immigration laws. The immigration of families has been made possible by the humane nature of the 1965 U.S. immigration law, which emphasized the reunion of immediate relatives.

The continuation of two- and often three-generation families in New York is another key factor in the proliferation of small businesses among Korean immigrants. First, family members who have come to New York are a major source of capital for small businesses. Some families bring considerable amounts of money from South Korea; others rely heavily on savings accumulated and pooled in New York for their first businesses (compare Kim and Hurh 1985:101–102 on Korean businesses in the Chicago area). The South Korean government allows each emigrant family to take a maximum of $100,000 to the United States in the form of settlement money. Family members planning to emigrate frequently gather a significant sum by combining their savings or by selling personal property. This settlement money represents one of the few ways a Korean family can enter the United States prepared to buy a small business or to pay initial living expenses. Second, many immigrants can rely on family labor in their enterprises in New York. Largely owing to the cultural legacy of Confucian familism, Korean immigrants subscribe to a family–centered success ethic that leads family members to be willing to devote themselves to the family business. That family members are willing to work long hours has been especially important in the greengrocer business, enabling Korean enterprises in New York to compete with supermarket chains (Illsoo Kim 1981:115–116). Here is one family story:

Mr. Yun, his wife, and their two teenage children entered the United States in 1974 after Mr. Yun's brother, a naturalized American citizen, had petitioned the U.S. Immigration and Naturalization Service on their behalf. Upon arrival, Mrs. Yun immediately sent for her parents on a tourist visa, and consequently a three-generation family was established at Mr. Yun's residence. Mr. Yun, a college graduate with a major in business management, had worked for the U.S. Army in South Korea. He had a good command of colloquial English and, when he arrived, was able to get a low-level clerical job in a New York City government agency. His wife and mother-in-law did piecework for New York garment factories. In two years they had saved $20,000, which they used to buy a fruit and vegetable store from another Korean who, in turn, had purchased it from an old Italian.

Thereafter, Mr. Yun arose at 4 A.M. every morning and drove to the Hunt's Point wholesale market in the Bronx to purchase the day's goods. His wife worked from 7 A.M. to 7 P.M. as the store's cashier. Mrs. Yun's mother washed, clipped, and sorted vegetables; her father, who was too old to engage in physical labor, regularly stationed himself on a chair at the store's entrance to help deter shoplifters. The teenagers, too, were part-time but regular workers, helping in the store before and after school. In Mr. Yun's words, "We worked and worked like hell." But he and and his family were successful. Mr. Yun found a Korean partner and in 1980 they bought a gas station on Route 4 in New Jersey. Mr. Yun continued to run the greengrocery business while leaving the management of the gas station to his partner, an auto mechanic.

SMALL BUSINESS AS AN ECONOMIC BASIS OF THE KOREAN COMMUNITY

The extent of Korean immigrants involvement in small business in New York is striking. It is true, of course, that Koreans are found in other occupational spheres in New York—many as medical professionals (doctors, nurses, pharmacists, and technicians) and as engineers, mechanics, and operatives (see Illsoo Kim 1981:40). Nonetheless, small businesses can be said to be the economic foundation of the Korean community in New York and in the United States in general.

Most Korean businesses, especially labor-intensive retail shops such as greengrocery businesses, fish stores, and discount stores want to hire, and actively recruit, Korean immigrants or *kyopo* (fellow countrymen). In the New York Korean community small businesses are the primary source of employment for newcomers or greenhorns who lack proficiency in English and skills that are marketable in the wider economy. These newcomers have no choice but to take jobs with Korean employers, working long hours without such benefits as medical insurance and overtime pay. The availability of this kind of labor is beneficial to business owners who, at the same time, can feel they are helping their compatriots. One Korean business leader, for example, boasted of the small business contribution to the community: "In our *kyopo* (fellow countrymen) society there is no unemployment problem thanks to the jobs created by *kyopo* businessmen. I have never seen unemployed Koreans." Indeed, it is also my observation that unemployed Korean immigrants are few in number.

The very proliferation and success of Korean small businesses has, in itself, had an independent effect in stimulating further business activity in the Korean community. Setting up a small business has become, in a sense, a "cultural fashion" among Koreans, a point that has not received sufficient attention in the literature on immigrant enterprises. A Korean aphorism has it that "running a *jangsa* (commercial business) is the fastest way to get ahead in America," and this saying is widespread among Korean immigrants, including those who have just arrived. In Korean gatherings such as church meetings, alumni meetings and picnics, Koreans devote much of their time to talk about *jangsa*. At one church meeting, a Korean immigrant, who had just opened a fine jewelry store in midtown Manhattan, talked to church members about his business: "Making money is a mysterious magic to me. I never expected such a good profit." Many Korean immigrants have been susceptible to this kind of glorification of small business and, impressed by the success of others, have entered small business. In addition, the ethnic media, especially Korean daily newspapers, frequently present stories about Korean Horatio Algers who have "made it" through small business and this, too, encourages Korean entry into small business. . . .

COMMUNITY INSTITUTIONS
AND BUSINESS ENTERPRISES

Korean community institutions play an important role in the proliferation and success of Korean small businesses in New York City, but these differ from the traditional ethnic associations that several works on immigrant enterprises in the United States have emphasized. . . .

In the case of Korean immigrants in New York, it is modern ethnic institutions, many derived from South Korea but all influenced by external forces in New York, that are crucial. These institutions serve many important functions for Korean enterpreneurs and stimulate Korean business activity in New York. The modern, ethnic institutions that support Korean enterprises in the New York metropolitan area include churches, the mass media, and business associations. The analysis below considers the extent to which each contributes to Korean business development.

The Protestant Church as a Community

Protestant churches have flourished among Koreans in New York partly because so many immigrants are drawn from the Christian, especially Protestant, population in South Korea. In addition, the churches have become important community centers for immigrants in the absence of discrete, residential enclaves among them. Indeed, at least for members, church communities have become the substitute for ethnic neighborhoods. . . .

Korean churches are much more than sites for religious services. Because they serve multiple, secular functions they are central places for community activities and they have, in fact, opened up membership to all segments of the Korean population. A Korean engineer living in a "white" New Jersey suburb said: "On Sunday I do not want my children watching TV all day long. At least one day a week I want them to intermingle with other Koreans and learn something about Korea. This is the reason why my family and I attend [Protestant] church even though I am a Buddhist. My offerings are nothing but the payment for the services my family has received from the church." Ministers in the churches perform numerous secular roles, and they are mainly judged by their congregations according to how well they do so. The ministers' extrachurch activities include: "matchmaking, presiding over marriage ceremonies, visiting hospitalized members, assisting moving families, making congratulatory visits to families having a new baby, making airport pick-ups of newly arrived family members, interpreting for "no-English" members, administering job referral and housing services, and performing other similar personal services" (Illsoo Kim 1981:200).

In this context, most Korean Protestants attend churches not only for religious salvation but also for secular—economic and social—reasons. They want to make and meet Korean friends; they are looking for jobs or job information; they want to obtain business information, make business contacts or conduct business negotiations; or they seek private loans or want to organize or participate in *gae,* a Korean rotating credit association.

Ethnic Media and the Business Community

The Korean ethnic media also play a decisive role in maintaining the Korean community in the New York metropolitan area. The Korean ethnic media go beyond delivering news. By informing geographically dispersed Korean immigrants of community events and meetings as well as of commercial sales and news, the media are a powerful means of integrating and sustaining the Korean community. What is pertinent here is that the ethnic media have been crucial in the rapid expansion of Korean enterprises. . . .

The contribution of the newspapers to Korean enterprises is twofold. First, they are an influential agency for socializing Korean immigrants into small business capitalism. They provide immigrants with all kinds of commercial information on tax guidelines, accounting, commercial issues, and prospects for new businesses. They carry articles or essays on successful *kyopo* (fellow countrymen) in business, who serve as role models for newcomers to emulate. They also quickly cover events affecting Korean small businessmen. For example, they have alerted Korean businessmen to immigration officials' crackdowns on Korean illegal aliens employed in Korean businesses and they have promptly published news of frequent conflicts between Korean businessmen and blacks. Second, the community media, especially the daily Korean language newspapers, facilitate the expansion of the Korean subeconomy by carrying advertising for ethnic business products, ethnic services, commodity sales, housing sales or rentals, jobs, and so forth.

Businessmen's Associations and Ethnic Solidarity

Korean businessmen's associations, as their name suggests, are clearly involved in Korean business development. They can be classified into two categories: (1) associations based on business type and (2) associations based on geographical area. Korean businessmen have formed associations of the first type in business lines in which they are active. There are, for example, associations of greengrocers, fish retailers, dry cleaners, garment retailers, garment subcontractors, and gas station operators. As for the second category, Korean businessmen have also established "prosperity associations" in major commercial areas of Korean business concentration. Korean prosperity associations can be found in the following areas of New York City: the South Bronx; Flushing, Sunnyside, and Jamaica in Queens; Church Avenue in Brooklyn; the Lower East Side, Central Harlem, and Washington Heights in Manhattan. . . .

Since Korean immigrants are "modernized" ethnics, they rely upon modern ethnic institutions—churches, the media, and businessmen's associations—in their development of small business capitalism. The Korean utilization of these modern institutions departs from the old pattern of Chinese and Japanese solidarity for business based upon kinship and regional associations. It is my view that studies of ethnic enterprise in America have not paid sufficient attention to the impact of "modern" ethnic community institutions on immigrant enterprises—or, for that matter, to the effect of homeland-derived class resources and economic opportunities in particular American urban contexts. These structural factors, so critical in Korean enterprises in New York, are, I would argue, bound to be important in understanding the involvement of other new immigrant groups in small businesses as well.

REFERENCES

Freedman, Marcia. 1983. "The Labor Market for Immigrants in New York City." *New York Affairs* 7:94–110.

Kim, Illsoo. 1981. *New Urban Immigrants: The Korean Community in New York.* Princeton: Princeton University Press.

———. 1984. "Korean Emigration Connections in Urban America: A Structural Analysis of Premigration Factors in South Korea." Paper presented to the Conference on Asia-Pacific Immigration to the United States, East-West Population Institute, Honolulu, Hawaii.

Kim, Kwang Chung and Won Moo Hurh. 1985. "Ethnic Resources Utilization of Korean Immigrant Entrepreneurs in the Chicago Minority Area." *International Migration Review* 19:82–111.

14

The Social Construction
of Gender

MARGARET L. ANDERSEN

In this essay, Margaret Andersen outlines the meaning of the "social construction of gender." She discusses the difference between the terms "sex" and "gender" and defines sexuality as it relates to both. After a brief discussion of the cultural basis of gender, the essay outlines the difference between a gender roles conceptualization of gender and the gendered institutions approach.

To understand what sociologists mean by the phrase *the social construction of gender,* watch people when they are with young children. "Oh, he's such a boy!" someone might say as he or she watches a 2-year-old child run around a room or shoot various kinds of play guns. "She's so sweet," someone might say while watching a little girl play with her toys. You can also see the social construction of gender by listening to children themselves or watching them play with each other. Boys are more likely to brag and insult other boys (often in joking ways) than are girls; when conflicts arise during children's play, girls are more likely than boys to take action to diffuse the conflict (McCloskey and Coleman, 1992; Miller, Danaber, and Forbes, 1986).

To see the social construction of gender, try to buy a gender-neutral present for a child—that is, one not specifically designed with either boys or girls in mind. You may be surprised how hard this is, since the aisles in toy stores are highly stereotyped by concepts of what boys and girls do and like. Even products such as diapers, kids' shampoos, and bicycles are gender stereotyped. Diapers for boys are packaged in blue boxes; girls' diapers are packaged in pink. Boys wear diapers with blue borders and little animals on them; girls wear diapers with pink borders with flowers. You can continue your observations by thinking about how we describe children's toys. Girls are said to play with dolls; boys play with action figures!

When sociologists refer to the **social construction of gender,** they are referring to the many different processes by which the expectations associated with being a boy (and later a man) or being a girl (later a woman) are passed on through society. This process pervades society, and it begins the minute a child is born. The exclamation "It's a boy!" or "It's a girl!" in the delivery room sets a

From: Margaret L. Andersen. 2000. *Thinking about Women: Sociological Perspectives on Sex and Gender.* Needham Heights, MA: Allyn and Bacon, pp. 19–24. Reprinted with permission.

course that from that moment on influences multiple facets of a person's life. Indeed, with the modern technologies now used during pregnancy, the social construction of gender can begin even before one is born. Parents or grandparents may buy expected children gifts that reflect different images, depending on whether the child will be a boy or a girl. They may choose names that embed gendered meanings or talk about the expected child in ways that are based on different social stereotypes about how boys and girls behave and what they will become. All of these expectations—communicated through parents, peers, the media, schools, religious organizations, and numerous other facets of society—create a concept of what it means to be a "woman" or be a "man." They deeply influence who we become, what others think of us, and the opportunities and choices available to us. The idea of the social construction of gender sees society, not biological sex differences, as the basis for gender identity. To understand this fully, we first need to understand some of the basic concepts associated with the social construction of gender and review some information about biological sex differences.

SEX, GENDER, AND SEXUALITY

The terms *sex, gender,* and *sexuality* have related, but distinct, meanings within the scholarship on women. **Sex** refers to the biological identity and is meant to signify the fact that one is either male or female. One's biological sex usually establishes a pattern of gendered expectations, although, . . . biological sex identity is not always the same as gender identity; nor is biological identity always as clear as this definition implies.

Gender is a social, not biological, concept, referring to the entire array of social patterns that we associate with women and men in society. Being "female" and "male" are biological facts; being a woman or a man is a social and cultural process—one that is constructed through the whole array of social, political, economic, and cultural experiences in a given society. Like race and class, gender is a social construct that establishes, in large measure, one's life chances and directs social relations with others. Sociologists typically distinguish sex and gender to emphasize the social and cultural basis of gender, although this distinction is not always so clear as one might imagine, since gender can even construct our concepts of biological sex identity.

Making this picture even more complex, **sexuality** refers to whole constellation of sexual behaviors, identities, meaning systems, and institutional practices that constitute sexual experience within society. This is not so simple a concept as it might appear, since sexuality is neither fixed nor unidimensional in the social experience of diverse groups. Furthermore, sexuality is deeply linked to gender relations in society. Here, it is important to understand that sexuality, sex, and gender are intricately linked social and cultural processes that overlap in establishing women's and men's experiences in society.

Fundamental to each of these concepts is understanding the significance of culture. Sociologists and anthropologists define **culture** as "the set of definitions of reality held in common by people who share a distinctive way of life" (Kluck-hohn, 1962:52). Culture is, in essence, a pattern of expectations about what are appropriate behaviors and beliefs for the members of the society; thus, culture provides prescriptions for social behavior. Culture tells us what we ought to do, what we ought to think, who we ought to be, and what we ought to expect of others. . . .

The cultural basis of gender is apparent especially when we look at different cultural contexts. In most Western cultures, people think of *man* and *woman* as di-chotomous categories—that is, separate and opposite, with no overlap between the two. Looking at gender from different cultural viewpoints challenges this as-sumption, however. Many cultures consider there to be three genders, or even more. Consider the Navaho Indians. In traditional Navaho society, the *berdaches* were those who were anatomically normal men but who were defined as a third gender and were considered to be intersexed. Berdaches married other men. The men they married were not themselves considered to be berdaches; they were defined as ordinary men. Nor were the berdaches or the men they married con-sidered to be homosexuals, as they would be judged by contemporary Western culture. . . .

Another good example for understanding the cultural basis of gender is the *hi-jras* of India (Nanda, 1998). Hijras are a religious community of men in India who are born as males, but they come to think of themselves as neither men nor women. Like berdaches, they are considered a third gender. Hijras dress as women and may marry other men; typically, they live within a communal subculture. An important thing to note is that hijras are not born so; they choose this way of life. As male ado-lescents, they have their penises and testicles cut off in an elaborate and prolonged cultural ritual—a rite of passage marking the transition to becoming a hijra. . . .

These examples are good illustrations of the cultural basis of gender. Even within contemporary U.S. society, so-called "gender bending" shows how the dichotomous thinking that defines men and women as "either/or" can be transformed. Cross-dressers, transvestites, and transsexuals illustrate how fluid gender can be and, if one is willing to challenge social convention, how easily gender can be altered. The cul-tural expectations associated with gender, however, are strong, as one may witness by people's reactions to those who deviate from presumed gender roles. . . .

In different ways and for a variety of reasons, all cultures use gender as a pri-mary category of social relations. The differences we observe between men and women can be attributed largely to these cultural patterns.

THE INSTITUTIONAL BASIS OF GENDER

Understanding the cultural basis for gender requires putting gender into a socio-logical context. From a sociological perspective, gender is systematically struc-tured in social institutions, meaning that it is deeply embedded in the social structure of society. Gender is created, not just within family or interpersonal re-lationships (although these are important sources of gender relations), but also within the structure of all major social institutions, including schools, religion, the economy, and the state (i.e., government and other organized systems of authority such as the police and the military). These institutions shape and mold the experiences of us all.

Sociologists define **institutions** as established patterns of behavior with a particular and recognized purpose; institutions include specific participants who share expectations and act in specific roles, with rights and duties attached to them. Institutions define reality for us insofar as they exist as objective entities in our experience. . . .

Understanding gender in an institutional context means that gender is not just an attribute of individuals; instead, institutions themselves are *gendered*. To say that an institution is gendered means that the whole institution is patterned on specific gendered relationships. That is, gender is "present in the processes, practices, images and ideologies, and distribution of power in the various sectors of social life" (Acker, 1992:567). The concept of a gendered institution was introduced by Joan Acker, a feminist sociologist. Acker uses this concept to explain not just that gender expectations are passed to men and women within institutions, but that the institutions themselves are structured along gendered lines. **Gendered institutions** are the total pattern of gender relations—stereotypical expectations, interpersonal relationships, and men's and women's different placements in social, economic, and political hierarchies. This is what interests sociologists, and it is what they mean by the social structure of gender relations in society.

Conceptualizing gender in this way is somewhat different from the related concept of gender roles. Sociologists use the concept of social roles to refer to culturally prescribed expectations, duties, and rights that define the relationship between a person in a particular position and the other people with whom she or he interacts. For example, to be a mother is a specific social role with a definable set of expectations, rights, and duties. Persons occupy multiple roles in society; we can think of social roles as linking individuals to social structures. It is through social roles that cultural norms are patterned and learned. **Gender roles** are the expectations for behavior and attitudes that the culture defines as appropriate for women and men.

The concept of gender is broader than the concept of gender roles. *Gender* refers to the complex social, political, economic, and psychological relations between women and men in society. Gender is part of the social structure—in other words, it is institutionalized in society. *Gender roles* are the patterns through which gender relations are expressed, but our understanding of gender in society cannot be reduced to roles and learned expectations.

The distinction between gender as institutionalized and gender roles is perhaps most clear in thinking about analogous cases—specifically, race and class. Race relations in society are seldom, if ever, thought of in terms of "race roles." Likewise, class inequality is not discussed in terms of "class roles." Doing so would make race and class inequality seem like matters of interpersonal interaction. Although race, class, and gender inequalities are experienced within interpersonal interactions, limiting the analysis of race, class, or gender relations to this level of social interaction individualizes more complex systems of inequality; moreover, restricting the analysis of race, class, or gender to social roles hides the power relations that are embedded in race, class, and gender inequality (Lopata and Thorne, 1978).

Understanding the institutional basis of gender also underscores the interrelationships of gender, race, and class, since all three are part of the institutional framework of society. As a social category, gender intersects with class and race; thus, gender is manifested in different ways, depending on one's location in the race and class system. For example, African American women are more likely than White women to reject gender stereotypes for women, although they are more accepting than White women of stereotypical gender roles for children. Although this seems contradictory, it can be explained by understanding that African American women may reject the dominant culture's view while also hoping their children can attain some of the privileges of the dominant group (Dugger, 1988).

Institutional analyses of gender emphasize that gender, like race and class, is a part of the social experience of us all—not just of women. Gender is just as important in the formation of men's experiences as it is in women's (Messner, 1998). From a sociological perspective, class, race, and gender relations are systemically structured in social institutions, meaning that class, race, and gender relations shape the experiences of all. Sociologists do not see gender simply as a psychological attribute, although that is one dimension of gender relations in society. In addition to the psychological significance of gender, gender relations are part of the institutionalized patterns in society. Understanding gender, as well as class and race, is central to the study of any social institution or situation. Understanding gender in terms of social structure indicates that social change is not just a matter of individual will—that if we changed our minds, gender would disappear. Transformation of gender inequality requires change both in consciousness and in social institutions. . . .

NOTES

Acker, Joan. 1992. "Gendered Institutions: From Sex Roles to Gendered Institutions." *Contemporary Sociology* 21 (September): 565–569.

Dugger, Karen. 1988. "The Social Location of Black and White Women's Attitudes." *Gender & Society* 2 (December): 425–448.

Kluckhohn, C. 1962. *Culture and Behavior.* New York: Free Press.

Lopata, Helene Z., and Barrie Thorne. 1978. "On the Term 'Sex Roles.'" *Signs* 3 (Spring): 718–721.

McCloskey, Laura A., and Lerita M. Coleman. 1992. "Difference Without Dominance: Children's Talk in Mixed- and Same-Sex Dyads." *Sex Roles* 27 (September): 241–258.

Messner, Michael A. 1998. "The Limits of 'The Male Sex Role': An Analysis of the Men's Liberation and Men's Rights Movements' Discourse." *Gender & Society* 12 (June): 255–276.

Miller, D., D. Danaber, and D. Forbes. 1986. "Sex-related Strategies for Coping with Interpersonal Conflict in Children Five and Seven." *Development Psychology* 22: 543–548.

Nanda, Serena. 1998. *Neither Man Nor Woman: The Hijras of India.* Belmont, CA: Wadsworth.

DISCUSSION QUESTIONS

1. Walk through a baby store. Can you easily identify products for girls and for boys? Could you easily purchase clothing appropriate for either a boy or a girl?

2. Consider an occupation that is traditionally men's work or traditionally women's work. What happens when a member of the opposite sex works in that field? What stereotypes and derogatory assumptions do we make about a woman working in a man's occupation or a man working in a woman's occupation?

INFOTRACT COLLEGE EDITION

You can use your access to InfoTrac College Edition to learn more about the subjects covered in this essay. Some suggested search terms include:

culture
gender roles
gendered institutions

sexuality
social construction of gender

15

Beauty and the Beast of Advertising

JEAN KILBOURNE

Another example of a powerful informal agent of socialization is advertising. Kilbourne provides a graphic description of informal socialization that takes place through advertising and discusses the sometimes negative effects that ads have on the images and treatment of women and men. Adolescents are especially vulnerable to the stereotypes of male and female images presented in ads.

Keep in mind the following questions as you read:

1. What impact does advertising have on our development as individuals?

2. How has advertising influenced your socialization and that of your friends?

GLOSSARY

Mass media Sources that reach a wide audience such as TV, magazines, newspapers.
Objectify To view one's face and body as an object separate from the real self.
Internalize Make an image part of oneself.
Self-fulfilling prophecy Actualize or make real these images by accepting them.

"YOU'RE A HALSTON WOMAN from the very beginning," the advertisement proclaims. The model stares provocatively at the viewer, her long blonde hair waving around her face, her bare chest partially covered by two curved bottles that give the illusion of breasts and a cleavage.

The average American is accustomed to blue-eyed blondes seductively touting a variety of products. In this case, however, the blonde is about five years old.

Advertising is an over $130 billion a year industry and affects all of us throughout our lives. We are each exposed to over 1500 ads a day, constituting perhaps the most powerful educational force in society. The average adult will spend one and one-half years of his/her life watching television commercials. But the ads sell a great deal more than products. They sell values, images, and concepts of success and worth, love and sexuality, popularity and normalcy. They tell us who we are and who we should be. Sometimes they sell addictions.

Advertising is the foundation and economic lifeblood of the mass media. The primary purpose of the mass media is to deliver an audience to advertisers.

Adolescents are particularly vulnerable, however, because they are new and inexperienced consumers and are the prime targets of many advertisements. They are in the process of learning their values and roles and developing their self-concepts. Most teenagers are sensitive to peer pressure and find it difficult to resist or even question the dominant cultural messages perpetuated and reinforced by the media. Mass communication has made possible a kind of nationally distributed peer pressure that erodes private and individual values and standards.

But what does society, and especially teenagers, learn from the advertising messages that proliferate in the mass media? On the most obvious level they learn the stereotypes. Advertising creates a mythical, WASP-oriented world in which no one is ever ugly, overweight, poor, struggling, or disabled either physically or mentally (unless you count the housewives who talk to little men in toilet bowls). And it is a world in which people talk only about products.

Reprinted by permission from Media & Values *(Winter 1989), published by the Center for Media Literacy, Los Angeles.*

Housewives or Sex Objects

The aspect of advertising most in need of analysis and change is the portrayal of women. Scientific studies and the most casual viewing yield the same conclusion: Women are shown almost exclusively as housewives or sex objects.

The housewife, pathologically obsessed by cleanliness and lemon-fresh scents, debates cleaning products and worries about her husband's "ring around the collar."

The sex object is a mannequin, a shell. Conventional beauty is her only attribute. She has no lines or wrinkles (which would indicate she had the bad taste and poor judgment to grow older), no scars or blemishes—indeed, she has no pores. She is thin, generally tall and long-legged, and, above all, she is young. All "beautiful" women in advertisements (including minority women), regardless of product or audience, conform to this norm. Women are constantly exhorted to emulate this ideal, to feel ashamed and guilty if they fail, and to feel that their desirability and lovability are contingent upon physical perfection.

Creating Artificiality

The image is artificial and can only be achieved artificially (even the "natural look" requires much preparation and expense). Beauty is something that comes from without: more than one million dollars is spent every hour on cosmetics. Desperate to conform to an ideal and impossible standard, many women go to great lengths to manipulate and change their faces and bodies. A woman is conditioned to view her face as a mask and her body as an object, as *things* separate from and more important than her real self, constantly in need of alteration, improvement, and disguise. She is made to feel dissatisfied with and ashamed of herself, whether she tries to achieve "the look" or not. Objectified constantly by others, she learns to objectify herself. (It is interesting to note that one in five college-age women has an eating disorder.)

"When *Glamour* magazine surveyed its readers in 1984, 75 percent felt too heavy and only 15 percent felt just right. Nearly half of those who were actually underweight reported feeling too fat and wanting to diet. Among a sample of college women, 40 percent felt overweight when only 12 percent actually were too heavy," according to Rita Freedman in her book *Beauty Bound.*

There is evidence that this preoccupation with weight begins at ever-earlier ages for women. According to a recent article in *New Age Journal,* "even grade-school girls are succumbing to stick-like standards of beauty enforced by a relentless parade of wasp-waisted fashion models, movie stars, and pop idols." A study by a University of California professor showed that nearly 80 percent of fourth-grade girls in the Bay Area are watching their weight.

A recent *Wall Street Journal* survey of students in four Chicago-area schools found that more than half the fourth-grade girls were dieting and three-quarters felt they were overweight. One student said, "We don't expect boys to be that handsome. We take them as they are." Another added, "But boys expect girls to be perfect and beautiful. And skinny."

Dr. Steven Levenkrom, author of *The Best Little Girl in the World,* the story of an anorexic, says his blood pressure soars every time he opens a magazine and finds an ad for women's fashions. "If I had my way," he said, "every one of them would have to carry a line saying, 'Caution: This model may be hazardous to your health.' "

Women are also dismembered in commercials, their bodies separated into parts in need of change or improvement. If a woman has "acceptable" breasts, then she must also be sure that her legs are worth watching, her hips slim, her feet sexy, and that her buttocks look nuder under her clothes ("like I'm not wearin' nothin' "). This image is difficult and costly to achieve and impossible to maintain—no one is flawless and everyone ages. Growing older is the great taboo. Women are encouraged to remain little girls ("because innocence is sexier than you think"), to be passive and dependent, never to mature. The contradictory message—"sensual, but not too far from innocence"—places women in a double bind: somehow we are supposed to be both sexy and virginal, experienced and naive, seductive and chaste. The disparagement of maturity is, of course, insulting and frustrating to adult women, and the implication that little girls are seductive is dangerous to real children.

Influencing Sexual Attitudes

Young people also learn a great deal about sexual attitudes from the media and from advertising in particular. Advertising's approach to sex is pornographic: it reduces people to objects and de-emphasizes human contact and individuality. This reduction of sexuality to a dirty joke and of people to objects is the real obscenity of the culture. Although the sexual sell, overt and subliminal, is at a fevered pitch in most commercials, there is at the same time a notable absence of sex as an important and profound human activity.

There have been some changes in the images of women. Indeed, a "new woman" has emerged in commercials in recent years. She is generally presented as superwoman, who manages to do all the work at home and on the job (with the help of a product, of course, not of her husband or children or friends); or as the liberated woman, who owes her independence and self-esteem to the products she uses. These new images do not represent any real progress but rather create a myth of progress, an illusion that reduces complex sociopolitical problems to mundane personal ones.

Advertising images do not cause these problems, but they contribute to them by creating a climate in which the marketing of women's bodies—the sexual sell and dismemberment, distorted body image ideal, and children as sex objects—is seen as acceptable.

This is the real tragedy, that many women internalize these stereotypes and learn their "limitations," thus establishing a self-fulfilling prophecy. If one accepts these mythical and degrading images, to some extent one actualizes them. By remaining unaware of the profound seriousness of the ubiquitous influence, the redundant message, and the subliminal impact of advertisements, we ignore one of the most powerful "educational" forces in the culture—one that greatly affects our self-images, our ability to relate to each other, and effectively destroys awareness and action that might help to change that climate.

16

Money Changes Everything

DAN CLAWSON, ALAN NEWSTADT, AND DENISE SCOTT

The United States claims to be a representative democracy. The implication of this reading is that our political representation is far narrower than trumpeted. What can be done to bring about our democratic claims? Do you think it will happen?

As you read, ask yourself the following questions:

1. *What effects have PACs had on campaign financing?*
2. *How would you change the financing of political campaigns?*

GLOSSARY

Hegemony Leadership dominance.

IN THE PAST TWENTY years political action committees, or PACs, have transformed campaign finance. . . .

Most analyses of campaign finance focus on the candidates who receive the money, not on the people and political action committees that give it. PACs are entities that collect money from many contributors, pool it, and then make donations to candidates. Donors may give to a PAC because they are in basic agreement with its aims, but once they have donated they lose direct control over their money, trusting the PAC to decide which candidates should receive contributions. . . .

Why Does the Air Stink?

Everybody wants clean air. Who could oppose it? "I spent seven years of my life trying to stop the Clean Air Act," explained the PAC director for a major corporation that is a heavy-duty polluter. Nonetheless, he was perfectly willing to

In Money Talks: Corporate PACs and Political Influence. *Basic Books, 1992. Reprinted with permission.*

use his corporation's PAC to contribute to members of Congress who voted for the act:

> How a person votes on the final piece of legislation often is not representative of what they have done. Somebody will do a lot of things during the process. How many guys voted against the Clean Air Act? But during the process some of them were very sympathetic to some of our concerns.

In the world of Congress and political action committees things are not always what they seem. Members of Congress want to vote for clean air, but they also want to receive campaign contributions from corporate PACs and pass a law that business accepts as "reasonable." The compromise solution to this dilemma is to gut the bill by crafting dozens of loopholes inserted in private meetings or in subcommittee hearings that don't receive much (if any) attention in the press. Then the public vote on the final bill can be nearly unanimous: members of Congress can assure their constituents that they voted for the final bill and their corporate PAC contributors that they helped weaken the bill in private. We can use the Clean Air Act of 1990 to introduce and explain this process.

The public strongly supports clean air and is unimpressed when corporate officials and apologists trot out their normal arguments: "corporations are already doing all they reasonably can to improve environmental quality"; "we need to balance the costs against the benefits"; "people will lose their jobs if we make controls any stricter." The original Clean Air Act was passed in 1970, revised in 1977, and not revised again until 1990. Although the initial goal of its supporters was to have us breathing clean air by 1975, the deadline for compliance has been repeatedly extended—and the 1990 legislation provides a new set of deadlines to be reached sometime far in the future.

Because corporations control the production process unless the government specifically intervenes, any delay in government action leaves corporations free to do as they choose. Not only have laws been slow to come, but corporations have fought to delay or subvert implementation. The 1970 law ordered the Environmental Protection Agency (EPA) to regulate the hundreds of poisonous chemicals that are emitted by corporations, but as William Greider notes, "in twenty years of stalling, dodging, and fighting off court orders, the EPA has managed to issue regulatory standards for a total of seven toxics."

Corporations have done exceptionally well politically, given the problem they face: the interests of business often are diametrically opposed to those of the public. Clean air laws and amendments have been few and far between, enforcement is ineffective, and the penalties for infractions are minimal. . . .

This corporate struggle for the right to pollute takes place on many fronts. One front is public relations: the Chemical Manufacturers Association took out a two-page Earth Day ad in the *Washington Post* to demonstrate its concern for the environment; coincidentally many of the corporate signers are also on the EPA's list of high-risk producers. Another front is research: expert studies delay action while more information is gathered. The federally funded National Acid Precipitation Assessment Program (NAPAP) took ten years and $600 million to figure out whether acid rain was a problem. Both business and the Reagan administration argued that no action should be taken until the study was completed. The study was discredited when its summary of findings minimized the impact of acid rain—even though this did not accurately represent the expert research in the report. But the key site of struggle has been Congress, where for years corporations have succeeded in defeating environmental legislation. In 1987 utility companies were offered a compromise bill on acid rain, but they "were very adamant that they had beat the thing since 1981 and they could always beat it," according to Representative Edward Madigan (R-Ill.). Throughout the 1980s the utilities defeated all efforts at change. . . .

The stage was set for a revision of the Clean Air Act when George Bush was elected as "the environmental president" and George Mitchell, a strong supporter of environmentalism, became the Senate majority leader. But what sort of clean air bill would it be? "What we wanted," said Richard Ayres, head of the environmentalists' Clean Air Coalition, "is a health-based standard— one-in-1-million cancer risk." Such a standard would require corporations to clean up their plants until the cancer risk from their operations was reduced to one in a million. "The Senate bill still has the requirement," Ayres said, "but there are forty pages of extensions and exceptions and qualifications and loopholes that largely render the health standard a nullity." Greider reports, for example, that "according to the EPA, there are now twenty-six coke ovens that pose a cancer risk greater than 1 in 1000 and six where the risk is greater than 1 in 100. Yet the new clean-air bill will give the steel industry another thirty years to deal with the problem."

This change from what the bill was supposed to do to what it did do came about through what corporate executives like to call the "access" process. The main aim of most corporate political action committee contributions is to help corporate executives attain "access" to key members of Congress and their staffs. Corporate executives (and corporate PAC money) work to persuade the member of Congress to accept a carefully pre-designed loophole that sounds innocent but effectively undercuts the stated intention of the bill. Representative Dingell (D-Mich.), chair of the House Committee on Energy and Commerce, is a strong industry supporter; one of the people we interviewed called him "the point man for the Business Roundtable on clean air." Representative Waxman (D-Calif.), chair of the Subcommittee on Health and the Environment, is an environmentalist. Observers of the Clean Air Act legislative process expected a confrontation and contested votes on the floor of Congress.

The problem for corporations was that, as one Republican staff aide said, "If any bill has the blessing of Waxman and the environmental groups, unless it is totally in outer space, who's going to vote against it?" But corporations successfully minimized public votes. Somehow Waxman was persuaded to make behind-the-scenes compromises with Dingell so members didn't have to publicly side with business against the environment during an election year. Often the access process leads to loopholes that protect a single corporation, but for "clean" air most special deals targeted entire industries, not specific companies. The initial bill, for example, required cars to be able to use strictly specified cleaner fuels. But the auto industry wanted the rules loosened, and Congress eventually modified the bill by incorporating a variant of a formula suggested by the head of General Motors' fuels and lubricants department.

Nor did corporations stop fighting after they gutted the bill through amendments. Business pressed the EPA for favorable regulations to implement the law: "The cost of this legislation could vary dramatically, depending on how EPA interprets it," said William D. Fay, vice president of the National Coal Association, who headed the hilariously misnamed Clean Air Working Group, an industry coalition that fought to weaken the legislation. An EPA aide working on acid rain regulations reported, "We're having a hard time getting our work done because of the number of phone calls we're getting" from corporations and their lawyers.

Corporations trying to convince federal regulators to adopt the "right" regulations don't rely exclusively on the cogency of their arguments. They often exert pressure on a member of Congress to intervene for them at the EPA or other agency. Senators and representatives regularly intervene on behalf of constituents and contributors by doing everything from straightening out a social security problem to asking a regulatory agency to explain why it is pressuring a company. This process—like campaign finance—usually follows accepted etiquette. In addressing a regulatory agency the senator does not say, "Lay off my campaign contributors, or I'll cut your budget." One standard phrasing for letters asks regulators to resolve the problem "as quickly as possible within applicable rules and regulations." No matter how mild and careful the inquiry, the agency receiving the request is certain to give it extra attention; only after careful consideration will they refuse to make any accommodation.

The power disparity between business and environmentalists is enormous during the legislative process but even larger thereafter. When the Clean Air Act passed, corporations and industry groups offered positions, typically with large pay increases, to congressional staff members who wrote the law. The former congressional staff members who work for corporations know how to evade the law and can persuasively claim to EPA that they know what Congress intended. Environmental organizations pay substantially less than Congress and can't afford large staffs. They are rarely able to become involved in the details of the administrative process or influence implementation and enforcement.

Having pushed Congress for a law, and the Environmental Protection Agency for regulations, allowing as much pollution as possible, business then went to the Quayle Council for rules allowing even more pollution. Vice President J. Danforth Quayle's Council, technically the Council on Competitiveness, was created by President Bush specifically to help reduce regulations on business. Quayle told the *Boston Globe* "that his council has an 'open door' to business groups and that he has a bias against regulations." The Council reviews, and can override, all federal regulations, including those by the EPA setting the limits at which a chemical is subject to regulation. The council also recommended that corporations be allowed to increase their polluting emissions if a state did not object within seven days of the proposed increase. Corporations thus have multiple opportunities to win. If they lose in Congress, they can win at the regulatory agency; if they lose there, they can try again at the Quayle Council. If they lose there, they can try to reduce the money available to enforce regulations, tie up the issue in the courts, or accept a minimal fine.

The operation of the Quayle Council probably would have received little publicity, but reporters discovered that the executive director of the Council, Allan Hubbard, had a clear conflict of interest. Hubbard chaired the biweekly White House meetings on the Clean Air Act. He owns half of World Wide Chemical, received an average of more than a million dollars a year in profits from it while directing the Council, and continues to attend quarterly stockholder meetings. According to the *Boston Globe,* "Records on file with the Indianapolis Air Pollution Control Board show that World Wide Chemical emitted 17,000 to 19,000 pounds of chemicals into the air last year." The company "does not have the permit required to release the emissions," "is putting out nearly four times the allowable emissions without a permit, and could be subject to a $2,500-a-day penalty," according to David Jordan, director of the Indianapolis Air Pollution Board. . . .

The real issue is the system of business-government relations, and especially of campaign finance, that offers business so many opportunities to craft loopholes, undermine regulations, and subvert enforcement. Still worse, many of these actions take place outside of public scrutiny.

THE CANDIDATES' PERSPECTIVE

. . . Money has always been a critically important factor in campaigns, but the shift to expensive technology has made it the dominant factor. Today money is the key to victory and substitutes for everything else—instead of door-to-door canvassers, a good television spot; instead of a committee of respected long-time party workers who know the local area, a paid political consultant and media expert. To be a viable political candidate, one must possess—or be able to raise—huge sums. Nor is this a one-time requirement; each reelection campaign requires new infusions of cash.

The quest for money is never ending. Challengers must have money to be viable contenders; incumbents can seldom predict when they might face a tight race. In 1988 the average winning candidate for the House of Representatives spent $388,000; for the Senate, $3,745,000. Although the Congress, especially the Senate, has many millionaires, few candidates have fortunes large enough to finance repeated campaigns out of their own pockets. It would take the entire congressional salary for

3.1 years for a member of the House, or 29.9 years for a senator, to pay for a single reelection campaign. Most members are therefore in no position to say, "Asking people for money is just too big a hassle. Forget it. I'll pay for it myself." They must raise the money from others, and the pressure to do so never lets up. To pay for an average winning campaign, representatives need to raise $3,700 and senators $12,000 during *every week* of their term of office.

Increasingly incumbents use money to win elections before voters get involved. Senator Rudy Boschwitz (R-Minn.) spent $6 million getting reelected in 1984 and had raised $1.5 million of it by the beginning of the year, effectively discouraging the most promising Democratic challengers. . . .

Fundraising isn't popular with the public, but candidates keep emphasizing it because it works: the champion money raiser wins almost regardless of the merits. *Almost* is an important qualifier here, as Boschwitz would be the first to attest: in his 1990 race he outspent his opponent by about five to one and lost nonetheless. . . .

It is not only that senators leave committee hearings for the more crucial task of calling people to beg for money. They also chase all over the country because reelection is more dependent on meetings with rich people two thousand miles from home than it is on meetings with their own constituents.

. . . Do members of Congress incur any obligations in seeking and accepting these campaign contributions? Bob Dole, Republican leader in the Senate and George Bush's main rival for the 1988 Republican presidential nomination, was quoted by the *Wall Street Journal* as saying, "When the Political Action Committees give money, they expect something in return other than good government." One unusually outspoken business donor, Charles Keating, made the same point: "One question among the many raised in recent weeks had to do with whether my financial support in any way influenced several political figures to take up my cause. I want to say in the most forceful way I can, I certainly hope so." . . .

THE CURRENT LAW

The law, however, regulates fundraising and limits the amount that any one individual or organization may (legally) contribute. According to current law:

1. A *candidate* may donate an unlimited amount of personal funds to his or her *own* campaign. The Supreme Court has ruled this is protected as free speech.
2. Individuals may not contribute more than $1,000 per candidate per election, nor more than $25,000 in total in a given two-year election cycle.
3. Political action committees may contribute up to $5,000 per candidate per election. Since most candidates face primaries, an individual may contribute $2,000 and a PAC $10,000 to the candidate during a two-year election cycle. PACs may give to an unlimited number of candidates and hence may give an unlimited amount of money.
4. Individuals may contribute up to $5,000 per year to a political action committee.
5. Candidates must disclose the full amount they have received, the donor and identifying information for any individual contribution of $200 or more, the name of the PAC and donation amount for any PAC contribution however small, and all disbursements. PACs must disclose any donation they make to a candidate, no matter how small. They must also disclose the total amount received by the PAC and the names and positions of all contributors who give the PAC more than $200 in a year.
6. Sponsoring organizations, including corporations and unions, may pay all the expenses of creating and operating a PAC. Thus a corporation may pay the cost of the rent, telephones, postage, supplies, and air travel for all PAC activities; the salaries of full-time corporate employees who work exclusively on the PAC; and the salaries of all managers who listen to a presentation about the PAC. However, the PAC money itself— the money used to contribute to

candidates—must come from voluntary donations by individual contributors. The corporation may not legally take a portion of its profits and put it directly into the PAC.

7. Corporations may establish and control the PAC and solicit stockholders and/or managerial employees for contributions to the PAC. It is technically possible for corporations to solicit hourly (or nonmanagerial) employees and for unions to solicit managers, but these practices are so much more tightly regulated and restricted that in practice cross-solicitation is rare.

8. The Federal Election Commission (FEC) is to monitor candidates and contributors and enforce the rules.

These are the key rules governing fundraising, but the history of campaign finance is that as time goes on, loopholes develop. . . . What is generally regarded as the most important current loophole is that there are no reporting requirements or limits for contributions given to political parties as opposed to candidates. Such money is ostensibly to be used to promote party building and get-out-the-vote drives; in 1988 literally hundreds of individuals gave $100,000 or more in unreported "soft money" donations. Many of these loopholes are neither accidents nor oversights. Three Democrats and three Republicans serve as federal election commissioners, and commissioners are notorious party loyalists. Because it requires a majority to investigate a suspected violation, the FEC not only fails to punish violations, it fails to investigate them.

CORPORATE PACS

The Federal Election Commission categorizes PACs as corporate, labor, trade-health-membership, and nonconnected. Nonconnected PACs are unaffiliated with any other organization: they are formed exclusively for the purpose of raising and contributing money. Most subsist by direct-mail fundraising targeted at people with a commitment to a single issue (abortion or the environment) or philosophical position (liberalism or conservatism). Other PACs are affiliated with an already existing organization, and that organization—whether a corporation, union, trade, or membership association—pays the expenses associated with operating the PAC and decides what will happen to the money the PAC collects.

Candidates increasingly rely on PACs because they can easily solicit a large number of PACs, each of which is relatively likely to make a major contribution. "From 1976–88, PAC donations rose from 22 per cent to 40 per cent of House campaign receipts, and from 15 per cent to 22 per cent of Senate receipts." Almost half of all House members (205 of the 435) "received at least 50 per cent of their campaign contributions from PACs." The reliance of PACs is greater in the House than in the Senate: PACs give more to Senate candidates, but Senate races are more expensive than House races, so a larger fraction of total Senate-race receipts comes from individual contributions.

Although other sorts of PACs deserve study, we believe the most important part of this story concerns corporate PACs, the subject of this book. We focus on corporate PACs for three interrelated reasons. First, they are the largest concentrated source of campaign money and the fastest growing. In 1988 corporate PACs contributed more than $50 million, all trade-membership-health PACs combined less than $40 million, labor PACs less than $35 million, and nonconnected PACs less than $20 million. Moreover, these figures understate the importance of corporate decisions about money because industry trade associations are controlled by corporations and follow their lead. In addition, corporate executives have high incomes and make many individual contributions; a handful of labor leaders may attempt to do the same on a reduced scale, but rank-and-file workers are unlikely to do so. Second, corporations have disproportionate power in U.S. society, magnifying the importance of the money they contribute. Finally, corporate PACs have enormous untapped fundraising potential. They are in a position to coerce their donors in a way no other kind of PAC can and, if the need arose, could dramatically increase the amount of money they raise. . . .

Corporate PACs follow two very different strategies, pragmatic and ideological. . . .

Pragmatic donations are given specifically to advance the short-run interests of the donor, primarily to enable the corporation to gain a chance to meet with the member and argue its case. Because the aim of these donations is to gain "access" to powerful members of Congress, the money is given without regard to whether or not the member needs it and with little consideration of the member's political stance on large issues. The corporation's only concern is that the member will be willing and able to help them out—and virtually all members, regardless of party, are willing to cooperate in this access process. Perhaps the most memorable characterization of this strategy was by Jay Gould, nineteenth-century robber baron and owner of the Erie Railroad: "In a Republican district I was a Republican; in a Democratic district, a Democrat; in a doubtful district I was doubtful; but I was always for Erie."

Ideological donations, on the other hand, are made to influence the political composition of the Congress. From this perspective, contributions should meet two conditions: (1) they should be directed to politically congenial "pro-free enterprise" candidates who face opponents unsympathetic to business (in practice, these are always conservatives); and (2) they should be targeted at competitive races where money can potentially influence the election outcome. The member's willingness to do the company favors doesn't matter, and even a conservative "free enterprise" philosophy wouldn't be sufficient: if the two opponents' views were the same, then the election couldn't influence the ideological composition of Congress. Most incumbents are reelected: in some years as many as 98 percent of all House members running are reelected. Precisely because incumbents will probably be reelected even without PAC support, ideological corporations usually give to nonincumbents, either challengers or candidates for open seats.

Virtually all corporations use some combinations of pragmatic and ideological strategies. The simplest method of classifying PACs is by the proportion of money they give to incumbents: the higher this proportion, the more pragmatic the corporation. . . . In 1988 about a third (36 percent) of the largest corporate PACs gave more than 90 percent of their money to incumbents, and another third (34 percent) gave 80 to 90 percent to incumbents. Although roughly a third gave less than 80 percent to incumbents, only eight corporate PACs gave less than 50 percent of their money to incumbents (that is, more than 50 percent to nonincumbents). . . . The pragmatic emphasis of recent years is a change from 1980, when a large number of corporations followed an ideological approach.

Our Research

. . . Our quantitative analyses concentrate on Democrats and Republicans in general-election contests for congressional seats. We focus on the 309 corporate PACs that made the largest contributions in the period from 1975 to 1988. As might be expected, these are almost exclusively very large corporations: on average in 1984 they had $6.7 billion in sales and 48,000 employees. . . . Moreover, not all firms with large PACs have huge sales, so our sample includes about twenty-five "small" firms with 1984 revenues of less than $500 million. . . .

On average, in 1988 these PACs gave 52.7 percent of their money to Republicans and 47.3 percent to Democrats. They gave 83.6 percent of their money to incumbents, 10.2 percent to candidates for open seats, and 6.2 percent to challengers.

The PAC officials we interviewed were selected from this set of the 309 largest corporate PACs and were representative of the larger sample in terms of both economic and political characteristics. . . .

A third source of original data supplements our quantitative analyses of the 309 largest corporate PACs and our 38 in-depth interviews. In November and December of 1986 we mailed surveys to a random sample of ninety-four directors of large corporate PACs, achieving a response rate of 58 percent. For the most part, we use this to place our interview comments in context: if a PAC director tells us a story of being pressured by a candidate, how typical is this? How many other PAC directors report similar experiences? Finally, our original data also are supplemented by books, articles, and newspaper accounts about campaign finance. . . .

Overview and Background

. . . We argue that corporate PACs differ from other PACs in two ways: (1) as employees, managers can be—and are—coerced to contribute; and (2) corporate PACs are not democratically controlled by their contributors (even in theory). . . .

We argue that PAC contributions are best understood as gifts, not bribes. They create a generalized sense of obligation and an expectation that "if I scratch your back you scratch mine." . . .

A corporation uses the member of Congress's sense of indebtedness for past contributions to help it gain access to the member. In committee hearings and private meetings the corporation then persuades the member to make "minor" changes in a bill, which exempt a particular company or industry from some specific provision.

Even some corporations are troubled by this "access" approach, and . . . consider the alternative: donations to close races intended to change the ideological composition of the Congress. In the late 1980s and early 1990s only a small number of corporations used this as their primary strategy, but most corporations make some such donations. In the 1980 election a large group of corporations pursued an ideological strategy. We argue this was one of the reasons for the conservative successes of that period. . . .

Do competing firms or industries oppose each other in Washington, such that one business's political donations oppose and cancel out those of the next corporation or industry? More generally, how much power does business have in U.S. society, and how does its political power relate to its economic activity? . . .

The PAC directors we interviewed are not very worried about reform: they don't expect meaningful changes in campaign funding laws, and they assume that if "reforms" are enacted, they will be easily evaded. . . .

Three interrelated points . . . . First, power is exercised in many loose and subtle ways, not simply through the visible use of force and threats. Power may in fact be most effective, and most limiting, when it structures the conditions for action—even though in these circumstances it may be hard to recognize. Thus PAC contributions can and do exercise enormous influence through creating a sense of obligation, even if there is no explicit agreement to perform a specific service in return for a donation. Second, business is different from, and more powerful than, other groups in the society. As a result, corporations and their PACs are frequently treated differently than others would be. Other groups could not match business power simply by raising equivalent amounts of PAC money. Third, this does not mean that business always wins, or that it wins automatically. If it did, corporate PACs would be unnecessary. Business must engage in a constant struggle to maintain its dominance. This is a class struggle just as surely as are strikes and mass mobilizations, even though it is rarely thought of in these terms.

WHAT IS POWER?

Our analysis is based on an understanding of power that differs from that usually articulated by both business and politicians. The corporate PAC directors we interviewed insisted that they have no power. . . .

The executives who expressed these views used the word *power* in roughly the same sense that it is usually used within political science, which is also the way the term was defined by Max Weber, the classical sociological theorist. Power, according to this common conception, is the ability to make someone do something against his or her will. If that is what power means, then corporations rarely have power in relation to members of Congress. As one corporate senior vice president said to us, "You certainly aren't going to be able to buy anybody for $500 or $1,000 or $10,000. It's a joke." In this regard we agree with the corporate officials we interviewed: a PAC is not in a position to say to a member of Congress, "Either you vote for this bill, or we will defeat your bid for reelection." Rarely do they even say, "Vote for this bill, or you won't get any money from us." . . . Therefore, if power is the ability to make someone do something against his or her will, then PAC donations rarely give corporations power over members of Congress.

This definition of power as the ability to make someone do something against his or her will is what Steven Lukes calls a *one-dimensional view of power. A two-dimensional view* recognizes the existence of nondecisions: a potential issue never gets articulated or, if articulated by someone somewhere, never receives serious consideration. . . . A two-dimensional view of power makes the same point: in some situations no one notices power is being exercised—because there is no overt conflict.

Even this model of power is too restrictive, however, because it still focuses on discrete decisions and nondecisions. . . . Such models do not recognize "the idea that the most fundamental use of power in society is its use in structuring the basic manner in which social agents interact with one another." . . . Similarly, the mere presence of a powerful social agent alters social space for others and causes them to orient to the powerful agent. One of the executives we interviewed took it for granted that "if we go see the congressman who represents [a city where the company has a major plant], where 10,000 of our employees are also his constituents, we don't need a PAC to go see him." The corporation is so important in that area that the member has to orient himself or herself in relation to the corporation and its concerns. In a different sense, the mere act of accepting a campaign contribution changes the way a member relates to a PAC, creating a sense of obligation and need to reciprocate. The PAC contribution has altered the member's social space, his or her awareness of the company and wish to help it, even if no explicit commitments have been made.

BUSINESS IS DIFFERENT

Power therefore is not just the ability to force people to do something against their will; it is most effective (and least recognized) when it shapes the field of action. Moreover, business's vast resources, influence on the economy, and general legitimacy place it on a different footing from other so-called special interests. Business donors are often treated differently from other campaign contributors. When a member of Congress accepts a $1,000 donation from a corporate PAC, goes to a committee hearing, and proposes "minor" changes in a bill's wording, those changes are often accepted without discussion or examination. The changes "clarify" the language of the bill, perhaps legalizing higher levels of pollution for a specific pollutant or exempting the company from some tax. The media do not report on this change, and no one speaks against it. . . .

Even groups with great social legitimacy encounter more opposition and controversy than business faces for proposals that are virtually without public support. Contrast the largely unopposed commitment of more than $500 billion for the bailout of savings and loan associations with the sharp debate, close votes, and defeats for the rights of men and women to take *unpaid* parental leaves. Although the classic phrase for something noncontroversial that everyone must support is to call it a "motherhood" issue, and it would cost little to guarantee every woman the right to an unpaid parental leave, nonetheless this measure generated intense scrutiny and controversy, ultimately going down to defeat. Few people are prepared to publicly defend pollution or tax evasion, but business is routinely able to win pollution exemptions and tax loopholes. Although cumulatively these provisions may trouble people, individually most are allowed to pass without scrutiny. *No* analysis of corporate political activity makes sense unless it begins with a recognition that the PAC is a vital element of corporate power, but it does not operate by itself. The PAC donation is always backed by the wider range of business power and influence.

Corporations are different from other special-interest groups not only because business has far more resources, but also because of this acceptance and legitimacy. When people feel that "the system" is screwing them, they tend to blame politicians, the government, the media—but rarely business. Although much of the public is outraged at the way money influences elections and public policy, the issue is almost always posed in terms of what politicians do or don't do. This pervasive double standard largely exempts business from criticism. . . .

Many people who are outraged that members of Congress recently raised their pay to $125,100 are apparently unconcerned about corporate executives' pay. One study calculated that CEOs at the largest U.S. companies are paid an average of $2.8 million a year, 150 times more than the average U.S. worker and 22 times as much as members of Congress. More anger is directed at Congress for delaying new environmental laws than at the companies who fight every step of the way to stall and subvert the legislation. When members of Congress do favors for large campaign contributors, the anger is directed at the senators who went along, not at the business owner who paid the money (and usually initiated the pressure). The focus is on the member's receipt of thousands of dollars, not on the business's receipt of millions (or hundreds of millions) in tax breaks or special treatment. It is widely held that "politics is dirty," but companies' getting away with murder—quite literally—generates little public comment and condemnation. This disparity is evidence of business's success in shaping public perceptions. Lee Atwater, George Bush's campaign manager for the 1988 presidential election, saw this as a key to Republican success:

> In the 1980 campaign, we were able to make the establishment, insofar as it is bad, the government. In other words, big government was the enemy, not big business. If the people think the problem is that taxes are too high, and the government interferes too much, then we are doing our job. But, if they get to the point where they say that the real problem is

that rich people aren't paying taxes . . . then the Democrats are going to be in good shape.

. . . We argue corporations are so different, and so dominant that they exercise a special kind of power, what Antonio Gramsci called *hegemony*. Hegemony can be regarded as the ultimate example of a field of power that structures what people and groups do. It is sometimes referred to as a world view—a way of thinking about the world that influences every action and makes it difficult to even consider alternatives. But in Gramsci's analysis it is much more than this; it is a culture and set of institutions that structure life patterns and coerce a particular way of life. . . .

Hegemony is most successful and most powerful if it is unrecognized. . . . In some sense gender relations in the 1950s embodied a hegemony even more powerful than that of race relations. Betty Friedan titled the first chapter of *The Feminine Mystique* "The Problem That Has No Name" because women literally did not have a name for and did not recognize the existence of their oppression. Women as well as men denied the existence of inequality or oppression and denied the systematic exercise of power to maintain unequal relations.

We argue that today business has enormous power and exercises effective hegemony, even though (perhaps because) this is largely undiscussed and unrecognized. *Politically* business power today is similar to white treatment of blacks in 1959: business may sincerely deny its power, but many of the groups it exercises power over recognize it, feel dominated, resent this, and fight the power as best they can. *Economically* business power is more similar to gender relations in 1959: virtually no one sees this power as problematic. If the issue is brought to people's attention, many still don't see a problem: "Well, so what? How else could it be? Maybe we don't like it, but that's just the way things are." . . .

Hegemony is never absolute. . . . A hegemonic power is usually opposed by a counter-hegemony. . . .

THE LIMITS TO BUSINESS POWER

We have argued that power is more than winning an open conflict, and business is different from other groups because of its pervasive influence on our society—the way it shapes the social space for all other actors. These two arguments, however, are joined with a third: a recognition of, in fact an insistence on, the limits to business power. We stress the power of business, but business does not feel powerful. . . .

Executives believe that corporations are constantly under attack, primarily because government simply doesn't understand that business is crucial to everything society does but can easily be crippled by well-intentioned but unrealistic government policies. A widespread view among the people we interviewed is that "far and away the vast majority of things that we do are literally to protect ourselves from public policy that is poorly crafted and nonresponsive to the needs and realities and circumstances of our company." These misguided policies, they feel, can come from many sources—labor unions, environmentalists, the pressure of unrealistic public-interest groups, the government's constant need for money, or the weight of its oppressive bureaucracy. Simply maintaining equilibrium requires a pervasive effort: if attention slips for even a minute, an onerous regulation will be imposed or a precious resource taken away. . . . But evidently the corporation agrees . . . since it devotes significant resources to political action of many kinds, including the awareness and involvement of top officials. Chief executive officers and members of the board of directors repeatedly express similar views.

Both of these views—the business view of vulnerability and our insistence on their power—are correct. . . .

Perhaps once upon a time business could simply make its wishes known and receive what it wanted; today corporations must form PACs, lobby actively, make their case to the public, run advocacy ads, and engage in a multitude of behaviors that they wish were unnecessary. From the outside we are impressed with the high success rates over a wide range of issues and with the lack of a credible challenge to the general authority of business. From the inside they are impressed with the serious consequences of occasional losses and with the continuing effort needed to maintain their privileged position.

Business power does not rest *only* on PAC donations, but the PAC is a crucial aspect of business power. A football analogy can be made: business's vast resources and its influence on the economy may be equivalent to a powerful offensive line that is able to clear out the opposition and create a huge opening, but someone then has to take the ball and run through that opening. The PAC and the government relations operation are, in this analogy, like a football running back. When they carry the ball they have to move quickly, dodge attempts to tackle them, and if necessary fight off an opponent and keep going. The analogy breaks down, however, because it implies a contest between two evenly matched opponents. Most of the time the situation approximates a contest between an NFL team and high school opponents. The opponents just don't have the same muscle. Often they are simply intimidated or have learned through past experience the best thing to do is get out of the way. Occasionally, however, the outclassed opponents will have so much courage and determination that they will be at least able to score, if not to win.

17

The Myth of a Liberal Media

MICHAEL PARENTI

It is a widely accepted belief in this country that the media suffer from a liberal bias. Television pundits, radio talk-show hosts, and political leaders—including presidents of both parties—help propagate this belief, and their views are widely disseminated in the media. On the other hand, dissident critics—those who maintain that the corporate-owned press exercises a conservative grip on news and commentary—are afforded almost no exposure in this same supposedly liberal media.

Consider the case of David Horowitz. When Horowitz was a radical author and editor of

Ramparts, the mainstream press ignored his existence. But after he and former *Ramparts* colleague Peter Colliers surfaced as new-born conservatives, the *Washington Post Magazine* gave prominent play to their "Lefties for Reagan" pronunciamento. Horowitz and Colliers soon linked up with the National Forum Foundation, which dipped into deep conservative pockets and came up with hundreds of thousands of dollars to enable the two ex-radicals to do ideological battle with the left. Today Horowitz is a rightist media critic with his own radio show, who appears with dismaying frequency on radio and television to whine about how radio and television shut out conservative viewpoints.

Then there are the many talk-show hosts, of whom Rush Limbaugh is only the best known, who rail against the "pinko press" on hundreds of local television stations and thousands of radio stations owned by wealthy conservatives or underwritten by big business firms. To complain about how the media are dominated by liberals, Limbaugh has an hour a day on network television, an hour on cable, and a radio show syndicated by over 600 stations.

Then there are the well-financed right-wing media-watch organizations like Reed Irvine's Accuracy in Media (AIM). In a syndicated column appearing in over 100 newspapers and on a radio show aired on some 200 stations, Irvine and his associates complain that conservative viewpoints are frozen out of the media. Many left critics would like to be frozen out the way AIM, Limbaugh, and Horowitz are.

Not to be overlooked is National Empowerment Television (NET), a new cable network available in all 50 states, offering round-the-clock conservative political commentary. In the words of its founder Paul Weyrich, NET is dedicated to countering media news that "is riddled with a far-left political bias" and "unacceptable" notions about "gender-norming, racial quotas, global warming, and gays in the military."

Political leaders do their share to reinforce the image of a liberal press. During the Iran–contra affair, President Reagan likened the "liberal" media to a pack of sharks. More recently President Clinton complained that he has "not

gotten one damn bit of credit from the knee-jerk liberal press." Clinton is confused; almost all the criticism hurled his way by the so-called liberal press is coming from conservatives.

HE WHO PAYS THE PIPER

There is no free and independent press in the United States. The notion of a "free market of ideas" is just as mythical as the notion of a free market of goods. Both conjure up an image of a bazaar in which many small producers sell their wares on a more or less equal footing. In fact—be it commodities or commentary—to reach a mass market you need huge sums of money for production, exposure, and distribution. Those who are without big bucks end up with a decidedly smaller clientele, assuming they survive at all.

Who owns the big media? The press lords who come to mind are William Randolph Hearst, Henry Luce, Rupert Murdock, Arthur Sulzberger, Walter Annenberg, and the like—personages of markedly conservative hue who regularly leave their ideological imprint on both news and editorial content.

The boards of directors of print and broadcast news organizations are populated by representatives from Ford, General Motors, General Electric, Dow Corning, Alcoa, Coca-Cola, Philip Morris, ITT, IBM, AT&T, and other corporations in a system of interlocking directorates that resemble the boards of other corporations. Among the major stockholders of the three largest broadcast networks are Chase Manhattan, J. P. Morgan, and Citibank. NBC is owned outright by GE. The prime stockholder of this country's most far-reaching wire service, Associated Press, is Merrill Lynch.

Not surprisingly, this pattern of ownership affects how news and commentary are manufactured. Virtually all the chief executives of mainstream news organizations are drawn from a narrow, high-income segment of the population and tilt decidedly to the right in their political preferences. Rupert Murdoch was once asked in an interview: "You're considered to be politically conservative. To what extent do you influence the editorial posture of your newspapers?" He responded with refreshing candor: "Considerably . . . my editors have input, but I make the final decisions."

Corporate advertisers exercise an additional conservative influence on the media. They cancel accounts not only when stories reflect poorly on their product but, as is more often the case, when they perceive liberal tendencies creeping into news reports and commentary.

As might be expected, the concerns of labor are regularly downplayed. Jonathan Tasini, head of the National Writers Union, studied all reports dealing with workers' issues carried by ABC, CBS, and NBC evening news during 1989, including child care and minimum wage: it came to only 2.3 percent of total coverage. No wonder one survey found that only 6 percent of business leaders thought the media treatment accorded them was "poor," while 66 percent said it was "good" or "excellent."

Religious media manifest the same gross imbalance of right over left. The fundamentalist media—featuring homophobic, sexist, reactionary televangelists like Pat Robertson—comprise a $2-billion-a-year industry, controlling about 10 percent of all radio outlets and 14 percent of the nation's television stations. In contrast, tens of thousands of liberal and often radically oriented Christians and their organizations lack the financial backing needed to gain media access.

THE PETROLEUM BROADCASTING SYSTEM

A favorite conservative hallucination is that the Public Broadcasting System is a leftist stronghold. In fact, more than 70 percent of PBS's prime-time shows are funded wholly or in major part by four giant oil companies, earing it the sobriquet of "Petroleum Broadcasting System." PBS's public-affairs programs are underwritten by General Electric, General Motors, Metropolitan Life, Pepsico, Mobil, Paine Webber, and the like. One media watchdog group found that corporate representatives constitute 44 percent of the

sources about the economy; activists account for only 3 percent, while labor representatives are virtually shut out. Guests on NPR and PBS generally are as ideologically conservative as any found on commercial networks. Even "Frontline" and Bill Moyers' "Listening to America"—favorite GOP targets—use Republicans far more frequently than Democrats.

Conservatives like Horowitz make much of the occasional muckraking documentary that is aired on public television. But most PBS documentaries are politically nondescript or centrist. Progressive works rarely see the light of day. Documentaries like *Faces of War* (revealing the brutality of the U.S.-backed counterinsurgercy in El Salvador), *Building Bombs* (on nuclear proliferation), *Coverup* (on the Iran-contra conspiracy), *Deadly Deception* (an Academy Award–winning critique of General Electric and the nuclear arms industry), and *The Panama Deception* (an Academy Award–winning expose of the United States' invasion of Panama) were, with a few local exceptions, denied broadcast rights on both commercial and public television.

A rightist perspective dominates commentary shows like NBC's "McLaughlin Group," PBS's "One on One" (with John McLaughlin as host), CNBCs "McLaughlin Show" (with guess who), PBS's "Firing Line" (with William F. Buckley, Jr.), CNN's "Evans and Novak" and "Capital Gang," and ABC's "This Week with David Brinkley." The spectrum of opinion on such programs, as on the pages of most newspapers, ranges from far right to moderate center. In a display of false balancing, right-wing ideologues are pitted against moderates and centrists. Facing Pat Buchanan on CNN's "Crossfire" Michael Kinsley correctly summed it up: "Buchanan is much further to the right than I am to the left."

On foreign affairs, the press's role as a cheerleader of the national security state and free-market capitalism seems almost without restraint. Virtually no favorable exposure has ever been given to indigenous Third World revolutionary or reformist struggles or to protests at home and abroad against U.S. overseas interventions. The media's view of the world is much the same as the view from the State Department and the Pentagon. The horrendous devastation wreaked upon the presumed beneficiaries of U.S. power generally goes unmentioned and unexplained—as do the massive human-rights violations perpetrated by U.S.-supported forces in dozens of free-market client states.

WHY DO CONSERVATIVES COMPLAIN?

If news and commentary are so preponderantly conservative, why do rightists blast the press for its supposed leftist bias? For one thing, attacks from the right help create a climate of opinion favorable to the right. Railing against the press's "liberalism" is a way of putting the press on the defensive, keeping it leaning rightward for its respectability, so that liberal opinion in this country is forever striving for credibility within a conservatively defined framework.

Ideological control is not formal and overt as with a state censor but informal and usually implicit. Hence it works with imperfect effect. Editors sometimes are unable to see the troublesome implications of particular stories. As far as right-wingers are concerned, too much gets in that should be excluded. Their goal is not partial control but perfect control, not an overbearing advantage (which they already have) but total dominance of the communication universe. Anything short of unanimous support for a rightist agenda is treated as evidence of liberal bias. Expecting the press corps to be a press chorus, the conservative ideologue, like any imperious maestro, reacts sharply to the occasionally discordant note.

The discordant notes can be real. The news media never challenge freemarket ideology, but they do occasionally report things that might put business and the national security state in a bad light: toxic-waste dumping by industrial firms, price-gouging by defense contractors, bodies piling up in Haiti, financial thievery on Wall Street, and the like. These exposures are more than rightists care to hear and are perceived by them as a liberal vendetta.

The conservative problem is that reality itself is radical. The Third World really is poor and oppressed; the United States usually does side with Third World oligarchs; our tax system really is regressive; millions of Americans do live in poverty; the corporations do plunder and pollute the environment; real wages for blue-collar workers definitely have declined; and the rich really are increasing their share of the pie. Despite their best efforts, there are limits to how much the media can finesse these kinds of realities.

The limits of reality sometimes impose limits on propaganda, as Dr. Goebbels discovered when trying to explain to the German public how invincible Nazi armies could win victory after victory while retreating on both fronts in 1944 and 1945. Although they see the world through much the same ideological lens as do corporate and government elites, the media must occasionally report some of the unpleasantness of life—if only to maintain credibility with a public that is not always willing to buy the official line. On such occasions, rightists complain bitterly about a left bias.

Rightist ideologues object not only to what the press says but to what it omits. They castigate the media for failing to tell the American people that federal bureaucrats, "cultural elites," gays, lesbians, feminists, and abortionists are destroying the nation, that the U.S. military and corporate America are our only salvation, that there is no health-care problem, that eco-terrorists stalk the land, that the environment is doing just fine—and other such loony tunes.

SELF-CENSORSHIP

Reporters often operate in a state of self-censorship and anticipatory response. They frequently wonder aloud how their boss is taking things. They recall instances when superiors have warned them not to antagonize big advertisers and other powerful interests. They can name journalists who were banished for turning in the wrong kind of copy. Still, most newspeople treat these incidents as aberrant departures from a basically professional news system and insist they owe their souls to no one. They claim they are free to say what they like, not realizing it is because their superiors like what they say. Since they seldom cross any forbidden lines, they are not reined in and they remain unaware that they are on an ideological leash.

While incarcerated in Mussolini's dungeons from 1928 to 1937, Antonio Gramsci wrote about politics and culture in his prison notebooks. But he had to be careful not to antagonize the fascist censor. Today most of our journalists and social commentators exercise a similar caution. However, unlike Gramsci, they are not in prison. They don't need a fascist censor breathing down their necks because they have a mainstream one implanted in their heads.

These internalized forms of self-censorship are far more effective in preserving the dominant ideology than any state censor could hope to be. Gramsci knew he was being censored. Many of our newspeople and pundits think they are as free as birds—and they are, as long as they fly around in the right circles.

For conservative critics, however, the right circles are neither right enough nor tight enough. Anything to the left of themselves, including moderate right and establishment centrist, is defined as "liberal." Their campaign against the media helps to shift the center of political gravity in their direction. By giving such generous publicity to conservative preachments and pronouncements while amputating everything on the left, the media limit public debate to a contest between right and center. In doing so, they are active accomplices in maintaining a rightward bent.

On the American political scene, the center is occupied by conservative Democrats like Bill Clinton, who are happy to be considered the only alternative to the ultra-right. This center is then passed off as "liberal." Meanwhile, real liberalism and everything progressive remain out of the picture—which is just what the mainstream pundits, publishers, politicians, and plutocrats want.

• • •

18

Toward a 24-Hour Economy

HARRIET B. PRESSER

Analysis of employment data indicates that few in the United States are working a "typi-cal" forty-hour work week. This change is being driven by the changing economy, the chang-ing demography of the workplace, and changing technology. Harriet Presser discusses the effects of the increase in working hours on families.

Americans are moving toward a 24-hour, 7-day-a-week economy. Two-fifths of all employed Americans work mostly during the evenings or nights, on rotating shifts, or on weekends. Much more attention has been given to the number of hours Americans work[1,2] than to the issue of which hours—or days—Americans work. Yet the widespread prevalence of nonstandard work schedules is a significant social phenomenon, with important implications for the health and well-being of individuals and their families and for the imple-mentation of social policies. Here I discuss recent national data on the widespread prevalence of nonstandard work schedules, explain why this has come about, and highlight some of the important social implications.

PREVALENCE

As of 1997, only 29.1% of employed U.S. citizens worked a "standard work week," defined as 35 to 40 hours a week, Monday through Friday, on a fixed daytime schedule. For employed men, the proportion is 26.5%; for employed women, 32.8%. Only 54.4%—a bare majority—regularly work a fixed daytime schedule, all five weekdays, for any number of hours.

These figures are derived from the May 1997 Current Population Survey (CPS), a representative sample of about 48,000 U.S. households. I selected for further study a subset of about 50,000 employed Americans ages 18 and over in these households with nonagricultural occupations and who reported on their specific work hours and/or work days.

Of the people in this group, one in five work other than on a fixed daytime schedule, and one in three work on weekends (and, for most, on weekdays as well). Men and women are similar in their prevalence of evening employment,

From: *Science* 284 (June 1999): 1778–1779. Reprinted with permission.

but a somewhat higher proportion of men than women work fixed nights, rotating and variable hours, and weekends. The most marked differences are between those working full time and part-time. More part-timers work other than a fixed day (29.6%) than do full-timers (17.0%); evening employment is especially high among part timers. The difference between full- and part-timers is less marked for weekend employment (30.7% and 34.7%, respectively).

For the modal U.S. family—the two-earner couple—the prevalence of nonstandard work schedules is especially high, because either the husband or wife may be working nondays or weekends. (Rarely do both work the same nonstandard schedules.) Among two-earner couples, 27.8% include at least one spouse who works other than a fixed daytime schedule, and 54.6% include at least one spouse working weekends. When children under age 14 are in the household the respective percentages are 31.1 and 46.8%. Indeed of all two-earner couples with children, those with both spouses working fixed daytime schedules and weekdays are a minority; 57.3% do not fit this description. Thus, the temporal context in which millions of American couples are raising their children today is diverse and is likely to become even more so in the future.

ORIGINS AND CAUSES

At least three interrelated factors are increasing the demand for Americans to work late hours and weekends: a changing economy, changing demography, and changing technology. With regard to the changing economy, an important aspect is the growth of the service sector with its high prevalence of nonstandard work schedules relative to the goods-producing sector. In the 1960s, employees in manufacturing greatly exceeded those in service industries, whereas by 1995 the percentage was about twice as high in services as in manufacturing[3]. In particular, there is an interaction between the growth of women's employment and the growth of the service sector because there is a disproportionately high percentage of female occupations in this sector. In turn, the increasing participation of women in the labor force contributes to the growth of the service economy. For example, the decline in full-time homemaking has generated an increase in family members eating out and purchasing other services. Moreover, women's increasing daytime labor force participation has generated a demand for services during nondaytime hours and weekends[4].

Demographic changes also have contributed. The postponement of marriage, along with the rise in real family income resulting from two earners, has increased the demand for recreation and entertainment during late hours and weekends. The aging of the population has increased the demand for medical services over a 24-hour day, 7 days a week.

Finally, technological change, along with reduced costs, has moved us to a global 24-hour economy. The ability to be "on call" at all hours of the day and night to others around the world at low cost generates a need to do so. For example, the rise of multinational corporations, along with the use of computers, faxes, and other forms of rapid communication, increases the demand for branch offices to operate at the same time that corporate headquarters are open. Similarly, international financial markets are expanding their hours of operation. Express mailing companies such as United Parcel Service require round-the-clock workers all days of the week.

We do not have precise national estimates of the amount of growth over recent decades in the prevalence of nonstandard work schedules as a consequence of these changes. Questions on work hours have been asked differently by the Bureau of Labor Statistics in each of the CPSs since 1980; questions on work days were not even asked until 1991.

Most of the top 10 occupations projected by the Bureau of Labor Statistics to have the largest job growth between 1996 and 2006 are service occupations[5]. Using the May 1997 CPS data. I calculated the percentages in the top growth occupations for which nonstandard schedules are prevalent and considered their gender and racial composition.

The data suggest that not only will future job growth generate an increase in employment during nonstandard hours and weekends, but also that this increase will be experienced disproportionately by females and blacks. Many of the top growth occupations that tend to have nonstandard work schedules also have high percentages of female workers: cashiers, registered nurses, retail salespersons, nurses' aides, orderlies, and attendants combined with home health aides. The top growth occupations that disproportionately include blacks and tend to have nonstandard work schedules are cashiers, truck drivers, nurses' aides, orderlies, and attendants combined with home health aides.

Although nonstandard work schedules are pervasive throughout the occupational structure, such schedules are disproportionately concentrated in jobs low in the occupational hierarchy[6]. This fact, combined with the expectation that women and blacks will disproportionately increase their participation in nonstandard work schedules, suggests that this phenomenon will increasingly affect the working poor.

Effects on Families

The physical consequences of working non-standard hours, particularly night and rotating hours, have been well documented[7]. Such work schedules alter one's circadian rhythms, often leading to sleep disturbances, gastrointestinal disorders, and chronic malaise. The social consequences of such employment have received less attention, although working nonstandard schedules may be significantly altering the structure and stability of family life. Some of the consequences can be viewed as positive, others negative, and both may vary by family member. Moreover, short-term benefits may be offset by long-term costs and vice versa.

Consider, for example, the care of children among dual-earner couples. As noted above, one-third of such couples with preschool-aged children are split-shift couples with one spouse working days and the other evenings, nights, or rotating schedules. A national study of American couples with preschool-aged children showed that in virtually all cases in which mothers and fathers are employed different hours and neither are on rotating schedules, fathers are the primary caregivers of children when their wives are employed[8]. Insofar as we view the greater involvement of fathers in child care as desirable, and considering the economic benefits to the family of reduced child care expenses resulting from this arrangement, such split-shift parenting may be a positive outcome.

However, these gains may be more than offset by the longer term costs to the marriage. New research shows that among couples with children, when men work nights (and are married less than 5 years) the likelihood of separation or divorce 5 years later is some six times that when men work days. When women work nights (and are married more than 5 years) the odds of divorce or separation are three times as high. Moreover, the data suggest that the increased tendency for divorce is not because spouses in troubled marriages are more likely to opt for night work; the causality seems in the opposite direction[9].

Single as well as married mothers often engage in a split-shift caregiving arrangement with grandmothers. More than one-third of grandmothers who provide care for preschool-aged children are otherwise employed[10]. Here, too, there may be both positive and negative aspects of such arrangements, but this has not been studied. The observation that single mothers are more likely than married mothers to work long as well as nonstandard hours and are more likely to be among the working poor [11,12] suggests that the problems of managing time and money are especially stressful for such mothers.

Policymakers and scholars must take a more realistic view of the temporal nature of family life among Americans. With regard to welfare reform, for example, close to half (43.3%) of employed mothers with a high school education or less, ages 18 to 34, work other than a fixed daytime schedule, weekdays only[13]. If mothers on welfare are to move into jobs similar to these mothers, a key policy issue is how to improve the fit between the availability of child care and these working mothers' schedules. Expanding day care alone will not be satisfactory.

The movement toward a 24-hour economy is well underway, and will continue into the next century. Although driven by factors external to individual families, it will affect the lives of family members in profound ways. The home-time structure of families is becoming temporally very complex. We need to change our conception of family life to include such complexities. This should help to improve social policies that seek to ease the economic and social tensions that often result from the dual demands of work and family, particularly among the working poor.

REFERENCES AND NOTES

1. J. Schor, *The Overworked American* (Basic Books, New York, 1991).

2. J. P. Robinson and G. Godbey. *Time for Life: The Surprising Ways Americans Use Their Time* (Pennsylvania State Univ. Press, University Park, PA, 1997).

3. J. R. Meisenheimer II, *Mon. Labor Rev.* **121,** 22 (February 1998).

4. H. B. Presser, *Demography* **26,** 523 (1989).

5. G. T. Silvestri, *Mon. Labor Rev.* **120,** 58 (November 1997).

6. H. B. Presser, *Demography* **32,** 577 (1995).

7. *Biological Rhythms: Implications for the Worker* (OTA-BA-463, Office of

Technological Assessment, Washington, DC, 1991).

8. H. B. Presser, *J. Marr. Fam.* **50,** 133 (1988).

9. —— *ibid.,* in press.

10. —— *ibid.,* **51,** 581 (1989).

11. A. G. Cox, thesis, University of Maryland (1994).

12. —— and H. B. Presser, in *Work and Family: Research Informing Policy.* T. Parcel and D. B. Cornfield, Eds. (Sage. Thousand Oaks, CA, in press.).

13. H. B. Presser and A. G. Cor, *Mon. Labor Rev.* **120,** 25 (April 1997).

DISCUSSION QUESTIONS

1. What factors does Presser identify as leading to increases in the working hours of employed people? What impact are these changes likely to have on the labor force experiences of two-earner households?

2. Sociologists have often argued that work and family structures are mutually interdependent. How is this evidenced by the effects of increasing work hours on families' experiences? What evidence of this have you seen in your own life?

INFOTRAC COLLEGE EDITION

You can use your access to InfoTrac College edition to learn more about the subjects covered in this essay. Some suggested search terms include:

flex-time
part-time work
time-budget studies
women's labor force participation

work hours
worker stress
working poor

19

The McDonaldization
of Society

GEORGE RITZER

The success of fast food chains is used by Ritzer as a metaphor for some general trends characterizing contemporary American society. We have become a nation driven by concerns for rationality, speed, and efficiency that are so well illustrated by the McDonalds' style of operation. Food, packaging, and service are designed to move quickly and cheaply through and out of these restaurants, giving customers the most modern eating experience. Speed, convenience, and standardization have replaced the flair of design and creation in cooking, the comfort of relationships in serving, and the variety available in choice. McDonaldization has become so pervasive that one can travel to nearly any city or town in America and find familiar chain-style restaurants, shops, hotels, and other avenues for commercial exchange. This has fostered the homogenization of American culture and life, streamlined along a set of rational, efficient, and impersonal principles. How has the McDonaldization phenomenon affected your life? What types of commercial exchanges are affected by this process? What are the benefits of this for society? What are some of the detriments that you see?

A wide-ranging process of *rationalization* is occurring across American society and is having an increasingly powerful impact in many other parts of the world. It encompasses such disparate phenomena as fast-food restaurants, TV dinners, packaged tours, industrial robots, plea bargaining, and open-heart surgery on an assembly-line basis. As widespread and as important as these developments are, it is clear that we have barely begun a process that promises even more extraordinary changes (e.g. genetic engineering) in the years to come. We can think of rationalization as a historical process and rationality as the end result of that development. As a historical process, rationalization has distinctive roots in the western world. Writing in the late nineteenth and early twentieth centuries, the great German sociologist Max Weber saw his society as the center

From the *Journal of American Culture*, V. 6, No. 1, 1983, pp. 100–107. Reprinted by permission of the publisher.

of the ongoing process of rationalization and the bureaucracy as its paradigm case. The model of rationalization, at least in contemporary America, is no longer the bureaucracy, but might be better thought of as the fast-food restaurant. As a result, our concern here is with what might be termed the "McDonaldization of Society." While the fast-food restaurant is not the ultimate expression of rationality, it is the current exemplar for future developments in rationalization.

A society characterized by rationality is one which emphasizes *efficiency, predictability, calculability, substitution of nonhuman for human technology,* and *control over uncertainty.* In discussing the various dimensions of rationalization, we will be little concerned with the gains already made, and yet to be realized, by greater rationalization. These advantages are widely discussed in schools and in the mass media. In fact, we are in danger of being seduced by the innumerable advantages already offered, and promised in the future, by rationalization. The glitter of these accomplishments and promises has served to distract most people from the grave dangers posed by progressive rationalization. In other words, we are ultimately concerned here with the irrational consequences that often flow from rational systems. Thus, the second major theme of this essay might be termed "the irrationality of rationality." . . .

EFFICIENCY

The process of rationalization leads to a society in which a great deal of emphasis is placed on finding the best or optimum means to any given end. Whatever a group of people define as an end, and everything they so define, is to be pursued by attempting to find the best means to achieve the end. Thus, in the Germany of Weber's day, the bureaucracy was seen as the most efficient means of handling a wide array of administrative tasks. Somewhat later, the Nazis came to develop the concentration camp, its ovens, and other devices as the optimum method of collecting and murdering millions of Jews and other people. The efficiency that Weber described in turn-of-the-century Germany, and which later came to characterize many Nazi activities, has become a basic principle of life in virtually every sector of a rational society.

The modern American family, often with two wage earners, has little time to prepare elaborate meals. For the relatively few who still cook such meals, there is likely to be great reliance on cookbooks that make cooking from scratch much more efficient. However, such cooking is relatively rare today. Most families take as their objective quickly and easily prepared meals. To this end, much use is made of prepackaged meals and frozen TV dinners.

For many modern families, the TV dinner is no longer efficient enough. To many people, eating out, particularly in a fast-food restaurant, is a far more efficient way of obtaining their meals. Fast-food restaurants capitalize on this by being organized so that diners are fed as efficiently as possible. They offer a limited, simple menu that can be cooked and served in an assembly-line fashion. The latest development in fast-food restaurants, the addition of drive-through windows, constitutes an effort to increase still further the efficiency of the dining experience. The family now can simply drive through, pick up its order, and eat it while driving to the next, undoubtedly efficiently organized, activity. The success of the fast-food restaurant has come full circle with frozen food manufacturers now touting products for the home modeled after those served in fast-food restaurants.

Increasingly, efficiently organized food production and distribution systems lie at the base of the ability of people to eat their food efficiently at home, in the fast-food restaurant, or in their cars. Farms, groves, ranches, slaughterhouses, warehouses, transportation systems, and retailers are all oriented toward increasing efficiency. A notable example is chicken production where they are mass-bred, force-fed (often with many chemicals), slaughtered on an assembly line, iced or fast frozen, and shipped to all parts of the country. Some may argue that such chickens do not taste as good as the fresh-killed, local variety, but their complaints are likely to be drowned in a flood of mass-produced chickens. Then there is bacon which is more efficiently shipped, stored, and sold when it is preserved by sodium nitrate, a chemical which is unfortunately thought by many to be carcinogenic. Whatever one may say about the quality or the danger of the products, the fact remains that they are all shaped by the drive for efficiency. . . .

One of the most interesting and important aspects of efficiency is that it often comes to be not a means but an end in itself. This "displacement of goals" is a major problem in a rationalizing society. We have, for example, the bureaucrats who slavishly follow the rules even though their inflexibility negatively affects the organization's ability to achieve its goals. Then there are the bureaucrats who are so concerned with efficiency that they lose sight of the ultimate goals the means are designed to achieve. A good example was the Nazi concentration camp officers who, in devoting so much attention to maximizing the efficiency of the camps' operation, lost sight of the fact that the ultimate purpose of the camps was the murder of millions of people.

PREDICTABILITY

A second component of rationalization involves the effort to ensure predictability from one place to another. In a rational society, people want to know what to expect when they enter a given setting or acquire some sort of commodity. They neither want nor expect surprises. They want to know that if they journey to another locale, the setting they enter or the commodity they buy will be essentially the same as the setting they entered or product they purchased earlier. Furthermore, people want to be sure that what they encounter is much like what they encountered at earlier times. In order to ensure predictability over time and place a rational society must emphasize such things as discipline, order, systemization, formalization, routine, consistency, and methodical operation.

One of the attractions of TV dinners for modern families is that they are highly predictable. The TV dinner composed of fried chicken, mashed potatoes, green peas, and peach cobbler is exactly the same from one time to another and one city to another. Home cooking from scratch is, conversely, a notoriously unpredictable enterprise with little assurance that dishes will taste the same time after time. However, the cookbook cannot eliminate all unpredictability. There are often simply too many ingredients and other variables involved. Thus the cookbook dish is far less predictable than the TV dinner or a wide array of other prepared dishes.

Fast-food restaurants rank very high on the dimension of predictability. In order to help ensure consistency, the fast-food restaurant offers only a limited menu. Predictable end products are made possible by the use of similar raw materials, technologies, and preparation and serving techniques. Not only the food is predictable; the physical structures, the logo, the "ambience," and even the personnel are as well.

The food that is shipped to our homes and our fast-food restaurants is itself affected by the process of increasing predictability. Thus our favorite white bread is indistinguishable from one place to another. In fact, food producers have made great efforts to ensure such predictability.

On packaged tours travelers can be fairly sure that the people they travel with will be much like themselves. The planes, buses, hotel accommodations, restaurants, and at least the way in which the sites are visited are very similar from one location to another. Many people go on packaged tours *because* they are far more predictable than travel undertaken on an individual basis.

Amusement parks used to be highly unpredictable affairs. People could never be sure, from one park to another, precisely what sorts of rides, events, foods, visitors, and employees they would encounter. All of that has changed in the era of the theme parks inspired by Disneyland. Such parks seek to ensure predictability in various ways. For example, a specific type of young person is hired in these parks, and they are all trained in much the same way, so that they have a robot-like predictability.

Other leisure-time activities have grown similarly predictable. Camping in the wild is loaded with uncertainties—bugs, bears, rain, cold, and the like. To make camping more predictable, organized grounds have sprung up around the country. Gone are many of the elements of unpredictability replaced by RVs, paved-over parking lots, sanitized campsites, fences and enclosed camp centers that provide laundry and food services, recreational activities, television, and video games. Sporting events, too, have in a variety of ways been made more predictable. The use of artificial turf in baseball makes for a more predictable bounce of a ball. . . .

CALCULABILITY OR QUANTITY RATHER THAN QUALITY

It could easily be argued that the emphasis on quantifiable measures, on things that can be counted, is *the* most defining characteristic of a rational society. Quality is notoriously difficult to evaluate. How do we assess the quality of a hamburger, or a physician, or a student? Instead of even trying, in an increasing number of cases, a rational society seeks to develop a series of quantifiable measures that it takes as surrogates for quality. This urge to quantify has given great impetus to the development of the computer and has, in turn, been spurred by the widespread use and increasing sophistication of the computer.

The fact is that many aspects of modern rational society, especially as far as calculable issues are concerned, are made possible and more widespread by the computer. We need not belabor the ability of the computer to handle large numbers of virtually anything, but somewhat less obvious is the use of the computer to give the illusion of personal attention in a world made increasingly impersonal in large part because of the computer's capacity to turn virtually everything into quantifiable dimensions. We have all now had many experiences where we open a letter personally addressed to us only to find a computer letter. We are aware that the names and addresses of millions of people have been stored on tape and that with the aid of a number of word processors a form letter has been sent to every name on the list. Although the computer is able to give a sense of personal attention, most people are nothing more than an item on a huge mailing list.

Our main concern here, though, is not with the computer, but with the emphasis on quantity rather than quality that it has helped foster. One of the most obvious examples in the university is the emphasis given to grades and cumulative grade point averages. With less and less contact between professor and student, there is little real effort to assess the quality of what students know, let alone the quality of their overall abilities. Instead, the sole measure of the quality of most college students is their grade in a given course and their grade point averages. Another blatant example is the emphasis on a variety of uniform exams such as SATs and GREs in which the essence of an applicant is reduced to a few simple scores and percentiles.

Within the educational institution, the importance of grades is well known, but somewhat less known is the way quantifiable factors have become an essential part of the process of evaluating college professors. For example, teaching ability is very hard to evaluate. Administrators have difficulty assessing teaching quality and thus substitute quantitative scores. Of course each score involves qualitative judgments, but this is conveniently ignored. Student opinion polls are taken and the scores are summed, averaged, and compared. Those who score well are deemed good teachers while those who don't are seen as poor teachers. There are many problems involved in relying on these scores such as the fact that easy teachers in "gut" courses may well obtain high ratings while rigorous teachers of difficult courses are likely to score poorly. . . .

In the workworld we find many examples of the effort to substitute quantity for quality. Scientific management was heavily oriented to turning everything work-related into quantifiable dimensions. Instead of relying on the "rule of thumb" of the operator, scientific management sought to develop precise measures of how much work was to be done by each and every motion of the worker. Everything that could be was reduced to numbers and all these numbers were then analyzable using a variety of mathematical formulae. The assembly line is similarly oriented to a variety of quantifiable dimensions such as optimizing the speed of the line, minimizing time for each task, lowering the price of the finished product, increasing sales and ultimately increasing profits. The divisional system pioneered by General Motors and thought to be one of the major reasons for its past success was oriented to the reduction of the performance of each division to a few, bottom-line numbers. By monitoring and comparing these numbers, General Motors was able to exercise control over the results without getting involved in the day-to-day activities of each division. . . .

Thus, the third dimension of rationalization, calculability or the emphasis on quantity rather than quality, has wide applicability to the social world. It is truly central, if not the central, component of a rationalizing society. To return to our favorite example, it is the case that McDonald's expends far more effort telling us how many billions of hamburgers it has sold than it does in telling us about the quality of those burgers. Relatedly, it touts the size of its product (the "Big Mac") more than the quality of the product (it is not the "Good Mac"). The bottom line in many settings is the number of customers processed, the speed with which they are processed, and the profits produced. Quality is secondary, if indeed there is any concern at all for it.

SUBSTITUTION OF NONHUMAN TECHNOLOGY

In spite of Herculean efforts, there are important limits to the ability to rationalize what human beings think and do. Seemingly no matter what one does, people still retain at least the ultimate capacity to think and act in a variety of unanticipated ways. Thus, in spite of great efforts to make human behavior more efficient, more predictable, more calculable, people continue to act in unforeseen ways. People continue to make home-cooked meals from scratch, to camp in tents in the wild, to eat in old-fashioned diners, and to sabotage the assembly lines. Because of these realities, there is great interest among those who foster increasing rationality in using rational technologies to limit individual independence and ultimately to replace human beings with machines and other technologies that lack the ability to think and act in unpredictable ways.

McDonald's does not yet have robots to serve us food, but it does have teenagers whose ability to act autonomously is almost completely eliminated by techniques, procedures, routines, and machines. There are numerous examples of this including rules which prescribe all the things a counterperson should do in dealing with a customer as well as a large variety of technologies which determine the actions of workers such as drink dispensers which shut themselves off when the cup is full; buzzers, lights, and bells which indicate when food (e.g., french fries) is done; and cash registers which have the prices of each item programmed in. One of the latest attempts to constrain individual action is Denny's use of pre-measured packages of dehydrated food that are "cooked" simply by putting them under the hot water tap. Because of such tools and machines, as well as the elaborate rules dictating worker behavior, people often feel like they are dealing with human robots when they relate to the personnel of a fast-food restaurant. When human robots are found, mechanical robots cannot be far behind. Once people are reduced to a few robot-like actions, it is a relatively easy step to replace them with mechanical robots. Thus, Burgerworld is reportedly opening a prototypical restaurant in which mechanical robots serve the food.

Much of the recent history of work, especially manual work, is a history of efforts to replace human technology with nonhuman technology. Scientific management was oriented to the development of an elaborate and rigid set of rules about how jobs were to be done. The workers were to blindly and obediently follow those rules and not to do the work the way they saw fit. The various skills needed to perform a task were carefully delineated and broken down into a series of routine steps that could be taught to all workers. The skills, in other words, were built into the routines rather than belonging to skilled craftspersons. Similar points can be made about the assembly line which is basically a set of nonhuman technologies that have the needed steps and skills built into them. The human worker is reduced to performing a limited number of simple, repetitive operations. However, the control of this technology over the individual worker is so great and omnipresent that individual workers have reacted negatively manifesting such things as tardiness, absenteeism, turnover, and even sabotage. We are now witnessing a new stage in this technological development with automated processes now totally replacing many workers with robots. With the coming of robots we have reached the ultimate stage in the replacement of humans with nonhuman technology.

Even religion and religious crusades have not been unaffected by the spread of nonhuman technologies. The growth of large religious organizations, the use of Madison Avenue techniques, and even drive-in churches all reflect the incursion of modern technology. But it is in the electronic church, religion through the TV screens, that replacement of human by nonhuman technology in religion is most visible and has its most important manifestation. . . .

CONTROL

This leads us to the fifth major dimension of rationalization—control. Rational systems are oriented toward, and structured to expedite, control in a variety of senses. At the most general level, we can say that rational systems are set up to allow for greater control over the uncertainties of life—birth, death, food production and distribution, housing, religious salvation, and many, many others. More specifically, rational systems are oriented to gaining greater control over the major source of uncertainty in social life—other people. Among other things, this means control over subordinates by superiors and control of clients and customers by workers.

There are many examples of rationalization oriented toward gaining greater control over the uncertainties of life. The burgeoning of the genetic engineering movement can be seen as being aimed at gaining better control over the production of life itself. Similarly, amniocentesis can be seen as a technique which will allow the parents to determine the kind of child they will have. The efforts to rationalize food production and distribution can be seen as being aimed at gaining greater control over the problems of hunger and starvation. A steady and regular supply of food can make life itself more certain for large numbers of people who today live under the threat of death from starvation.

At a more specific level, the rationalization of food preparation and serving at McDonald's gives it great control over its employees. The automobile assembly line has a similar impact. In fact, the vast majority of the structures of a rational society exert extraordinary control over the people who labor in them. But because of the limits that still exist on the degree of control that rational structures can exercise over individuals, many rationalizing employers are driven to seek to more fully rationalize their operations and totally eliminate the worker. The result is an automated, robot-like technology over which, barring some *2001* rebellion, there is almost total control.

In addition to control over employees, rational systems are also interested in controlling the customer/clients they serve. For example, the fast-food restaurant with its counter, the absence of waiters and waitresses, the limited seating, and the drive-through windows all tend to lead customers to do certain things and not to do others.

Irrationality of Rationality

Although not an inherent part of rationalization, the *irrationality of rationality* is a seemingly inevitable byproduct of the process. We can think of the irrationality of rationality in several ways. At the most general level it can simply be seen as an overarching label for all the negative effects of rationalization. More specifically, it can be seen as the opposite of rationality, at least in some of its senses. For example, there are the inefficiencies and unpredictabilities that are often produced by seemingly rational systems. Thus, although bureaucracies are constructed to bring about greater efficiency in organizational work, the fact is that there are notorious inefficiencies such as the "red tape" associated with the operation of most bureaucracies. Or, take the example of the arms race in which a focus on quantifiable aspects of nuclear weapons may well have made the occurrence of nuclear war more, rather than less, unpredictable.

Of greatest importance, however, is the variety of negative effects that rational systems have on the individuals who live, work, and are served by them. We might say that *rational systems are not reasonable systems*. As we've already discussed, rationality brings with it great dehumanization as people are reduced to acting like robots. Among the dehumanizing aspects of a rational society are large lecture classes, computer letters, pray TV, work on the automobile assembly line, and dining at a fast-food restaurant. Rationalization also tends to bring with it disenchantment leaving much of our lives without any mystery or excitement. Production by a hand craftsman is far more mysterious than an assembly-line technology where each worker does a single, very limited operation. Camping in an RV tends to suffer in comparison to the joys to be derived from camping in the wild. Overall a fully rational society would be a very bleak and uninteresting place.

CONCLUSION

Rationalization, with McDonald's as the paradigm case, is occurring throughout America, and, increasingly, other societies. In virtually every sector of society more and more emphasis is placed on efficiency, predictability, calculability, replacement of human by nonhuman technology, and control over uncertainty. Although progressive rationalization has brought with it innumerable advantages, it has also created a number of problems, the various irrationalities of rationality, which threaten to accelerate in the years to come. These problems, and their acceleration should not be taken as a case for the return to a less rational form of society. Such a return is not only impossible but also undesirable. What is needed is not a less rational society, but greater control over the process of rationalization involving, among other things, efforts to ameliorate its irrational consequences.

THE FAMILY:
Husbands and Wives

20

Playing Fair

BARBARA RISMAN

The research of Berkeley sociologist Arlie Hochschild in the 1980s on the "second shift" discouraged many American women when they realized they were not alone in having entered the labor market full-time only to be shouldering the brunt of the responsibility for a second full-time job running the household and family. Men offered help, to varying degrees, but essentially failed to assume ownership of the tasks and roles in this domain. Risman searched to find the groups in society where this inequality did not exist, where husbands and wives comanaged this realm equally. She found this pattern primarily among "educationally elite" American households whose members worked in white-collar professions. A phenomenon arising predominantly in the late 1980s, equal sharing and labor management occurred where men's incomes were too low to sustain the family lifestyle on their own and the wife's paycheck had real meaning. Risman examines the commonalities and different patterns characterizing these couples, how they moved into "playing fair," and the very high marital satisfaction they display. Her findings offer hope, in contrast to Nock's analysis, for the future of gender roles in marriage. How equitable do you want your relationship with your spouse to be? Is Risman's forecast only applicable to the "educationally elite" that she studied, or are these people on the forefront for how most husbands and wives will organize their marriages in the future? If we move more toward the egalitarian marriages described by Risman, will other parts of society have to change to accommodate this?

Much research on contemporary families focuses on the stalled revolution in most American homes: even when women spend as many hours in the paid labor force as their husbands do, they retain primary responsibility for homemaking and childrearing. The power of gender as a social structure is apparent in these typical families. To understand how and when the gender structure changes we must consider not only the typical family but also families who live on the cutting edge of social change. In this chapter we look at

From Barbara Risman, *Gender Vertigo*, pp. 93–94, 100–101, 106–108, 110–113, 114. Reprinted by permission of Yale University Press.

a statistically rare phenomenon—"fair" role-sharing families, those in which husbands and wives occupy breadwinner and nurturer roles equally.

There is a scarcity of research on couples who have redistributed family work equitably and without regard for the gendered division of responsibilities. There is a good reason for this dearth of research: such families are very rare in a statistical sense, and social scientists prefer to study more mainstream families. All of the research in this field is made up of qualitative studies of recruited volunteer families because there are not enough such families to survey in a random sample. The research that does exist leads me to believe that there have been major changes in egalitarian families in the past two decades. The most striking change is that now some such families actually exist. . . .

THE "FAIR FAMILY" STUDY

We sent a survey to the seventy-five families who had volunteered to participate and seemed eligible based on our screening conversation. The survey worked well: only once did our screening device let through a family in which the woman did more than her share. The problem was, however, that this screened group of seventy-five families yielded us only fifteen who met our criteria for inclusion. Only one of five families who identified themselves as equitable on the telephone, or 20 percent, actually shared the household labor in a 40/60 or better split, agreed that they shared equally the responsibility for breadwinning and childrearing, and felt that their relationship was fair. That alone tells us much about the strength of our gender structure for creating inequitable marriage. Yet I do not want to discredit the tendency toward egalitarianism in the rest of the families who volunteered to participate. The husbands and wives in the families we did not include in our sample were trying to share equally—they were challenging the gender structure. Even if they were not entirely successful they clearly are part of the massive social change that feminism has inspired. Still, as a social analyst, I find it remarkable that the taken-for-granted nature of female responsibility for family work hides a gendered division of labor even from many fair-minded couples themselves.

The fifteen families who met our criteria were educationally elite. More than half of the parents (eight men and nine women) had a Ph.D. or an M.D. Another eight parents had master's degrees (usually in education or business). Three fathers and one mother had a bachelor's degree only, and one mother had never completed college. These families were not necessarily rich, as many had given up high-paying jobs or occupations in order to care for their children equally. Others were college professors, a group with notoriously high educational attainment relative to their incomes. Nevertheless, these were the only families who met our criteria. . . .

Four relationships leading to an equitable division of household labor were identified: dual-career couples, dual-nurturer couples, post-traditionals, and those pushed by external circumstances. In dual-career marriages both partners had always been interested in their own career growth and success, as well as in co-parenting their children. Dual-nurturer couples were more child-centered than work centered, with both parents organizing their work lives almost exclusively around their parental responsibilities. Post-traditional couples had spent at least part of their adult lives in husband-breadwinner and wife-nurturer roles and had consciously rejected that model. And two couples had been pushed into "fair" relationships by circumstances beyond their control. In one such family, the wife's job was the organizing principle for the family's life because she earned nearly twice as much as her husband, who was not very career oriented. In the other family the wife's chronic illness was at least partly responsible for the husband's domestic labor.

DUAL-CAREER COUPLES

The most common route to peer marriage—and the one I had expected because it mirrors my own experience—was the partnership of two career-oriented professionals who both held egalitarian values. Two-thirds of the couples in this study (ten of fifteen) divided their labor "fairly" because both partners were career and equity oriented. Both parents compromised work goals to balance family and career priorities, but both remained committed to their careers as well as their childrearing responsibilities. In all but one of these ten couples, both partners had always studied or worked full-time, shared household responsibilities before parenthood, and never considered any childrearing style other than co-parenting. In one couple, the wife had stayed home for a year after the birth of their daughter while her husband held a temporary position; she remembered the experience as atypical and miserable. She was lonely and unhappy with no work other than mothering. These are families in which both husband and wife simply assume that a fulfilling life involves both paid and family work. No husband or wife articulated, without some probing, an ideological justification for this assumption; they simply had adopted the culturally available feminist view on equality as their own taken-for-granted reality.

A remarkable finding is the absence of gender expectations used as a basis for organizing labor. Not one of these couples mentioned that they had ever considered that the wife devote herself exclusively to family work. No husband or wife complained about consistently doing more than a fair share of housework, nor did the men wish that their wives were more traditionally domestic. Only two of the ten dual-career couples reported any serious conflict over division of labor, usually long in the past. Often the couples never had negotiated at all. One mother, a mathematician married to a public policy analyst explained,

> We didn't tend to do the "You'll do half of the time, I'll do half of the time." We tended to divide tasks up, [decide] who would do them. So Karl liked to cook. He cooked for himself before we ever married. I didn't cook for myself at all before we were married. I ate out or in the cafeteria where I worked, so we didn't really have to adapt ourselves in that way. If he had wanted to share the cooking because he didn't much like it, I probably would've divided it in

some way, half and half, but we tended to sort jobs. He didn't like to do laundry, I like to do laundry. I didn't mind cleaning up, I do the cleaning up . . . the dishes and wiping up counters and stuff. So we found a way that we considered equitable . . . but we did talk about it and we did consciously do it.

In another household the family tried to divide the cooking 50:50 but quickly reverted to sorting tasks by preference—here the mother cooked and father cleaned up afterward. . . .The one way that gender did manifest itself in the family labor of dual-career couples was that the wives sometimes came to the relationship with higher standards of cleanliness. But unlike more traditional families, these couples did not use this difference to justify an extra burden for the wife. Rather, differing standards were seen as a problem to be worked out equitably.

DUAL-NURTURER COUPLES

Two couples were dual nurturers, oriented to home, family, and lifestyle rather than career. They worked for pay so that they could spend time together and with their families. Only one of these couples was unequivocally dual nurturing, however. In the Woods family, neither parent has worked full-time consistently for years, and neither wants to do so. The father, an aspiring sculptor, works half-time as an editor; the mother is an accountant who sees clients three days a week. They try to organize their work schedules so that both are not working during the same day, even though their baby is in day care and their other child is in school and after-school programs. They feel that the evenings are too hectic if both arrive home at the same time after a full day away. Their work schedules and choice of jobs have varied with family needs. In many ways this looked like a home with two mothers in that neither parent was strongly attached to the labor force. This couple was particularly focused on the quality of their lives rather than material acquisition or career development. Yet the couple did not appear to be suffering economically from their career decisions. They lived in a modern, energy-efficient home they had designed themselves. Original artwork, painting, and pottery were in evidence in their rural, picturesque setting.

POST-TRADITIONAL COUPLES

The third route to a division of equitable labor was dissatisfaction with more traditional arrangements. Two of the couples in this study were post-traditional families. In the case of the Germanes, both partners' previous marriages had been organized around traditional gendered expectations and responsibilities. The woman stated clearly that she had left a previous marriage because her husband did not meet her needs for an equal partner. She had been married to a career diplomat and had moved every three years of her adult life. As a bookkeeper in government service she found it easy to relocate, and she had never been unemployed more than three months in her entire working life because of the "work ethic I grew up with." Paid work was important to her sense of self. When asked about her maternity leave, she answered, "I do feel that three months out of work—I don't care who I'm taking care of—is a lot of time." She cut back her work to thirty-two hours a week during her daughter's infancy, but only because her husband was on an assignment that involved much travel. Her current husband, who also had been a diplomat, had returned to school for another college degree when their daughter was in the early elementary grades. Ms. Germane enthusiastically recalled, "I liked the role reversal when he was the housewife. . . . He walked [our daughter] to school and I swear he knew every lady in the school. . . . He became a PTA mom." Both husband and wife reported having always shared work equally; the wife was very much aware that they seemed to share things "more in the middle" than other people. Even now that the husband is again working full-time in business management the couple continue to share labor equally. Both husband and wife had experienced less satisfying relationships, and they were, in Schwartz's (1994) language, very deep friends. Both wanted to keep things fair to protect their precious friendship.

The other post-traditional couple had renegotiated their gender-based roles when the youngest of their three boys entered kindergarten. It took this family three to four years to transform a decade-long male-breadwinner/female-homemaker pattern into a fair relationship. The wife was clearly the moving force behind this transformation. Ms. Potadman told us about her resentment at spending Saturdays doing housework after she returned to nursing full-time. Eventually her family—at her urging—divided the household tasks with a scheduling system. The mother explains it this way: "I had the idea, let's just list the tasks and we'll divide them up, and whenever he [her husband] gets his done, he gets them done." This wife still holds primary responsibility for the scheduling sessions. The entire family talked at length about the scheduling charts they used: each son cooked one day a week, the mother twice, and the father once, with dinner out every Friday. The sons were assigned cleanup tasks on days they did not cook.

COUPLES PUSHED INTO SHARING

The final route to a fair relationship was to be pushed by external forces. In one family the wife had a considerably better-paying job and a much less flexible schedule. In another family the wife was chronically ill. In both of these families gender equality was the conceptual framework that helped them make sense of their lives. In many ways they saw these external constraints in gender-neutral terms. In the Cody family the wife earned two-thirds of the household income. The husband had been passed over for a promotion that he had expected, and quit his job and changed careers. Mr. Cody was no longer work-focused and was pleased to have a flexible schedule. He enjoyed the freedom of owning a small business without the economic burden of supporting the family on his income.

When we decided that we were going to have children Marilyn's job situation was such that . . . she worked in a reasonably structured environment, and in that case you can't take time off to bring somebody to gymnastics and, you know, go to the school for plays and . . . give parties and do that kind of stuff. So we made a decision that I would do that, and what it does basically is it takes me out of, you know, being the high-powered career person and, you know, . . . I just do something that brings in some money, and [parenting] gives me satisfaction that I can do it. . . .

In summary, not one of the thirty parents interviewed even suggested that the husband's paid work was more important than the wife's. In fact, four of these families had moved to North Carolina because of the wife's work, and not one husband or wife mentioned this as unusual. Another four had relocated to North Carolina because of the husband's job; in two of these families the wife's ability to transfer was mentioned as a prerequisite for relocation. Another three families relocated because both partners found positions in the area. The other four couples were living there when they met. Not one of the thirty parents suggested that caring for their babies was or should have been more the mother's responsibility. Not one believed that housework should be the wife's responsibility, although half did admit to conflict at some point in their relationship about standards of cleanliness. It is to how conflict is negotiated and power exercised in fair families that I now turn.

Control refers to the cultural lines of authority and coercion, the status differential between men and women that is at the root of our gender structure. There are countless overt and subtle means by which male privilege is constructed in daily life. Women's fear of rape constrains their mobility in ways that men never experience. Fear of ridicule and social disapproval keeps women, from girlhood on, worried about their weight and physical attractiveness. The wage gap and sexual harassment in the workplace also reinforce male dominance. The normative belief that husbands should head the household also explicitly reinforces dominance and provides cultural authority for men to control their wives. Similarly, the continuing expectation that wifehood involves domestic service is yet another way that male privilege and female subordination is re-created in daily life. While such daily inequity appears to pale in comparison with fear of rape, the expectation that women provide domestic services to husbands and primary care for children not only creates inequitable marriages but also disadvantages women in the world of work.

Yet there are families—fair families—in which the marital control issues that reinforce male privilege appear to be moot. These women and men are both pioneers in and beneficiaries of the women's liberation movement.

REFERENCES

Blumstein, Phillip and Pepper Schwartz. 1983. *American Couples.* New York: William Morrow.

Schwartz, Pepper. 1994. *Peer Marriage.* New York: Free Press.

21

In the Name of the Family

JUDITH STACEY

The nuclear family evolved as the result of specific historical transformations, referred to here as modernization. Family patterns of male breadwinners and dependent women emerged in a particular context and are now being transformed by demographic and postindustrial trends. Yet, as Judith Stacey argues, nostalgia for families of the past often shapes family policies, leaving the society with inadequate supports for the diverse family forms that actually exist.

In most of Europe and North America the family has become nearly synonymous with the nuclear household unit made up of a married, heterosexual couple and their biological or adopted children. Although popular usage more fluidly adapts the concept to refer to all people related through blood marriage, or adoption, most Westerners do erroneously associate the family with nature and project it backward into a timeless past.

It is important to recognize . . . that the family is a product . . . of long historical transformations, generally referred to as modernization. Indeed, many historians employ the concept of the modern family, to describe the particular domestic arrangements which the family has come to designate. The modern family in the West developed historically out of a patriarchal, premodern family economy in which work and family life were thoroughly integrated. In the United States, the modern family system arose in the nineteenth century when industrialization turned men into breadwinners and women into homemakers by separating paid work from households. Beginning first among white middle-class people, this family pattern came to represent modernity and success. Indeed the American way of life came to be so identified with this family form that the trade union movement struggled for nearly a century to secure for male workers the material condition upon which it was based—the male breadwinner wage. However, not until the mid-twentieth century did significant percentages of industrial workers achieve this access to the male breadwinner nuclear family, and it has always exceeded the reach of the vast majority of African-Americans. Slaves were not allowed to marry and had no parental rights at all, and few African-American households have ever been able to afford a full-time homemaker. In fact, many African-American mothers have worked as domestic workers in the modern-family homes of relatively privileged whites.

The rise of the modern family system spelled the demise of the premodern, family economy which was explicitly patriarchal. Thus, it represented a shift in

From: Judith Stacey. 1997. *In the Name of the Family: Rethinking Values in the Postmodern Age.* Boston: Beacon Press, pp. 38–50. Reprinted with permission.

what sociologist Deniz Kanidyoti has called "patriarchal bargains." In the classical patriarchal bargain, women accept overt subordination in exchange for protection and secure social status. The modern patriarchal bargain sugarcoats this exchange by wrapping it in an ideology of separate spheres and romantic love. In place of premodern marriages, which were arranged, in whole or in part, by parents and kin for economic, political, and social purposes, modern men and women, seeking love and companionship, voluntarily bind themselves for life to the complementary object of their individual desires. Under the guise of a separate but equal division of labor between male breadwinners and female homemakers, women and children became increasingly dependent upon the earnings of men. The nineteenth century gave rise to cults of "true womanhood," celebrating domesticity and maternalism. This generated conceptions of femininity that continue to infuse Western family ideology. The development of analogous doctrines about the "tender years" of young children who need a specifically maternal form of love and care began to undermine earlier legal doctrines, which had treated children as patriarchal property.

U.S. family patterns became more predictable and homogeneous as the modern family system evolved in the nineteenth and twentieth centuries. High mortality and remarriage rates had kept premodern family patterns diverse and complex, but declines in mortality enabled increasing numbers of people to anticipate a normal family life course. By the mid-twentieth century, modern family life patterns, from birth through courtship, marriage, work, childrearing, and death had become so homogeneous, normative, and predictable that the family began to appear natural, universal and self-evident.

Social scientists are rarely impervious to the tacit cultural understandings of their times. During the post–World War II period, family sociologists in the United States developed a theory of family modernization that was rooted in the conviction that U.S. family history would prove to be a global model. Arguing that the modern nuclear family was ideally suited to support the functioning of industrial society, and that it was both a product of and handmaiden to Enlightenment progress and democracy, social scientists predicted that it would spread throughout the modernizing world. A product of Western cultural imperialism, the family modernization thesis presumed that the superiority of Western cultural forms would insure their eventual triumph over the "backward" nations and peoples of the globe. Indeed some family scholars came to argue that the early development of the modern nuclear family in the West facilitated the Western supremacy in developing capitalism.

So convinced have Western governments been of the superiority of their family patterns that they have often imposed their gender and family patterns on conquered peoples. The United States, for example, disrupted matrilineal and extended kin systems among several indigenous New World cultures by awarding land titles exclusively to male-headed, nuclear household units. In a similar fashion, Europeans have destructively imposed nuclear family principles on very different African kinship systems. In the Zambian copperbelt, for example, mineowners ignored and disrupted the actual extended kinship patterns of their workers by distributing benefits only to a worker's wife and children. More often, however, Westerners presumed that the global diffusion of the modern nuclear family system would come about automatically. These rather contradictory ideas about the family—that it is natural and universal, on the one hand, and that it is a sign and agent of Western superiority, on the other—continue to collide in popular and scholarly discourse.

CONTRADICTIONS OF THE FAMILY

We can gain some perspective on contemporary family turmoil by recognizing contradictions inherent in the ideology, principles, and practices of the modern family system, the most glaring of which is the tension between volition and coercion. The ideology of the modern family construes marital commitment as a product of the free will and passions of two equal individuals who are drawn to each other by romantic attraction and complementary emotional needs. However, the domestic division of labor of the modern family system, which made women economically dependent upon male earners, and the subordination of women, both de jure and de facto, provided potent incentives for women to choose to enter and remain in marriages, quite apart from their individual desires. And while men certainly have always enjoyed greater opportunities to pursue their emotional and sexual interests inside and outside of marriage, until quite recently cultural codes and material sanctions led most men to depend upon the personal, emotional, and social services of a full-time homemaker. Political satirist Barbara Ehrenreich has observed that the white middle classes in the United States are likely the only bourgeoisie in history to employ members of their own class as personal servants.

The relative acceptability of the contradiction between egalitarian principles of free love and companionship and inegalitarian forms of material and cultural coercion depended upon the availability and accessibility of a male breadwinner wage. Feminist historians have debated the degree to which working-class wives supported, resisted, or benefitted from the trade-union struggle that men conducted to earn wages sufficient to support fulltime homemakers and mothers. However, no matter who achieved this arrangement, which Heidi Hartmann has called a patriarchal-capitalist bargain negotiated between male factory owners and laborers, it has proven to be quite ephemeral. The majority of industrial workers did not earn enough to support a full-time housewife until the 1950s or 1960s, and soon after they did so, deindustrialization and post-industrialization conspired to eliminate their jobs and erode their earnings.

Thus, instability was written into the genetic code of the modern family system (on the "Y" chromosome), because its sustenance depended upon the wide availability of stable, liveable-wage jobs for men. As that strand of the bargain began to unravel during the 1970s and 1980s, the fragility of the entire gender and family order moved into full view, provoking widespread consternation over "family crisis" throughout advanced industrial societies.

During the past few decades, every developed industrial nation has experienced soaring divorce rates, falling birth rates, and rising rates of unmarried domestic partners, of step- and blended families, and of nonfamily households.

Alarmists who decry family decline in the United States often overlook the transnational character of these demographic trends. A 1977 Viennese study warned that if the rate of increase in European divorce rates during the 1970s were to continue until the year 2000, at that point 85 percent of all European marriages would end in divorce.

During this same period, the employment rates of women and men, formerly quite distinct, began to converge worldwide. Women, especially mothers of young children, now find it necessary to work for pay to support or contribute to the support of families that have been undermined by the loss of jobs and real earnings by men. The loss of steady work, or any work, for men at lower educational levels has been quite dramatic. While more than two-thirds of men with less than a high school education worked full time, year round during the 1970s, a decade later only half could find such steady work. A significant wage gap between men and women persists, but the normalization of female employment and the decline in jobs for men has reduced some of women's economic dependency on men, and thus, has weakened one coercive buttress of marriage.

That is one major reason why single motherhood is rising around the globe, and why increasing percentages of single mothers have never been married. Sitcom heroine Murphy Brown has become a controversial symbol of the family circumstances of a small, but rising number of affluent, professional women in the U.S. who are choosing to become single mothers rather than to forego motherhood entirely. In reality, the vast majority of single-mother families confront dire economic circumstances. At the same time that many women began choosing to become mothers alone, and for related reasons, birth rates were falling below replacement levels throughout the postindustrial world. It is particularly striking that women in Italy, an overwhelmingly Catholic country, now give birth to the smallest national average number of children in the advanced industrial world. On the other hand, birth rates have begun to rise in Sweden, despite its reputation as the leading country for family decline. The comparative level of security and confidence that prospective Swedish parents, particularly would-be mothers, derive from their nation's exceptionally progressive tax structure and social welfare provisions is the most likely explanation for this paradox. Meanwhile, *The New York Times* reports that "Eastern Germany's adults appear to have come as close to a temporary suspension of childbearing as any large population in the human experience," a response to the region's dire economic conditions since reunification. The state of Brandenburg has voted to offer parents a cash incentive of $650 per new child born.

Because global capitalism is governed by the endless search for profits through increased productivity and technological development, we can be certain that our only social constant is change. Social change is a permanent and endless feature of our world, and all we can know about the future of family life is that it too will continue to change. Recent developments in reproductive technology and genetic engineering offer glimpses of some of the most dramatic and radical implications of future family scenarios. *Junior*, a 1994 Christmas season family movie starring Arnold Schwarzenegger as a pregnant experimental scientist, (a movie which proved to be more popular with women than men), presages some of the redefinitions of family life in store as science completes its Faustian gift of separating sexuality, conception, gestation, procreation, marriage, childrearing, and parenting. Pregnant men and test-tube babies, once the standard fare of science fiction, now appear inevitable. We have already reached the point at which a man's sperm can fertilize one woman's ovum, which gestates in the uterus of a second woman, who, in turn, serves as a "surrogate" for yet a third woman, who plans to adopt and rear the offspring, with or without a second man or a fourth woman as co-parent. What and who is the mother, the father, or the family in such a world?

THE POSTMODERN FAMILY CONDITION

The astonishing transformations sketched above indicate that the particular patriarchal bargain of the modern family system has collapsed. Instead, we now forge our intimate lives within the terms of the postmodern family condition described earlier. At the current moment in Western family history, no single family pattern is statistically dominant, and our domestic arrangements have become increasingly diverse. Only a minority of U.S. households still contain married couples with children; and many of these include divorced and remarried adults. More children live with single mothers than in modern families containing a breadwinner dad and a full-time homemaker mom. Most features of the postmodern family condition are most prominent in the United States and Scandinavia. But demographic trends are similar throughout the highly industrialized world, with variations only in the degree, timing, and pace of the changes, but not in their direction. Once the family modernization thesis predicted that all the societies of the globe would converge toward a singular family system—the modern Western family system. Ironically, instead we are converging internationally toward the postmodern family condition of diversity, flux, and instability.

Under postmodern conditions, the social character of practices of gender, sexuality, parenting, and family life, which once appeared to be natural and immutable, become visible and politically charged. While similar demographic trends are dissolving the modern family system throughout the capitalist, industrialized world, national responses to the modern family crisis differ widely. Some societies have adapted to the decline of the male breadwinner family by devising generous social welfare policies that attempt to mitigate some of the destructive impact that marital fragility too often inflicts on children and the unequal burden it places on women. Again the Scandinavian countries, with Sweden and Norway in the lead, set the standards for innovative family support policies of this sort. In both nations, parents of either gender are entitled to apportion a full year's leave with 90 percent pay to take care of a newborn. Because so few fathers availed themselves of this benefit, both Sweden and Norway recently offered them added incentive to do so. Both countries now allow men, and only men, to receive an additional month of paid parental leave beyond the original twelve months, which men and women can allot as they choose. Moreover, Scandinavian workers enjoy paid leave to care for sick children and relatives, as well as universal family allowances, health care, including sex education, contraception, and abortion services, and subsidized high-quality daycare. There are few deadbeat dads in these Nordic nations, because the state assumes responsibility for collecting and distributing child care payments. As a result, while more than half of single-parent families in the United States live below the official poverty line, in Sweden only 2 percent do so. Most likely this is why Swedish women have been willing to bear more children in recent years. Likewise, Sweden and Norway also followed Denmark's lead in legalizing a form of marriage for same-sex couples before this became a visible political issue in the United States.

Other affluent societies, however, have proven far more hostile to postmodern demographic and cultural changes. They are far less willing to assume public responsibility for addressing the unjust and disruptive effects caused by these changes. The United States is far and away the most extreme in this regard. Reflecting an exceptionally privatized economy, an individualistic culture, and racial antagonisms, social welfare for the poor in the United States has always been comparatively stingy, punitive, and unpopular. Yet even this meager system is currently being dismantled. The United States alone, among 18 advanced industrial nations, does not provide its citizens with universal health coverage, family allowances, or paid parental leaves. In fact, it was not until the Family Leave Act of 1993 that the right to take an unpaid three-month maternity leave, which few families can afford to use, was mandated for workers in firms with at least 50 employees. Welfare provisions in the United States have always been means-tested, stigmatized, and niggardly. As a result, a higher percentage of single-mother families in the United States as well as a higher percentage of children in general, live in poverty than in any advanced industrial nation. Conservative estimates of the numbers that current welfare reform legislation will add to this disturbing record have even frightened Senator Moynihan, one of the original advocates of revising the welfare system.

While family support policies in the United States are the weakest in the industrial world, no society has yet to come close to our expenditure of politicized rhetoric over family crisis. The politics of gender, sexuality, reproduction, and family here are the most polarized, militant, and socially divisive in the world, precisely because social structural responses to the decline of the modern family system have been so weak. This is an important reason why feminism, gay liberation, and backlash "profamily" movements are so vocal and influential across the political spectrum.

Rampant nostalgia for the modern family system, or more precisely, for an idealized version of a 1950s Ozzie and Harriet image of the family, has become an increasingly potent ideological force in the United States, with milder versions evident in Canada and England. Fundamentalist Christians and right-wing Republicans spearheaded the profamily movement that abetted the Reagan "revolution" of the 1980s. By the 1994 electoral season, however, even President Clinton had embraced the ideology of an explicitly centrist campaign for family values led by a small group of social scientists. This ongoing campaign portrays family breakdown as the primary source of social malaise in the United States, blaming the decline of the married-couple family for everything from crime, violence, and declining educational standards to poverty, drug abuse, and sexually transmitted disease.

There seems to be nearly an inverse relationship between a nation's rhetorical concern over the plight of children in declining families and its willingness to implement policies to ease their suffering. This may appear paradoxical, if not hypocritical, but family support policies are consistent with the historical development of public responsibility for social welfare in each nation. They are strongest in parliamentary governments in which labor movements have achieved a significant voice. Lip service to the family, on the other hand, serves as a proxy for the private sphere and as a rationale for abdicating public responsibility for social welfare. Unfortunately, the more individualistic and market-oriented a society becomes, the more difficult it becomes to sustain family bonds. . . .

LET'S BURY "THE FAMILY"

The family indeed is dead, if what we mean by it is the modern family system in which units comprised of male breadwinner and female homemaker, married couples, and their offspring dominate the land. But its ghost, the ideology of the family, survives to haunt the consciousness of all those who refuse to confront it. It is time to perform a social autopsy on the corpse of the modern family system so that we may try to lay its troublesome sprit to rest. Perhaps, a proper memorial service for the family system we have lost can free us to address the diverse needs of people struggling to sustain intimate relationships under very difficult postmodern family conditions.

Adopting the pathologist's stance of hard-hearted, clinical detachment in this case can lead to an uncomfortable conclusion. Historically, all stable systems of marriage and family life have rested upon diverse measures of coercion and inequality. Family systems appear to have been most stable when women and men have been economically interdependent, when households served as units of production with sufficient resources to reproduce themselves, and when individuals lacked alternative means of economic, sexual, and social life. Family units of this sort have always been embedded in, supported, and sanctioned by wider sets of kinship, community, and religious ties. Disturbingly, all such family systems have been patriarchal. The stability of the modern family system, which represented a significant departure from several of these principles, depended upon the adequacy and reliability of the male family wage. However, the ceaseless development of capitalist industrialization, which disrupted the premodern patriarchal bargain, has now disrupted the modern one as well, and it will continue to disrupt postmodern familial regimes of any sort.

DISCUSSION QUESTIONS

1. What historical conditions shaped the development of the nuclear family and how have these changed in contemporary society?
2. Why does Stacey argue that there are contradictions in the ideology, principles, and practices of the modern family and what impact does this have on social policies on behalf of families?

INFOTRAC COLLEGE EDITION

You can use your access to InfoTrac College Edition to learn more about the subjects covered in this essay. Some suggested search terms include:

family diversity
male breadwinner
modern nuclear family

monogamy
postmodern families
single mothers

22

Sport as Religion

MICHAEL NOVAK

Over the years, many sport sociologists have recognized strong parallels between the social institutions of sport and religion. Some might say, in fact, that the decline in church attendance has shifted concomitantly with the rise in athletic attendance, and that sport has significant elements of religion. Novak draws out some parallels between these two strong components in our society, and we leave you to see for yourself if you think the comparison works. Is Novak's point a useful one in explaining the incredible popularity of sports in the United States and throughout the world? If sport has replaced religion, at least in part, what might be the long-term effects of this?

A sport is not a religion in the same way that Methodism, Presbyterianism, or Catholicism is a religion. But these are not the only kinds of religion. There are secular religions, civil religions. The United States of America has sacred documents to guide and to inspire it: The Constitution, the Declaration of Independence, Washington's Farewell Address, Lincoln's Gettysburg Address, and other solemn presidential documents. The President of the United States is spoken to with respect, is expected to exert "moral leadership"; and when he walks among crowds, hands reach out to touch his garments. Citizens are expected to die for the nation, and our flag symbolizes vivid memories, from Fort Sumter to Iwo Jima, from the Indian Wars to Normandy: memories that moved hard-hats in New York to break up a march that was "desecrating" the flag. Citizens regard the American way of life as though it were somehow chosen by God, special, uniquely important to the history of the human race.

The institutions of the state generate a civil religion; so do the institutions of sport. The ancient Olympic games used to be both festivals in honor of the gods and festivals in honor of the state—and that has been the classical position of sports ever since. The ceremonies of sports overlap those of the state on one side,

Reprinted by permission of the author.

and those of the churches on the other. . . . Going to a stadium is half like going to a political rally, half like going to church. Even today, the Olympics are constructed around high ceremonies, rituals, and symbols. The Olympics are not barebones athletic events, but religion and politics as well. . . .

I am saying that sports flow outward into action from a deep natural impulse that is radically religious: an impulse of freedom, respect for ritual limits, a zest for symbolic meaning, and a longing for perfection. The athlete may of course be pagan, but sports are, as it were, natural religions. There are many ways to express this radical impulse: by the asceticism and dedication of preparation; by a sense of respect for the mysteries of one's own body and soul, and for powers not in one's own control; by a sense of awe for the place and time of competition; by a sense of fate; by a felt sense of comradeship and destiny; by a sense of participation in the rhythms and tides of nature itself.

Sports, in the second place, are organized and dramatized in a religious way. Not only do the origins of sports, like the origins of drama, lie in religious celebrations; not only are the rituals, vestments, and tremor of anticipation involved in sports events like those of religions. Even in our own secular age and for quite sophisticated and agnostic persons, the rituals of sports really work. They do serve a religious function: they feed a deep human hunger, place humans in touch with certain dimly perceived features of human life within this cosmos, and provide an experience of at least a pagan sense of godliness. . . .

Sports are religious in the sense that they are organized institutions, disciplines, and liturgies; and also in the sense that they teach religious qualities of heart and soul. In particular, they recreate symbols of cosmic struggle, in which human survival and moral courage are not assured. To this extent, they are not mere games, diversions, pastimes. Their power to exhilarate or depress is far greater than that. To say "It was only a game" is the psyche's best defense against the cosmic symbolic meaning of sports events. And it is partly true. For a game is a symbol; it is not precisely identified with what it symbolizes. To lose symbolizes death, and it certainly feels like dying; but it is not death. The same is true of religious symbols like Baptism or the Eucharist; in both, the communicants experience death, symbolically, and are reborn, symbolically. If you give your heart to the ritual, its effects upon your inner life can be far-reaching. . . .

Sports are not merely fun and games, not merely diversions, not merely entertainment. A ballpark is not a temple, but it isn't a fun house either. A baseball game is not an entertainment, and a ballplayer is considerably more than a paid performer. No one can explain the passion, commitment, discipline, and dedication involved in sports by evasions like these. . . .

The motive for regarding sports as entertainment is to take the magic, mystification, and falsehood out of sports. . . .

At a sports event, there may be spectators, just as some people come to church to hear the music. But a participant is not a spectator merely, even if he does not walk among the clergy. At a liturgy, elected representatives perform the formal acts, but all believers put their hearts into the ritual. It is considered inadequate, almost blasphemous, to be a mere spectator. Fans are not mere spectators. If they wanted no more than to pass the time, to find diversion, there are cheaper and less internally exhausting ways. Believers in sport do not go to sports to be entertained; to plays and dramas, maybe, but not to sports. Sports are far more serious than the dramatic arts, much closer to primal symbols, metaphors, and acts, much more ancient and more frightening. Sports are mysteries of youth and aging, perfect action and decay, fortune and misfortune, strategy and contingency. Sports are rituals concerning human survival on this planet: liturgical enactments of animal perfection and the struggles of the human spirit to prevail. . . .

In order to be entertained, I watch television: prime-time shows. They slide effortlessly by. I am amused, or distracted, or engrossed. Good or bad, they help to pass the time pleasantly enough. Watching football on television is totally different. I don't watch football to pass the time. The outcome of the games affects me. I care. Afterward, the emotion I have lived through continues to affect me. Football is not entertainment. It is far more important than that. If you observe the passivity of television viewers being entertained, and the animation of fans watching a game on television, the difference between entertainment and involvement of spirit becomes transparent. Sports are more like religion than like entertainment. Indeed, at a contest in the stadium, the "entertainment"—the bands, singers, comedians, balloons, floats, fireworks, jets screaming overhead—pales before the impact of the contest itself.

On Monday nights, when television carries football games, police officers around the nation know that crime rates will fall to low levels otherwise reached only on Mother's Day and Christmas. . . .

Sports, in a word, are a form of godliness. That is why the corruptions of sports in our day, by corporations and television and glib journalism and cheap public relations, are so hateful. If sports were entertainment, why should we care? They are far more than that. So when we see them abused, our natural response is the rise of vomit in the throat.

It may be useful to list some of the elements of religions, to see how they are imitated in the world of sports.

If our anthropologists discovered in some other culture the elements they can plainly see in our own world of sports, they would be obliged to write monographs on the religions of the tribes they were studying. Two experiments in thought may make this plain.

Imagine that you are walking near your home and come upon a colony of ants. They move in extraordinary busy lines, a trail of brown bodies across the whitish soil like a highway underneath the blades of grass. The lanes of ants abut on a constructed mudbank oval; there the ants gather, 100,000 strong, sitting in a circle. Down below, in a small open place, eleven ants on one side and eleven on the other contest bitterly between two lines. From time to time a buzz arises from the 100,000 ants gathered in their sacred oval. When the game is over, the long lines of ants begin their traffic-dense return to their colonies. In one observation, you didn't have time to discover the rules of their ritual. Or who made them up, or when. Or what they mean to the ants. Is the gathering mere "escape"? Does it mirror other facets in the life of ants? Do all ants everywhere take part? Do the ants "understand" what they are doing, or do they only do it by rote, one of the things that ants do on a lovely afternoon? Do ants practice, and stay in shape, and perfect their arts?

Or suppose you are an anthropologist from Mars. You come suddenly upon some wild, adolescent tribes living in territories called the "United States of America." You try to understand their way of life, but their society does not make sense to you. Flying over the land in a rocket, you notice great ovals near every city. You descend and observe. You learn that an oval is called a "stadium." It is used, roughly, once a week in certain seasons. Weekly, regularly, millions of citizens stream into these concrete doughnuts, pay handsomely, are alternately hushed and awed and outraged and screaming mad. (They demand from time to time that certain sacrificial personages be "killed.") You see that the figures in the rituals have trained themselves superbly for their performances. The combatants are dedicated. So are the dancers and musicians in tribal dress who occupy the arena before, during, and after the combat. You note that, in millions of homes, at corner shrines in every household's sacred room, other citizens are bound by invisible attraction to the same events. At critical moments, the most intense worshipers demand of the less attentive silence. Virtually an entire nation is united in a central public rite. Afterward, you note exultation or depression among hundreds of thousands, and animation almost everywhere.

Some of the elements of a religion may be enumerated. A religion, first of all, is organized and structured. Culture is built on cult. Accordingly, a religion begins with ceremonies. At these ceremonies, a few surrogates perform for all. They need not even believe what they are doing. As professionals, they may perform so often that they have lost all religious instinct; they may have less faith than any of the participants. In the official ceremonies, sacred vestments are employed and rituals are prescribed. Customs develop. Actions are highly formalized. Right ways and wrong ways are plainly marked out; illicit behaviors are distinguished from licit ones. Professional watchdogs supervise formal correctness. Moments of silence are observed. Concentration and intensity are indispensable. To attain them, drugs or special disciplines of spirit might be employed; ordinary humans, in the ordinary ups and downs of daily experience, cannot be expected to perform routinely at the highest levels of awareness. . . .

Religions also channel the feeling most humans have of danger, contingency, and chance—in a word, Fate. Human plans involve ironies. Our choices are made with so little insight into their eventual effects that what we desire is often not the path to what we want. The decisions we make with little attention turn out to be major turning points. What we prepare for with exquisite detail never happens. Religions place us in the presence of powers greater than ourselves, and seek to reconcile us to them. The rituals of religion give these powers almost human shape, forms that give these powers visibility and tangible effect. Sports events in baseball, basketball, and football are structured so that "the breaks" may intervene and become central components in the action.

Religions make explicit the almost nameless dreads of daily human life: aging, dying, failure under pressure, cowardice, betrayal, guilt. Competitive sports embody these in every combat. . . .

Religions consecrate certain days and hours. Sacred time is a block of time lifted out of everyday normal routines, a time that is different, in which different laws apply, a time within which one forgets ordinary time. Sacred time is intended to suggest an "eternal return," a fundamental repetition like the circulation of the human blood, or the eternal turning of the seasons, or the wheeling of the stars and planets in their cycles: the sense that things repeat themselves, over and over, and yet are always a little different. Sacred time is more like eternity than like history, more like cycles of recurrence than like progress, more like a celebration of repetition than like a celebration of novelty. Yet sacred time is full of exhilaration, excitement, and peace, as though it were more real and more joyous than the activities of everyday life—as though it were *really living* to be in sacred time (wrapped up in a close game during the last two minutes), and comparatively boring to suffer the daily jading of work, progress, history.

To have a religion, you need to have heroic forms to try to live up to: patterns of excellence so high that human beings live up to them only rarely, even when they strive to do so; and images of perfection so beautiful that, living up to them or seeing someone else live up to them, produces a kind of "*ah!*"

You need to have a pattern of symbols and myths that a person can grow old with, with a kind of resignation, wisdom, and illumination. Do what we will, the human body ages. Moves we once could make our minds will but our bodies cannot implement; disciplines we once endured with suppressed animal desire are no longer worth the effort; heroes that once seemed to us immortal now age, become enfeebled, die, just as we do. The "boys of summer" become the aging men of winter. A religion celebrates the passing of all things: youth, skill, grace, heroic deeds.

To have a religion, you need to have a way to exhilarate the human body, and desire, and will, and the sense of beauty, and a sense of oneness with the universe and other humans. You need chants and songs, the rhythm of bodies in unison, the indescribable feeling of many who together "will one thing" as if they were each members of a single body.

All these things you have in sports.

23

Bowling Alone

ROBERT D. PUTNAM

The concern for community may be seen as one of the strongest themes faced in contemporary America. Putnam heralds this concern by articulating the decline of those social institutions and activities—the church, the family, labor unions, civic and political engagement, fraternal organizations, service clubs, parent-teacher associations—through which Americans traditionally fused together and created the fabric of community life. He whimsically focuses the title of this selection around an ironic shift in social behavior that he thinks reflects this trend toward the decline of traditional community: more Americans are bowling today than ever before, but bowling in organized leagues has plummeted. Putnam ponders this decline in "social capital" and its consequent erosion in good neighborliness and social trust. How likely are Americans to know their neighbors, to participate in community and civic events, and to belong to social clubs? Is Putnam right or wrong in his fears about the lack of community involvement of Americans? If he is right, how might this trend continue to affect the individual and group life of Americans?

Many students of the new democracies that have emerged over the past decade and a half have emphasized the importance of a strong and active civil society to the consolidation of democracy. Especially with regard to the postcommunist countries, scholars and democratic activists alike have lamented the absence or obliteration of traditions of independent civic engagement and a widespread tendency toward passive reliance on the state. To those concerned with the weakness of civil societies in the developing or postcommunist world, the advanced Western democracies and above all the Untied States have typically been taken as models to be emulated. There is striking evidence, however, that the vibrancy of American civil society has notably declined over the past several decades.

Ever since the publication of Alexis de Tocqueville's *Democracy in America*, the United States has played a central role in systematic studies of the links between

Reprinted from the *Journal of Democracy*, pp. 65–70, by permission of The Johns Hopkins University Press and National Endowment for Democracy.

democracy and civil society. Although this is in part because trends in American life are often regarded as harbingers of social modernization, it is also because America has traditionally been considered unusually "civic" (a reputation that, as we shall later see, has not been entirely unjustified).

When Tocqueville visited the United States in the 1830s, it was the Americans' propensity for civic association that most impressed him as the key to their unprecedented ability to make democracy work. "Americans of all ages, all stations in life, and all types of disposition," he observed, "are forever forming associations. There are not only commercial and industrial associations in which all take part, but others of a thousand different types—religious, moral, serious, futile, very general and very limited, immensely large and very minute. . . . Nothing, in my view, deserves more attention than the intellectual and moral associations in America.[1]

Recently, American social scientists of a neo-Tocquevillean bent have unearthed a wide range of empirical evidence that the quality of public life and the performance of social institutions (and not only in America) are indeed powerfully influenced by norms and networks of civic engagement. Researchers in such fields as education, urban poverty, unemployment, the control of crime and drug abuse, and even health have discovered that successful outcomes are more likely in civically engaged communities. Similarly, research on the varying economic attainments of different ethnic groups in the United States has demonstrated the importance of social bonds within each group. These results are consistent with research in a wide range of settings that demonstrates the vital importance of social networks for job placement and many other economic outcomes. . . .

The norms and networks of civic engagement also powerfully affect the performance of representative government. That, at least, was the central conclusion of my own 20-year, quasi-experimental study of subnational governments in different regions of Italy.[2] Although all these regional governments seemed identical on paper, their levels of effectiveness varied dramatically. Systematic inquiry showed that the quality of governance was determined by longstanding traditions of civic engagement (or its absence). Voter turnout, newspaper readership, membership in choral societies and football clubs—these were the hallmarks of a successful region. In fact, historical analysis suggested that these networks of organized reciprocity and civic solidarity, far from being an epiphenomenon of socioeconomic modernization, were a precondition for it.

No doubt the mechanisms through which civic engagement and social connectedness produce such results—better schools, faster economic development, lower crime, and more effective government—are multiple and complex. While these briefly recounted findings require further confirmation and perhaps qualification, the parallels across hundreds of empirical studies in a dozen disparate disciplines and subfields are striking. Social scientists in several fields have recently suggested a common framework for understanding these phenomena, a framework that rests on the concept of *social capital*.[3] By analogy with notions of physical capital and human capital—tools and training that enhance individual productivity—"social capital" refers to features of social organization such as networks, norms, and social trust that facilitate coordination and cooperation for mutual benefit.

For a variety of reasons, life is easier in a community blessed with a substantial stock of social capital. In the first place, networks of civic engagement foster sturdy norms of generalized reciprocity and encourage the emergence of social trust. Such networks facilitate coordination and communication, amplify reputations, and thus allow dilemmas of collective action to be resolved. When economic and political negotiation is embedded in dense networks of social interaction, incentives for opportunism are reduced. At the same time, networks of civic engagement embody past success at collaboration, which can serve as a cultural template for future collaboration. Finally, dense networks of interaction probably broaden the participants' sense of self, developing the "I" into the "we," or (in the language of rational-choice theorists) enhancing the participants' "taste" for collective benefits.

I do not intend here to survey (much less contribute to) the development of the theory of social capital. Instead, I use the central premise of that rapidly growing body of work—that social connections and civic engagement pervasively influence our public life, as well as our private prospects—as the starting point for an empirical survey of trends in social capital in contemporary America. I concentrate here entirely on the American case, although the developments I portray may in some measure characterize many contemporary societies.

WHATEVER HAPPENED TO CIVIC ENGAGEMENT?

We begin with familiar evidence on changing patterns of political participation, not least because it is immediately relevant to issues of democracy in the narrow sense. Consider the well-known decline in turnout in national elections over the last three decades. From a relative high point in the early 1960s, voter turnout had by 1990 declined by nearly a quarter; tens of millions of Americans had forsaken their parents' habitual readiness to engage in the simplest act of citizenship. Broadly similar trends also characterize participation in state and local elections.

It is not just the voting booth that has been increasingly deserted by Americans. A series of identical questions posed by the Roper Organization to national samples ten times each year over the last two decades reveals that since 1973 the number of Americans who report that "in the past year" they have "attended a public meeting on town or school affairs" has fallen by more than a third (from 22 percent in 1973 to 13 percent in 1993). Similar (or even greater) relative declines are evident in responses to questions about attending a political rally or speech, serving on a committee of some local organization, and working for a political party. By almost every measure, Americans' direct engagement in politics and government has fallen steadily and sharply over the last generation, despite the fact that average levels of education—the best individual-level predictor of political participation—have risen sharply throughout this period. Every year over the last decade or two, millions more have withdrawn from the affairs of their communities.

Not coincidentally, Americans have also disengaged psychologically from politics and government over this era. The proportion of Americans who reply that they "trust the government in Washington" only "some of the time" or "almost never" has risen steadily from 30 percent in 1966 to 75 percent in 1992.

These trends are well known, of course, and taken by themselves would seem amenable to a strictly political explanation. Perhaps the long litany of political tragedies and scandals since the 1960s (assassinations, Vietnam, Watergate, Irangate, and so on) has triggered an understandable disgust for politics and government among Americans, and that in turn has motivated their withdrawal. I do not doubt that this common interpretation has some merit, but its limitations become plain when we examine trends in civic engagement of a wider sort.

Our survey of organizational membership among Americans can usefully begin with a glance at the aggregate results of the General Social Survey, a scientifically conducted, national-sample survey that has been repeated 14 times over the last two decades. Church-related groups constitute the most common type of organization joined by Americans; they are especially popular with women. Other types of organizations frequently joined by women include school-service groups (mostly parent-teacher associations), sports groups, professional societies, and literary societies. Among men, sports clubs, labor unions, professional societies, fraternal groups, veterans' groups, and service clubs are all relatively popular.

Religious affiliation is by far the most common associational membership among Americans. Indeed, by many measures America continues to be (even more than in Tocqueville's time) an astonishingly "churched" society. For example, the United States has more houses of worship per capita than any other nation on Earth. Yet religious sentiment in America seems to be becoming somewhat less tied to institutions and more self-defined.

How have these complex crosscurrents played out over the last three or four decades in terms of Americans' engagement with organized religion? The general pattern is clear: The 1960s witnessed a significant drop in reported weekly churchgoing—from roughly 48 percent in the late 1950s to roughly 41 percent in the early 1970s. Since then, it has stagnated or (according to some surveys) declined still further. Meanwhile, data from the General Social Survey show a modest decline in membership in all "church-related groups" over the last 20 years. It would seem, then, that net participation by Americans, both in religious services and in church-related groups, has declined modestly (by perhaps a sixth) since the 1960s.

For many years, labor unions provided one of the most common organizational affiliations among American workers. Yet union membership has been falling for nearly four decades, with the steepest decline occurring between 1975 and 1985. Since the mid–1950s, when union membership peaked, the unionized portion of the nonagricultural work force in America has dropped by more than half, falling from 32.5 percent in 1953 to 15.8 percent in 1992. By now, virtually all of the explosive growth in union membership that was associated with the

New Deal has been erased. The solidarity of union halls is now mostly a fading memory of aging men.[4]

The parent-teacher association (PTA) has been an especially important form of civic engagement in twentieth-century America because parental involvement in the educational process represents a particularly productive form of social capital. It is, therefore, dismaying to discover that participation in parent-teacher organizations has dropped drastically over the last generation, from more than 12 million in 1964 to barely 5 million in 1982 before recovering to approximately 7 million now.

Next, we turn to evidence on membership in (and volunteering for) civic and fraternal organizations. These data show some striking patterns. First, membership in traditional women's groups has declined more or less steadily since the mid-1960s. For example, membership in the national Federation of Women's Clubs is down by more than half (59 percent) since 1964, while membership in the League of Women Voters (LWV) is off 42 percent since 1969.[5]

Similar reductions are apparent in the numbers of volunteers for mainline civic organizations, such as the Boy Scouts (off by 26 percent since 1970) and the Red Cross (off by 61 percent since 1970). But what about the possibility that volunteers have simply switched their loyalties to other organizations? Evidence on "regular" (as opposed to occasional or "drop-by") volunteering is available from the Labor Department's Current Population Surveys of 1974 and 1989. These estimates suggest that serious volunteering declined by roughly one-sixth over these 15 years, from 24 percent of adults in 1974 to 20 percent in 1989. The multitudes of Red Cross aides and Boy Scout troop leaders now missing in action have apparently not been offset by equal numbers of new recruits elsewhere.

Fraternal organizations have also witnessed a substantial drop in membership during the 1980s and 1990s. Membership is down significantly in such groups as the Lions (off 12 percent since 1983), the Elks (off 18 percent since 1979), the Shriners (off 27 percent since 1979), the Jaycees (off 44 percent since 1979), and the Masons (down 39 percent since 1959). In sum, after expanding steadily throughout most of this century, many major civic organizations have experienced a sudden, substantial, and nearly simultaneous decline in membership over the last decade or two.

The most whimsical yet discomfiting bit of evidence of social disengagement in contemporary America that I have discovered is this: more Americans are bowling today than ever before, but bowling in organized leagues has plummeted in the last decade or so. Between 1980 and 1993 the total number of bowlers in America increased by 10 percent, while league bowling decreased by 40 percent. (Lest this be thought a wholly trivial example, I should note that nearly 80 million Americans went bowling at least once during 1993, *nearly a third more than voted in the 1994 congressional elections* and roughly the same number as claim to attend church regularly. Even after the 1980s' plunge in league bowling, nearly 3 percent of American adults regularly bowl in leagues.) The rise of solo bowling threatens the livelihood of bowling-lane proprietors because those who bowl as members of leagues consume three times as much beer and pizza as solo bowlers, and the money in bowling is in the beer and pizza, not the balls and shoes. The broader social significance, however, lies in the social interaction and even occasionally civic conversations over beer and pizza that solo bowlers forgo. Whether or not bowling beats balloting in the eyes of most Americans, bowling teams illustrate yet another vanishing form of social capital.

NOTES

1. Alexis de Tocqueville, *Democracy in America,* ed. J. P. Maier, trans. George Lawrence (Garden City, N.Y.: Anchor Books, 1969), 513–17.

2. Robert D. Putnam, *Making Democracy Work: Civic Traditions in Modern Italy* (Princeton: Princeton University Press, 1993).

3. James S. Coleman deserves primary credit for developing the "social capital" theoretical framework. See his "Social Capital in the Creation of Human Capital," *American Journal of Sociology* (Supplement) 94 (1988): S95–S120, as well as his *The Foundations of Social Theory* (Cambridge: Harvard University Press, 1990), 300–21. See also Mark Granovetter, "Economic Action and Social Structure: The Problem of Embeddedness," *American Journal of Sociology* 91 (1985): 481–510; Glenn C. Loury, "Why Should We Care About Group Inequality?" *Social Philosophy and Policy* 5 (1987): 249–71; and Robert D. Putnam, "The Prosperous Community: Social Capital and Public Life," *American Prospect* 13 (1993): 35–42. To my knowledge, the first scholar to use the term "social capital" in its current sense was Jane Jacobs, in

The Death and Life of Great American Cities (New York: Random House, 1961), 138.

4. Any simplistically political interpretation of the collapse of American unionism would need to confront the fact that the steepest decline began more than six years before the Reagan administration's attack on PATCO. Data from the General Social Survey show a roughly 40-percent decline in reported union membership between 1975 and 1991.

5. Data for the LWV are available over a longer time span and show an interesting pattern: a sharp slump during the Depression, a strong and sustained rise after World War II that more than tripled membership between 1945 and 1969, and then the post-1969 decline, which has already erased virtually all the postwar gains and continues still. This same historical pattern applies to those men's fraternal organizations for which comparable data are available—steady increases for the first seven decades of the century, interrupted only by the Great Depression, followed by a collapse in the 1970s and 1980s that has already wiped out most of the postwar expansion and continues apace.

24

The Genius of the Civil Rights Movement:

Can It Happen Again?

ALDON MORRIS

The Civil Rights Movement is arguably the most influential movement in the United States during the twentieth century. Aldon Morris reviews the development of the civil rights movements and notes the products of this movement, including the mobilization of other national and international movements and the transformations in academic scholarship that the movement generated. By identifying the particular historical and social circumstances in which the civil rights movement developed, he also asks whether such a movement is possible again.

It is important for African Americans, as well as all Americans, to take a look backward and forward as we approach the turn of a new century, indeed a new millennium. When a panoramic view of the entire history of African Americans is taken into account, it becomes crystal clear that African American social protest has been crucial to Black liberation. In fact, African American protest has been critical to the freedom struggles of people of color around the globe and to progressive people throughout the world.

The purpose of this essay is: 1) to revisit the profound changes that the modern Black freedom struggle has achieved in terms of American race relations; 2) to assess how this movement has affected the rise of other liberation movements both nationally and internationally; 3) to focus on how this movement has transformed how scholars think about social movements; 4) to discuss the lessons that can be learned from this groundbreaking movement pertaining to future African American struggles for freedom in the next century.

It is hard to imagine how pervasive Black inequality would be today in America if it had not been constantly challenged by Black protests throughout each century since the beginning of slavery. The historical record is clear that slave resistance and slave rebellions and protest in the context of the Abolitionist movement were crucial to the overthrow of the powerful slave regime.

The establishment of the Jim Crow regime was one of the great tragedies of the late nineteenth and early twentieth centuries. The overthrow of slavery represented one of those rare historical moments where a nation had the opportunity

From: Aldon Morris, Northwestern University. Reprinted by permission of author.

to embrace a democratic future or to do business as usual by reinstalling undemocratic practices. In terms of African Americans, the White North and South chose to embark along undemocratic lines.

For Black people, the emergence of the Jim Crow regime was on of the greatest betrayals that could be visited upon a people who had hungered for freedom so long; what made it even worse for them is that the betrayal emerged from the bosom of a nation declaring to all the world that it was the beacon of democracy.

The triumph of Jim Crow ensured that African Americans would live in a modern form of slavery that would endure well into the second half of the twentieth century. The nature and consequences of the Jim Crow system are well known. It was successful in politically disenfranchising the Black population and in creating economic relationships that ensured Black economic subordination. Work on wealth by sociologists Melvin Oliver and Thomas Shapiro (1995), as well as Dalton Conley (1999), are making clear that wealth inequality is the most drastic form of inequality between Blacks and Whites. It was the slave and Jim Crow regimes that prevented Blacks from acquiring wealth that could have been passed down to succeeding generations. Finally, the Jim Crow regime consisted of a comprehensive set of laws that stamped a badge of inferiority on Black people and denied them basic citizenship rights.

The Jim Crow regime was backed by the iron fist of southern state power, the United States Supreme Court, and white terrorist organizations. Jim Crow was also held in place by white racist attitudes. As Larry Bobo has pointed out, "The available survey data suggests that anti-Black attitudes associated with Jim Crow were once widely accepted . . . [such attitudes were] expressly premised on the notion that Blacks were the innate intellectual, cultural, and temperamental inferior to Whites (Bobo, 1997:35)." Thus, as the twentieth century opened, African Americans were confronted with a powerful social order designed to keep them subordinate. As long as the Jim Crow order remained intact, the Black masses could breathe neither freely nor safely. Thus, nothing less than the overthrow of a social order was the daunting task that faced African Americans during the early decades of the twentieth century.

The voluminous research on the modern civil rights movement has reached a consensus: That movement was the central force that toppled the Jim Crow regime. To be sure, there were other factors that assisted in the overthrow including the advent of the television age, the competition for Northern Black votes between the two major parties, and the independence movement in Africa which sought to overthrow European domination. Yet it was the Civil Rights movement itself that targeted the Jim Crow regime and generated the great mass mobilizations that would bring it down.

What was the genius of the Civil Rights movement that made it so effective in fighting a powerful and vicious opposition? The genius of the Civil Rights movement was that its leaders and participants recognized that change could occur if they were able to generate massive crises within the Jim Crow order—crises of such magnitude that the authorities of oppression must yield to the demands of the movement to restore social order. Max Weber defined power as the ability to realize one's will despite resistance. Mass disruption generated power. That was the strategy of nonviolent direct action. By utilizing tactics of disruption, implemented by thousands of disciplined demonstrators who had been mobilized through their churches, schools, and voluntary associations, the Civil Rights movement was able to generate the necessary power to overcome the Jim Crow regime. The famous crises created in places like Birmingham and Selma, Alabama, coupled with the important less visible crises that mushroomed throughout the nation, caused social breakdown in Southern business and commerce, created unpredictability in all spheres of social life, and strained the resources and credibility of Southern state governments while forcing white terrorist groups to act on a visible stage where the whole world could watch. At the national level, the demonstrations and repressive measures used against them generated foreign policy nightmares because they were covered by foreign media in Europe, the Soviet Union, and Africa. Therefore what gave the mass-based sit-ins, boycotts, marches, and jailing their power was their ability to generate disorder.

As a result, within ten years—1955 to 1965—the Civil Rights movement had toppled the Jim Crow order. The 1964 Civil Rights Bill and the 1965 Voting Rights Act brought the regime of formal Jim Crow to a close.

The Civil Rights movement unleashed an important social product. It taught that a mass-based grass roots social movement that is sufficiently organized, sustained, and disruptive is capable of generating fundamental social change. In other words, it showed that human agency could flow from a relatively powerless and despised group that was thought to be backward, incapable of producing great leaders.

Other oppressed groups in America and around the world took notice. They reasoned that if American Blacks could generate such agency they should be able to do likewise. Thus the Civil Rights movement exposed the agency available to oppressed groups. By agency I refer to the empowering beliefs and action of individuals and groups that enable them to make a difference in their own lives and in the social structures in which they are embedded.

Because such agency was made visible by the Civil Rights movement, disadvantaged groups in America sought to discover and interject their agency into their own movements for social change. Indeed, movements as diverse as the Student movement, the Women's movement, the Farm Worker's movement, the Native American movement, the Gay and Lesbian movement, the Environmental movement, and the Disability Rights movement all drew important lessons and inspiration from the Civil Rights movement. From that movement other groups discovered how to organize, how to build social movement organizations, how to mobilize large numbers of people, how to devise appropriate tactics and strategies, how to infuse their movement activities with cultural creativity, how to confront and defeat authorities, and how to unleash the kind of agency that generates social change.

For similar reasons, the Black freedom struggle was able to effect freedom struggles internationally. For example, nonviolent direct action has inspired oppressed groups as diverse as Black South Africans, Arabs of the Middle East, and pro-democracy demonstrators in China to engage in collective actions. The sit-in tactic made famous by the Civil Rights movement, has been used in liberation movements throughout the third world, in Europe, and in many other foreign countries. The Civil Rights movement's national anthem "We Shall Overcome" has been interjected into hundreds of liberation movements both nationally and internationally. Because the Civil Rights movement has been so important to international struggles, activists from around the world have invited civil rights participants to travel abroad. Thus early in Poland's Solidarity movement Bayard Rustin was summoned to Poland by that movement. As he taught the lessons of the Civil Rights movement, he explained that "I am struck by the complete attentiveness of the predominantly young audience, which sits patiently, awaiting the translations of my words." (Rustin, undated)

Therefore, as we seek to understand the importance of the Black Freedom Struggle, we must conclude the following: the Black Freedom Struggle had provided a model and impetus for social movements that have exploded on the American and international landscapes. This impact has been especially pronounced in the second half of the twentieth century.

What is less obvious is the tremendous impact that the Black Freedom Struggle has had on the scholarly study of social movements. Indeed, the Black freedom struggle has helped trigger a shift in the study of social movements and collective action. The Black movement has provided scholars with profound empirical and theoretical puzzles because it has been so rich organizationally and tactically and because it has generated unprecedented levels of mobilization. Moreover, this movement has been characterized by a complex leadership base, diverse gender roles, and it has revealed the tremendous amount of human agency that usually lies dormant within oppressed groups. The empirical realities of the Civil Rights movement did not square with the theories used by scholars to explain social movements prior to the 1960s.

Previous theories did not focus on the organized nature of social movements, the social movement organizations that mobilize them, the tactical and strategic choices that make them effective, nor the rationally planned action of leaders and participants who guide them. In the final analysis, theories of social movements lacked a theory that incorporated human agency at the core of their conceptual apparatuses. Those theories conceptualized social movements as spontaneous, largely unstructured, and discontinuous with institutional and organizational behavior. Movement participants were viewed as reacting to various forms of strain and doing so in a non-rational manner. In these frameworks, human agency was conceptualized as reactive, created by uprooted individuals seeking to reestablish a modicum of personal and social stability. In short, social movement theories prior to the Civil Rights movement operated with a vague, weak vision of agency to explain phenomena that are driven by human action.

The predictions and analytical focus of social movement theories prior to the 1970s stood in sharp contrast to the kind of theories that would be needed to capture the basic dynamics that drove the Civil Rights movement. It became apparent to social movement scholars that if they were to understand the Civil Rights movement and the multiple movements it spun, the existing theoretical landscape would have to undergo a radical process of reconceptualization.

As a result, the field of social movements has been reconceptualized and this retheoritization will effect research well into the new millennium. To be credible in the current period any theory of social movements must grapple conceptually with the role of rational planning and strategic action, the role of movement leadership, and the nature of the mobilization process. How movements are gendered, how movement dynamics are bathed in cultural creativity, and how the interactions between movements and their opposition determine movement outcomes are important questions. At the center of this entire matrix of factors must be an analysis of the central role that human agency plays in social movements and in the generation of social change.

Thanks, in large part, to the Black freedom struggle, theories of social movements that grapple with real dynamics in concrete social movements are being elaborated. Intellectual work in the next century will determine how successful scholars will be in unraveling the new empirical and theoretical puzzles thrust forth by the Black freedom movement. Although it was not their goal, Black demonstrators of the Civil Rights movement changed an academic discipline.

A remaining question is: Will Black protest continue to be vigorous in the twenty-first century, capable of pushing forward the Black freedom agenda? It is not obvious that Black protest will be as sustainable and as paramount as it has been in previous centuries. To address this issue we need to examine the factors important to past protests and examine how they are situated in the current context.

Social movements are more effective when they can identify a clear-cut enemy. Who or what is the clear-cut enemy of African Americans of the twenty-first century? Is it racism, and if so, who embodies it? Is it capitalism, and if so, how is this enemy to be loosened from its abstract perch and concretized? In fact, we do not currently have a robust concept that grasps the modern form of domination that Blacks currently face. Because the modern enemy has become opaque, slippery, illusive, and covert, the launching of Black protest has become more difficult because of conceptual fuzziness.

Second, during the closing decades of the twentieth century the Black class structure has become more highly differentiated and it is no longer firmly anchored in the Black community. There is some danger, therefore, that the cross fertilization between different strata within the Black class structure so important to previous protest movements may have become eroded to the extent that it is no longer fully capable of launching and sustaining future Black protest movements.

Third, will the Black community of the twenty-first century possess the institutional strength required for sustaining Black protest? Black colleges have been weakened because of the racial integration of previously all white institutions of higher learning and because many Black colleges are being forced to integrate. The degree of institutional strength of the church has eroded because some of them have migrated to the suburbs in an attempt to attract affluent Blacks. In other instances, the Black Church has been unable to attract young people of the inner city who find more affinity with gangs and the underground economy. Moreover, a great potential power of the Black church is not being realized because its male clergy refuse to empower Black women as preachers and pastors. The key question is whether the Black church remains as close to the Black masses—especially to poor and working classes—as it once was. That closeness determines its strength to facilitate Black protest.

In short, research has shown conclusively that the Black church, Black colleges and other Black community organizations were critical vehicles through which social protest was organized, mobilized and sustained. A truncated class structure was also instrumental to Black protest. It is unclear whether during the twenty-first century these vehicles will continue to be effective tools of Black protest or whether new forces capable of generating protest will step into the vacuum.

In conclusion, I foresee no reason why Black protest should play a lesser role for Black people in the twenty-first century. Social inequality between the races will continue and may even worsen especially for poorer segments of the Black communities. Racism will continue to effect the lives of all people of color. If future changes are to materialize, protest will be required. In 1898 as Du Bois glanced toward the dawn of the twentieth century, he declared that in order for Blacks to achieve freedom they would have to protest continuously and energetically. This will become increasingly true for the twenty-first century. The question is whether organizationally, institutionally, and intellectually the Black community will have the wherewithal to engage in the kind of widespread and effective social protest that African Americans have utilized so magnificently. If previous centuries are our guide, then major surprises on the protest front should be expected early in the new millennium.

REFERENCES

Bobo, L. 1997. "The Color Line, the Dilemma, and the Dream: Race Relations in America at the Close of the Twentieth Century." In *Civil Rights and Social Wrongs: Black-White Relations since World War II,* edited by J. Higham, pp. 31–55. University Park, PA: Penn State University Press.

Conley, Dalton. 1999. *Being Black, Living in the Red: Race, Wealth, and Social Policy in*

America. Berkeley: University of California Press.

Rustin, Bayard. no date. *Report on Poland.* New York: A. Philip Randolph Institute.

Oliver, Melvin, and Thomas E. Shapiro. 1995. *Black Wealth / White Wealth: A New Perspective on Racial Inequality.* New York: Routledge.

DISCUSSION QUESTIONS

1. What does Morris mean by "the genius of the Civil Rights movement?" Can you imagine such a strategy being an effective means of combating the oppression of racial groups today? If so, how; if not, why not?

2. What does Morris identify as the products of the Civil Rights movement? What does this teach you about the connections between contemporary social movements and the Civil Rights movement?

INFOTRAC COLLEGE EDITION

You can use your access to InfoTrac College Edition to learn more about the subjects covered in this essay. Some suggested search terms include:

Black Panther Party   disability rights
Black power movement   Jim Crow segregation
Black protest   Montgomery Bus Boycott
Civil Rights movement